What People are Saying About
Reforming Sports Before the Clock Runs Out

RICK TELANDER, *Chicago Sun Times* and author of *The 100 Yard Lie.*

"Bruce Svare is one of the thinkers who recognizes that sports and the culture around them keep spinning into stranger and stranger lands. His thoughtful solutions are well worth paying attention to."

ROBERT LIPSYTE, *New York Times*

"In clear, urgent prose, Svare spotlights the crisis then offers a daring plan for reform. This is a thoughtful yet bracing call for action whose time has come."

ALEXANDER WOLFF, *Sports Illustrated* and author of *Big Game Small World: A Basketball Adventure.*

"Bruce Svare draws on his extensive experience at the grass roots in cataloging the many ways amateur sports are failing our youth and society. You may not agree with every one of his proposals for fixing pre-professional sports—I didn't—but Svare offers a starting point for an important debate with this comprehensive, personal and urgent book."

JAY WEINER, *Minneapolis Star-Tribune*

"Part indictment, part idealism, completely provocative, Bruce Svare doesn't merely argue for reform. He passionately demands it. Getting to where he wants to go won't be easy. But he offers a road map that is worthy of close inspection and sure to trigger debate."

DR. CHARLES YESALIS, Professor of Health Science and Administration and Exercise and Sport Science, Penn State University, author of *The Steroids Game.*

"Dr. Svare has delivered an accurate and hard-hitting description of the problems of our present sport culture, especially how those problems impact our children. This book goes beyond chronicling the ills of sport in that Dr. Svare has the courage to offer solutions, many of which might be viewed as radical and controversial. As a result some parents and coaches might feel uncomfortable as the rock covering the many dark aspects of sport is lifted. However, that is just what is needed. For too many decades, far too many of us have found it easier to look the other way. This book will help us educate ourselves about the breadth and depth of this dilemma and encourage discussion about what we need to do to fix it."

Bob Bigelow, youth sports activist and reformer, author of *Just Let the Kids Play*

"If you like the American 'Amateur' sports as currently constructed, read this book. If you love sports, devour these words and ideas. You may not agree with everything Bruce Svare writes, but his proposals for change are a wonderfully healthy addition to some much-needed discourse and debate on the direction of sports ages 3–22 in this country."

Dr. Jon Ericson, Professor Emeritus and Former Provost, Drake University.

"For Bruce Svare, a life-long love of sports has been betrayed by a sports culture turned dark. Fighting back, Svare exposes the destructive forces in sports—from pee wee to pro—and proposes reforms that are both far reaching and practical.

Reforming Sports Before the Clock Runs Out

One Man's Journey Through Our Runaway Sports Culture

BRUCE B. SVARE

Bordalice Publishing, Inc.
Sports Reform Press
Delmar, New York

Published by Sports Reform Press
An imprint of Bordalice Publishing, Inc.
218 Murray Avenue
Delmar, New York 12054

Web address: www.bordalicepublishing.com
Email address: bpi218@aol.com

Library of Congress Control Number: 2003099332
ISBN   0-9666323-6-2

This book is dedicated to the parents of our next generation of young athletes. Their wisdom, perseverance, and desire to create a better environmnet for their children will be the turning point in efforts to reform sports in our country. This book is also dedicated to the millions of young American athletes—past, present, and future—who continue to be affected by a sports culture that fails them. It is my hope that this book and the creation of the National Institute for Sports Reform (NISR) will improve their lives as they seek educational and athletic enrichment during their development.

Sports is a vital character builder. It molds the youth of our country for their roles as custodians of the republic. It teaches them to be strong enough to know they are weak and brave enough to face themselves when they are afraid. It teaches them to be proud and unbending in honest defeat, but humble and gentle in victory. It gives them a predominance of courage over timidity, of appetite for adventure over loss of ease.

GENERAL DOUGLAS MACARTHUR, from Chu, *The Character of American Higher Education and Intercollegiate Sport*

Organized sport in America is not all bad. There are plenty of coaches and athletic programs committed to instilling positive values in participants. There are thousands of athletes who benefit greatly from athletic participation. And there is a degree of value in sports' entertainment function. But while it is not all bad, it is clearly not what it is supposed to be. The fact is, an honest, rational argument can be made that organized sports' overall influence within our culture has become more negative than positive, that the moral basis upon which it was built has crumbled to dust and, as a result, has left it devoid of meaning. Merely the fact that such an argument can be made should certainly give us reason to pause.

JOHN GERDY, *Sports: The All-American Addiction*

Sports are over because they no longer have any moral resonance.

ROBERT LIPSYTE, *The Emasculation of Sports*

Those things that we have long valued in sport—its ability to promote good health, develop character, encourage sportsmanship, and bring people together—are simply no longer important.

JOHN GERDY, *Sports: The All-American Addiction*

At the heart of these problems (in sports) is a profound change in the American culture of sports itself. At one time, that culture was defined by colleges, high schools, summer leagues, and countless community recreational programs. Amateurism was a cherished ideal. In such a context, it made sense to regard athletics as an educational undertaking. Young people were taught values ranging from fitness, cooperation, teamwork, and perseverance to sportsmanship as moral endeavor. All of that seems somehow archaic and quaint today.

The Knight Commission, *A Call to Action*

I believe with all my heart that athletics is one of the finest preparations for most of the intricacies and darknesses a human life can throw at you. Athletics provide some of the richest fields of both metaphor and cliché to measure our lives against the intrusions and aggressions of our people.

PAT CONROY, *My Losing Season*

CONTENTS

Acknowledgments   ix

Note to the Reader   xiii

Preface   xv

Part One FOUNDATIONS

1   The Way We Were   5
2   A Father's Wisdom   13
3   Less is More   19
4   Passing Through the Age of Innocence   23
5   Throwbacks   29

Part Two   SERVING OUR YOUTH

6   Forgotten Values of the Game   39
7   On to Disneyworld   44
8   Backyard Reform   47
9   The Professionalization of Peter   61
10 The Athletic Scholarship Chase   67

Part Three   BE TRUE TO YOUR SCHOOL

11 Jock Culture 101   75
12 Scholastic Recruiting Wars   79
13 Suburban Council Rules   84
14 The Endless Season   90
15 Your High School Sports Hall of Fame   95
16 School Budget Blues   100

Part Four   SPORTS CASUALTIES

17 Fitness Failures   109

18 ACL Epidemic   128

19 Peaking at 15   132

20 Signing Day   138

21 Collegiate Gamblers Anonymous   145

22 A Courtship with Anabolic Steroids   153

23 The Up Side and the Down Side of Title IX   157

Part Five   ROOT FOR YOUR TEAM

24 About Second, Third, and Fourth Chances   170

25 The Ephs Versus the Lord Jeffs   177

26 The Cheating Dome   183

27 Pulling the Plug on Baseball   190

28 Naming the Sports Complex   195

29 Moving Up to Division I Athletics   201

Part Six   TRAVELING THE ROAD TO REFORM

30 Lessons from Singapore and Australia   210

31 Problem Areas   229

32 Needed Reforms   249

Epilogue   267

Essential Reading in Sports Reform   275

About the Author   279

Appendix I   The National Institute for Sports Reform   281

Appendix II   Sports Reform Resources   285

Index   293

ACKNOWLEDGMENTS

There are many people to thank for supporting me in my decision to author a book on my sports experiences and the field of sports reform. Let me mention a few of them.

Most important, my family has been incredibly supportive and patient with me while I have worked on this manuscript. My wife Maryalice and my two sons John and Mark provided helpful advice and critiques at every step of the way. I also want to thank my brother-in-law Jay Gearan, an outstanding journalist and exemplary teacher, who offered words of encouragement from the inception of this book so long ago. I also thank my brother-in-law Mark Gearan, an outstanding leader in government and education, who offered important insights to some of the issues discussed in this volume.

I especially want to thank my Bethlehem friends, better known as the "Breakfast Club." Mort Borzykowski, Bill Cushing, Al Russell, and Tom Venter reviewed earlier drafts of my book and provided a frequent sounding board for my ideas. They lived through many of the events I have reported on here and their eyes and ears helped me to reconstruct and interpret some of my sports experiences. Their steadfast encouragement and friendship have been instrumental in bringing this book to fruition. To repay them for their help, I will gladly foot the bill for future early morning meetings at the Four Corners Luncheonette.

I am also indebted to Alexander Wolff from *Sports Illustrated,* Robert Lipsyte from the *New York Times,* Jay Weiner from the *Minneapolis Star Tribune,* Rick Telander from the *Chicago Sun Times,* Chuck Yesalis from Penn State University, Jon Ericson from Drake University, and Bob Bigelow for reading portions of the manuscript and making comments. Their suggestions have improved the final product in many ways.

A source of inspiration while writing this book was my experiences with the many athletes I have either coached or have known through the years. In particular, I want to thank Chuck Abba Jr., Sean Battle, Ross Borzykowski, Marc Borzykowski, Leo Bresnahan, Josh Burnett, Rich Capeless, Dan Conway, Will Cushing, Cory Czajka, Joe D'Angelo,

Brian Davies, Willie Dean, Mike Gearan, Jack Gearan, Mike Del-Giacco, Steve Doran, Matt Fiedler, Seamus Gallagher, Chris Gerber, Erik Gill, Mike Grasso, Jason Gutman, Tom Hitter, Erik Hjeltnes, Pat Hughes, Geoff Hunter, Nate Kosoc, Mitchel Layne, Geoff Linstruth, Chris Marotta, Rory McInerney, David Musella, Chris Myer, Pat O'Connor, Dennis Pitaniello, Matt Quatraro, Brian Rowan, Kevin Russell, Marcus Rotundi, Steve Sgambelluri, Kyle Snyder, Mike Soronen, Bill Soronen, Tim Staniels, Aaron Thorpe, Matt Tulloch, Ryan Venter, Chris Wenger, Tim Wenger, Matt Wing, Mark Winterhoff, Matt Winterhoff, and Brian Yovine.

I also wish to thank my fellow sports reformers that serve on the advisory board of the NISR. They include Linda Bensel-Meyers, Bob Bigelow, Dale Brown, Dan Doyle, Fred Engh, Jon Ericson, John Gerdy, Michael Gray, Ramogi Huma, Marc Isenberg, David Janda, Brian Porto, Cathy Redmond, Ken Reed, Alan Sack, Marcia Sage, Ellen Stauronsky, Jim Thompson, and Chuck Yesalis. Their willingness to take a stand on difficult issues in the field of sports reform inspired me when I wrestled with certain questions raised in this book.

For helping me to understand the sports gambling atmosphere on college campuses, I thank two anonymous college students, "Steve" and "Mike," who provided me with candid information.

I thank Nicole Conway for her friendship and candor in discussing her high school, collegiate, and professional basketball career.

I am indebted to Pete Hogan for helping me to understand the decline of health and fitness as well as the de-emphasis of physical education in our sports culture.

For help in understanding ACL injuries in woman, I thank orthopedic specialist Dr. John Czajka from Albany Associates. I especially want to thank Peter and Texan Corrigan and Chuck and Cathy St. Lucia for sharing information about their daughters' ACL injuries.

I also thank former NFL football player Steve Courson for sharing with me his personal story on anabolic steroid abuse.

For giving me a different perspective on my own sports culture in the United States, I thank Nick Aplin and Steve Wright, my sports friends in Singapore at the National Institute for Education, and Alan Roberts and Mark Peters, sports colleagues at the University of Canberra and the Australian Sports Commission.

For his creative and professional artwork in developing cartoons for this book I thank Mark Parisi of the Atlantic Feature Syndicate. I also thank Bookcomp Inc., for their help in producing this book. In particular, I thank David den Boer for book layout and cover design as well as Maria den Boer for book editing.

For use of copyrighted material, I thank the *Albany Times Union* Newspaper, Providence College, Susquehanna University, New York Roadrunners, and Linda Bensel-Meyers.

Lastly, I want to thank my father, Myron L. Svare, who provided me with an idyllic youth. Though he passed long ago, his spirit continues to guide me in my thinking about what sports can and should be about.

These individuals are the reason why this book has finally reached its completion five years after it was started. To all of them, I owe my most sincere and heartfelt gratitude.

NOTE TO THE READER

In certain places in this book, I have tried to maintain the confidentiality of some of the individuals I have written about. This has been done on several occasions by using fictitious first names or by using composites of more than one individual. Also, the positions I have advanced do not necessarily reflect the official policies, mission, goals, and initiatives of the National Institute for Sports Reform (NISR).

PREFACE

I have two confessions to make at the outset of this book. First, I have a passionate love for sports. I loved athletics from the first day that I remember my father throwing a football to me on the front lawn of our home in New Hampshire. Sports were a new way to express myself. They enabled me to understand who I was and they provided a way for me to assess my limits. They also afforded me endless enjoyment in organized team situations as well as recreational play. And, after my playing days were over, I converted my love for sports to other areas, especially that of coaching and just being a fan.

The second confession that I have to make is that I find it more difficult with each passing year to maintain the same level of passionate love for sports that I once experienced. Sports are in turbulent times right now. What I see on our playing fields and what is revealed through countless newspaper stories, television programs, magazine articles, and Internet postings, is a sports landscape in crisis. My fear is that everything that was once good about athletics will be ruined unless significant change occurs in the near future. With these two feelings in mind—that of love and concern—I have produced a book to convey my thoughts to readers who may be experiencing similar emotions.

Reforming Sports Before the Clock Runs Out: One Man's Journey Through Our Runaway Sports Culture is part memoir and part critical analysis. It chronicles my sports experiences in Upstate New York and New England through a collection of short essays. As the son of a man who loved sports, as an athlete of only modest accomplishment, as the father of two athletes, as a college professor, as a coach, and as a sports administrator, I have a story that I need to tell. It is the story of an average American whose love affair with sports is being challenged almost daily by an increasingly dark side to our athletic landscape.

The essays you are about to read recount observations and experiences that are not unique to me. Because our sports culture sends mixed messages to its athletes at all levels of sports in every community of our country, it is also the universal story of countless other conflicted Americans who have similar experiences in their communities. The only difference between me and so many others is that I felt compelled to tell my story before our sports culture becomes sadly unrecognizable and completely irrelevant.

A more detailed examination of the issues raised here can be found in the soon to be published companion volume entitled *Crisis on Our Playing Fields: What Everyone Should Know About Our Out of Control Sports Culture and What We Can Do to Change It.* The reader is encouraged to examine this work for a better understanding of the systemic organizational problems that presently plague our sports landscape. The book provides thorough documentation of the major problem areas in preprofessional sports and analyzes the important legal and social events that may soon take place to reorder the organization of athletics in our country.

The solutions to life's most deep-rooted problems require patience, persistence, and systematic study. They also require what my fellow sports reformer, Jon Ericson, calls "truth-telling." It is popular now to engage in telling the truth about our institutions that have failed. Whether it is Enron or the Catholic Church or the institutions that promote and house our sports culture, telling the truth can have a cleansing effect. Solutions to problems can only come about by first telling the truth about what goes on in our sports culture. We can't explain away, rationalize, or deny the problems once the facts are exposed for all to see. And reform can come only when there is accountability by those who organize, administer, and supervise our athletes. Truth-telling about our sports culture can be liberating, especially when seen through the eyes of someone who has lived through the peaks and valleys of athletics for five decades.

This book tells the truth about how sports have become very serious business and how immense pressure is now placed upon the early specialization and professionalization of young athletes, about the intense promotion of athletic achievement for the reward of an athletic scholarship or professional contract, and about winning at all costs.

This book tells the truth about how academic corruption is pervasive in our public schools and institutions of higher learning that house big-time sports programs.

This book tells the truth about how commercialism and the big business of preprofessional sports is increasing and threatening the integrity of our academic institutions.

This book tells the truth about how the utilization of supplements and performance enhancing drugs is pervasive and has been fueled by a culture of winning at all costs.

This book tells the truth about how declining sportsmanship, elevated violence, and the general misbehavior of athletes, coaches, parents, and fans threaten to compromise the essence of athletic competition.

This book tells the truth about sports injuries and other health related issues that are increasing for almost all levels of athletics and that not enough is being done to prevent them.

This book tells the truth about how the media act irresponsibly and at times unethically in the manner in which they hype, overexpose, and glamorize the accomplishments of young athletes and popularize their misbehavior both on and off the field.

This book tells the truth about sports gambling and the printing of point spread information and how it threatens to undermine the integrity of sports.

This book tells the truth about how sports opportunities are shifting dramatically and producing severe inequities in many segments of our sports culture.

This book tells the truth about how competitive sports, which satisfy the needs of a small group of elite athletes, is the dominant theme in our sports culture while recreational and fitness-based sports, which satisfy the needs of the vast majority, have been deemphasized.

This book tells the truth about how existing sports governing bodies, youth and amateur organizations, and educational institutions have done a poor job of protecting the health and welfare of athletes who are increasingly abused and exploited by our present sports culture.

This book tells the truth about how our sports-loving parents, many of whom are well intentioned but are not sufficiently armed with important information, may not be aware of the threat posed to their children if our runaway sports culture is not reformed before it is too late.

The intent of this book is to tell the truth about the many difficult issues swirling about our sports culture at the present time. This is done by bringing these issues to life through my observations and experiences. My goal is also to provide some solutions for the difficult problems faced by those involved with sports at all levels. This is a daunting task but one that must be started if we are to reverse the negative culture of sports before it is too late. Lastly, and most important, my goal is to spur discussion and prompt action at the local, regional, and national levels about a crisis that presently undermines our most important possession—our kids.

Part One

FOUNDATIONS

Once upon a time—not long ago, really—kids were left to their own devices to play sports on sandlots after school. The two oldest kids acted as captains and chose equal teams. Everybody played. There were no uniforms, no refs, no scoreboards, no league standings, no trophies, and perhaps best of all—no parents. It was just like Charlie Brown's All-Stars. If a dispute occurred, the game stopped, and after a few moments of debate, the teams would declare a compromise—a "do-over." The disputed play was repeated, and the game went on as before. (In this age of ultra-organized participation, how many kids even know what a "do-over" is?) When the score became too lopsided in those sandlot games of yore, the two captains would rearrange the teams. Even then, as kids ourselves, we knew it was more exciting to play in a close game than in a rout. But the bottom line was that we had fun. Pure, simple, competitive fun.

Rick Wolf, *Sports Illustrated*

———————

I was a first-round draft pick and played in the National Basketball Association for four years, toe-to-toe and elbow-to-elbow with the stars of the game. I played basketball at an Ivy League college, in high school and in the driveways of my hometown, where children of my generation got the best education in sports there is: from each other.

Bob Bigelow, *Just Let the Kids Play*

———————

Organized sports has changed dramatically since I was a boy playing pick-up basketball, football, and baseball in the streets and fields of northern New Jersey. It has become too everything — too large, too important, too much money involved, too much pressure to win, and all too soon. It has assumed a place in our culture of far too much importance.

John Gerdy, *Sports: The All-American Addiction*

———————

The vast majority of the organized games our children play on the field and in the gym tend to be similar to the games we see on television played by adults. There is no reason that this should be so. In fact, it often makes little sense for children to attempt to play the same games as adults. It has been difficult for us, the adults, to change this pattern. We've been trying since 1938. Yet parents still enjoy seeing their children compete in sports that mimic those played by professionals. In many ways, the current state of organized sports programs for children meets the needs of parents rather than those of children. It's not too late to change this state of affairs. My hope is that parent by parent, family by family, school by school, and community by community, we can change our programs to meet the needs of our children.

Shane Murphy, *The Cheers and the Tears*

———————

offthemark.com

1

The Way We Were

As many adults often do as they grow older, I have romanticized about my early athletic days growing up in New England. My sports involvement was rather typical for a youngster in the 1950s and 1960s and was hardly the pressure cooker that it is today. There was a simple, predictable pattern—a rhythm—to sports activities during that time. The fall was for football, the winter was for basketball, and the spring and summer were for baseball. No one played a single sport all year round as they do today and many of us played several sports, oftentimes all three; once a playing season was over, we moved on to the next. When school let out in the spring, it was a whole different sports experience. Summer sports camps were few in number and intensive playing schedules with competitive club teams were virtually nonexistent. Instead, summers were for pickup games, hanging out with friends, family vacations, and lots of unstructured time. Summers were a time to meet yourself.

I have fond memories of my youth and scholastic playing days, but mostly I remember the playground games on vacant fields and neighborhood driveways. Those games meant everything to me because we called all the shots and adults weren't involved. We played with boys and girls of all ages and we had time to create our own games with our own rules. The unstructured nature of those sports activities produced spontaneity, creativity, and an ability to solve our own problems. We didn't need adult intervention. In fact, we did everything we could to avoid it. If we made mistakes, we only had ourselves to blame so we made sure that we got it right the first time.

The simplicity of my own sports activities during that time was paralleled by the primitive early stages of professional sports. There were 4 major professional leagues: Major League Baseball (MLB) consisted of 16 teams, the National Football League (NFL) consisted of 12 teams, the National Basketball Association (NBA) consisted of 8 teams, and the National Hockey League (NHL) consisted of only 6 teams. Likewise, college football and basketball were in their infancy and were just beginning to evolve into the minor leagues of their respective professional sports.

Sports entertainment in those days was hardly the multibillion-dollar business that it is today. Television broadcasting of sporting events was limited to only a few games a week on the major networks and usually this was restricted to weekend telecasts. Special television emphasis was placed on the World Series, the Olympics, college football bowl games, and tournament play such as the National Invitational Tournament (NIT) for college basketball. The amount of print devoted to sports in daily newspapers and magazines was small. *Sports Illustrated* and *Sport Magazine* were among the few publications devoted strictly to athletics. Daily newspapers included national, state, and local scores but the coverage typically gave the basics and little else.

So, what has happened since that uncomplicated time of the 1950s and 1960s and why have sports grown at such an exponential pace? The development of youth, scholastic, collegiate, and amateur sports was, more than anything, a by-product of the vast cultural, economic, and sociological changes that took place in our country at the turn of the century. While most of us assume that athletics have been a part of our American culture forever, it is important to note that this is not true. Indeed, prior to the urbanization and industrialization of America in the early 1900s, the amount of leisure time available for both kids and adults was relatively limited. Hence, participation in sports and attendance at sporting events was not a major activity occupying the lives of Americans. Likewise, the involvement of parents in the sports activities of young children was virtually unheard of at the time. The end result was that sports simply were not an important part of the fabric of every day living as they are today.

Intercollegiate sports began for track and field, baseball, soccer, rugby, and American Football between 1852 and 1880. These teams were an outgrowth of intramural competition on campuses and were managed and funded exclusively by undergraduates. At the time, participation in collegiate sports was strictly for recreation and there was no such thing as recruitment of students for their athletic abilities. However, following the Civil War, sport became a major commercial venture at both the collegiate and professional levels. As they became a formal part of our institutions of higher learning, intercollegiate sports increasingly were viewed as a method to market universities to the broader public and attract students as well as alumni support. The recruitment and the subsidizing of students who played sports therefore became a major focus of colleges and universities. Coincidentally, as the popularity of intercollegiate sports grew, more resources were devoted to building the necessary infrastructure such as gymnasiums, fieldhouses, and football fields.

The growth of institutionalized high school-sponsored sports in this country was due in part to the growing population of immigrants at the turn of the twentieth century. Because of an anti-immigrant sentiment in our culture, many began to express concern about the disorderliness and disorganization of student athletic associations and privately run sports teams and leagues. Wishing to "Americanize" newly arrived immigrants, many officials believed that schools would be the best place for this acculturation process. Hence, civic and school officials believed that sports clubs housed in schools would be the ideal place to teach the American virtues of hard work, fair play, and competition. At the same time, public officials denounced student-run leagues as unsafe. As a result, educational officials soon placed sports under the direct supervision of high school principals. This ushered in the true beginning of interscholastic sports in this country.

The growth of youth sports paralleled the development of collegiate and interscholastic athletics. The Young Men's Christian Association (YMCA) was one of the first organizations to provide sports activities for boys in 1851. This was followed in the 1920s and 1930s by organizations like Little League Baseball and Pop Warner Football. Presently, there are youth leagues for every sport offered in the United States and increasingly they follow a professional model with extensive local, regional, and national competition. Youth sports programs have become immensely popular and they are now the backbone of American family life.

The explosion of sports in the past 50 years and the attendant insanity that surrounds much of it can be attributed directly or indirectly to four simultaneous developments during the prosperous years following World War II. First, the amount of leisure time for adults dramatically increased and their involvement in organizing and overseeing sports escalated as a result. Second, colleges and universities started to grant athletic scholarships to promising student-athletes. Overseen by the National Collegiate Athletic Association (NCAA), such aid was based upon athletic potential in contrast to financial need or academic giftedness. As a result, athletic scholarships sparked many young athletes (and their parents) to devote much of their young lives to specializing in a single sport at a very early age. Third, salaries for professional athletes grew exponentially. Fueled by corporate sponsorships, television dollars, shrewd product marketing and an insatiable paying public, professional sports evolved into a multimillion dollar entertainment business. Consequently, the elevated attractiveness of salaries became an important incentive for those ultimately seeking careers as professional athletes. Fourth, television and media exposure rapidly expanded. This served to popularize the entertainment value of athletic activities to a point where they became the focal point of many people's lives.

Fast forwarding to the present can best be described as a lesson in sports culture shock. Sweeping changes in athletics have produced a sports culture today that is almost unrecognizable from what it was 40 to 50 years ago. The expansion of sports opportunities makes the 1950s and 1960s look like the prehistoric age of athletics in this country.

The nationwide figures today regarding sports participation are truly staggering. Roughly 22 million 6-to 18-year-olds participate in youth programs like Little League and Pop Warner; approximately 16 million athletes participate in community recreation programs; 10 million athletes are involved in intramural or interscholastic sports; 2 million are involved in club or fee-based programs; 332,000 are involved in intercollegiate athletics.

The growth in sports participation is especially remarkable in the case of soccer, where 500,000 new youths registered to play in the year following the 1994 World Cup in the United States. The American Youth Soccer Organization has more than doubled its membership to 607,000 over the past decade. Interestingly, the percentage of girl participants, the fastest-growing segment of athletics in this country, has jumped from 25 to 40 percent.

Youngsters are heading into sports programs at earlier and earlier ages. For example, some gymnastics, swimming, baseball, and soccer programs allow enrollment starting at 3 to 5 years of age. Likewise, summer sports camps, which have proliferated in this country over the past decade, allow enrollment as early as 5 years of age. A burgeoning growth area of sports is the proliferation of specialized sports academies such International Management Group (IMG) in Florida. For a hefty fee, young athletes can receive intensive year-round sports training and simultaneously attend classes at the academy.

A change in sports opportunities can also been seen in the avail-
ability of sports for both female and disabled athletes. Title IX of the
Educational Amendments Act was passed in 1972. It prohibits gender-
based discrimination in educational settings that receive federal funds.
As a result, there has been a dramatic increase in the number of females
playing organized, school-based, and collegiate sports at just about
every level of athletics and every type of sport. At one time, girls were
restricted to sports like gymnastics, tennis, and cheerleading. However,
now women are seen competing in soccer, baseball, lacrosse, and basketball to name just a few. Likewise, through the 1990 Americans with
Disabilities Act, athletic opportunities are now more available to those
who are physically or mentally challenged. Programs such as Buddy
Ball, the Little League Challenger Division, and Special Olympics have
provided countless new opportunities for those who historically were
excluded from the enjoyment of sports participation.

Another flourishing aspect of sports opportunities for young athletes can be seen in recent developments within the Amateur Athletic
Union (AAU). This organization forged a partnership with Walt Disney
World in 1996 in which AAU relocated its national headquarters to
Orlando. At Disney's Wide World of Sports Complex, the AAU now conducts 40 of its national events. The complex features a double-deck
7,500-seat stadium and quadraplex, a fieldhouse that accommodates up
to six full-size courts, a softball quadraplex, two youth baseball fields, a
tennis complex, a track and field complex, and four multipurpose performance fields that can accommodate sports ranging from international
soccer to sand volleyball.

Expansion of the professional leagues and increased opportunities
for athletes have also taken place. Major League baseball now has 30
teams, the National Hockey League now has 28 teams, the National
Football League now has 32 teams, and the National Basketball Association now has 29 teams. This represents a dramatic increase from the
fledgling days of some of these leagues only a relatively short time ago.

The established professional sports leagues have clearly grown and
are continuing to expand as I write. However, an equally important
development has been the growth of new professional sports leagues
such as Major League Soccer (10 teams), the Woman's National Basketball Association (12 teams), the Arena Football League (15 teams),
the United States Basketball League (12 teams), the National Professional Indoor Soccer League (13 teams), the World Team Tennis

League (7 teams), and the newly formed Major League Lacrosse (6 teams).

Sports marketing at the college and professional levels has become big business and the revenue dollars generated from gate receipts, advertising, and television pumps millions of dollars into the economy every year. In the NCAA, television contracts alone were worth approximately $147 million for the 1997–1998 season. Sports marketing of apparel, sneakers, team logos, and other merchandise also produces millions of dollars in revenue for both professional and college coffers. Estimates in 1995 indicate that the sports industry in the United States produced revenues in excess of $85 billion. Estimates for the year 2000 indicate that revenues approached $120 billion. These figures do not even take into consideration revenues from global sports advertising and marketing, which surely provide billions more.

The news and information we receive on sports has also greatly expanded in the past 20 to 30 years. Each day we are bombarded with sports information from television, radio, print media, and the Internet. At virtually any hour of the day, Fox Sports, Madison Square Garden (MSG), ESPN 1 and 2, ESPN Sports Classics, and the Golf Channel televise some sort of sporting event. All day sports talk is also available from radio stations like WFAN out of New York City and syndicated shows like *ESPN Radio* and the *Jim Rome Show*.

Major national newspapers such as *USA Today*, the *New York Times*, the *Boston Globe*, the *Washington Post*, the *Los Angeles Times*, and the *Chicago Sun-Times* have progressively increased the number of pages devoted to sports in the past 20 years. Sports magazines and daily publications are also on the increase. They include those that are mainly statistics-based (e.g., *Baseball Weekly*, *Sporting News*) to those that provide in-depth analysis of sports figures and game analysis (e.g., *Sports Illustrated*), to those that are involved with instruction, fitness, and preparation for athletic competition (e.g., *Health and Fitness*), to those that focus on individual sports (e.g., *Tennis*, *Golf Digest*). There are even sports magazines specifically written for kids (e.g., *Sports Illustrated for Kids*) women (e.g. *Woman's Sports and Fitness*), high school sports (e.g., *Indiana High School Basketball*, *Ohio Baseball*), and recruiting (e.g., *Superprep*, *Prepstar*).

The most startling development in sports information, however, is the Internet. Accessible 24 hours a day, it provides information instantaneously regarding game results, instruction, analysis, and sports information in general for just about every sport at every level of competition. Professional, college, and high school athletic programs maintain their own web sites and update them daily for the latest schedules, recruiting information, scores, and statistics. Even youth programs, such as Little League, maintain their own web sites where information of every kind can be obtained. There are web sites specialized for kids, women, and individual sports. Fan-driven websites for specific sports teams, especially at the collegiate level, have also proliferated.

Our present sports landscape hardly resembles what I was exposed to as a youngster. I don't think that we will ever return to that simpler era, and I am not advocating that we should, but the innocence of it all is gone. Our country has changed significantly in that period of time and much of it has been for the better, but I am not convinced that the changes in sports have necessarily been an improvement over my era. Sports are not just for fun anymore. Kids no longer participate for the sheer joy of the game because now there is a more important material motive: to win, to get a scholarship, or, better yet, to sign a pro contract.

These changes, which are the key motivating factors behind participation in many of America's athletic programs today, force us to reflect upon a sports landscape convulsing with major problems. Indeed, those of us growing up 40 to 50 years ago could not have imagined in our wildest dreams that we would be seeking remedies for the problems we have today: professionalization and specialization at an early age, exploitation and academic corruption, rampant commercialization of sport at all levels, sports gambling, performance-enhancing drugs, escalating poor sportsmanship by fans, parents, and players, increasing violence, unbalanced and inappropriate media coverage, escalating sports injuries, and declining health and fitness.

If we do not overhaul our present sports system soon, we will be well on our way to ruining the many positive things that athletic participation can provide. While I remain an optimist, there are many who fear that it is simply too late.

2

A Father's Wisdom

Throughout my involvement in sports, there is hardly a day that goes by when I don't think about my father, Myron L. Svare, and how I was brought up to enjoy athletics for what they really represent: participation, enjoyment, fitness, ethics, fair play, and sportsmanship. My own rather unspectacular performance as an athlete through my youth and high school days embodied all of these factors and my father made certain that I never lost sight of it. In particular, three events stick out in my mind that served to remind me that there is a larger purpose in life than learning how to throw a football, hit a baseball, or shoot a basketball. These moments really had little to do with the winning and losing of games or my individual performance, but rather they had more to do with keeping perspective and balancing athletics with more important life pursuits.

One event that I will never forget was my last season in Little League Baseball in which I lobbied the coaches to be a pitcher on our team. I was the biggest player on our squad and could throw a baseball harder than anybody. In my own immature logic, I reasoned that I should take the mound for most of our games. Although my coach caved in to my demands, he should have stuck with his own gut feeling. With my father watching from his usual spot way out in left field where few people could even see him, I proceeded to give up nine runs in the first inning of the opening day game by walking player after player and giving up a grand slam to one of my best friends. Yanked in the first inning for a better pitcher on the team, I caught for the rest of the season, and made the all-star team at that position. Upon arriving home after the opening day debacle with reddened eyes and tears, my father consoled me and simply said, "It wasn't a good day for you but don't worry about it. Catching is more fun, and you'll help the team more in that position." Those words meant a lot to me then because I was ready to ditch my glove and uniform and quit baseball altogether. Instead, I focused more on team success as opposed to fulfilling my own ego to be the next Whitey Ford or Warren Spahn.

A second event that changed my way of thinking about sports occurred when I was in the seventh grade. I was becoming addicted to basketball and I was spending almost every spare moment in the summer playing on the playgrounds and in my friends' driveways. It became a ritual each summer day to play all morning, then go swimming in the afternoon, and later return to the courts in the evening for two-on-two or three-on-three games. The Boston Celtics were sponsoring a one-week basketball camp for boys in New Hampshire and I desperately wanted to go. Instead, my father had made plans for me to attend a Boy Scouts camp on Lake Winnepasaukee. In retrospect it was a wonderful decision, but at the time I was devastated. My father tried to convince me that I would learn about a lot of other activities including sports but I wanted no part of it because all I wanted to do was play hoops with my friends. Needless to say, I came back from two weeks of camp having broadened my horizons. I learned how to dive, sail a boat, row a canoe and kayak, make a campfire, set up a tent, and cook food outdoors on an open fire. I also learned more about sports because for the first time I played tennis and golf, and even gave archery a try. Upon my return, I was able to demonstrate some of my new skills to my parents. Clearly, my father was proven right again.

However, the most transforming event in my athletic life occurred in my senior year of high school. I seriously injured my knee early in the football season and was forced to have surgery. As a result, I missed almost my entire senior football and basketball seasons. Feeling miserable and sorry for myself, I focused almost all of my mental energy on the painful fact that I had something taken away from me that I truly loved more than anything. I was an angry person then with a lot of "why me" selfish behavior. Like many, I had visions of playing in college someday but I knew that this dream was now all but over.

With his timing and good instincts, my father felt my pain but also helped me to see beyond it. He reminded me that not many are able to continue on in sports after high school and that the end comes sooner or later for everyone. I recall now that those were very hard facts of life to swallow, especially for a 16-year-old boy, but at the same time they eventually softened my anger and allowed me to turn a negative into a positive.

My father told me that I could look at my situation as an end or as a beginning. It eventually sunk in and for the first time in my life I started to apply myself to my subjects in school. My focus was now on academics and intellectual curiosity, an emphasis that has stayed with me through the rest of my life. Looking back, I am almost certain that my father was more proud of my academic accomplishments than he ever was of anything I did on the basketball court or football field. His wisdom helped me through a difficult time in my life.

Through the days of my involvement in sports, I don't remember my father ever saying anything negative to me about my athletic performances nor do I remember him second-guessing a coach, criticizing one of my teammates, grousing about my playing time or the position I played, chastising an official, or boasting to other parents. He enjoyed the fact that I liked athletics and had some success with it but he never reveled in it. Before I left the house for most games he would simply say, "Play hard and have some fun." Upon returning home, he would say, "Good game. You and your team were fun to watch" or "Nice game. I sat with (so and so) and we got caught up with things." I was never asked how many points I scored, how many hits I had, or whether or not I scored a touchdown or made an important tackle.

From my way of viewing things, my father's style was perfect. I knew he was at my games to support me regardless of the outcome individually or teamwise. I realized that my success in sports would not overly impress him nor would my failures unnecessarily provoke him to think that I was not going to be a success or a good person later in life. In other words, I learned from him that the results weren't so important but rather the process of participation was central to having a positive experience.

I tried to follow my father's example with my boys, John and Mark. Both were athletes and experienced some success in their youth and scholastic days. Sometimes I was successful in my role as unconditional supporter but I know that at other times I was as guilty as any overinvolved sport parent today. I had my moments when occasionally I became critical of a coach or overfocused on winning. There were also times when I ended up preaching a little too much about dedication and hard work and lost sight of the true meaning of sports participation. It's a trap that many parents fall into and I was no different. I was thankful that I had my father's low-key style to fall back on when I was about to go over the edge.

I did not learn until after my father's passing in 1978 how good an athlete he really was in his high school and amateur years. My uncles had frequently commented on how their younger brother had been an excellent athlete, an "incredible competitor" in their words, but they were always short on the details. Fortunately, my grandmother had compiled a scrapbook for my father in which I was able to fully document their claims. Looking through the articles for the first time was a revelation of sorts. I couldn't believe that my father had never shared any of it before, but in retrospect, it would not have been his style to drag them out along with yearbooks or any other memorabilia he possessed.

As a high school athlete, he was a star basketball and football player in Fergus Falls, Minnesota. According to his 1934 senior *Otter* yearbook, he played on both varsity teams beginning in his sophomore year. In his senior year of football, his team went 4–2-1 and shut out their last five opponents. In one story from the *Fergus Falls Daily Journal*, the writer noted that " 'My' Svare hauled in a 55 yard pass for a touchdown" in a 64–0 stomping of nearby Barnesville. In his senior year of basketball, his high school team finished 18–4, eventually losing in the district championship game when one of their best players, Neal Morstad, fractured a foot in the semifinal game. From all accounts in the newspaper clippings in his scrapbook, the 1934 season was one of the best ever logged by a Fergus Falls team up to that time. My father appeared to have a stellar senior season. In one game against the Breckridge Cowboys in which Fergus Falls won 37–29, the write-up in the paper says: "Svare led his teammates in field goals as he looped the ball for six baskets, and playing a fine game throughout, retrieving the ball repeatedly on backboard plays."

In a section of his yearbook entitled "Senior Stars", there is a picture of him in a three-point stance in his football uniform with the following written: "Myron Svare (end), 'Streamlined.' He was a bearcat under passes and was a hand tackler. He was steady, losing his temper at no time. His berth will be hard to fill next year." Likewise, in a picture of my father in his basketball uniform holding a ball in a chest pass position, these words were written: "My Svare (forward). Could be relied upon at any crisis with a set shot. He was a good steady player and good team man."

While his basketball and football exploits appeared to be considerable, it was baseball where he really achieved his greatest success. In those years, baseball in Minnesota was not a scholastic sport. He played American Legion baseball in the spring and summer and his team won the district championship each year from 1931 to 1933. After graduating from high school in 1934, he attended Interstate Business College in Fargo, North Dakota, and played for the Fergus Falls Red Sox amateur traveling team during his next three summers. At one point he served as manager and secretary-treasurer for the team.

The box scores for his games are interesting because they show that he always batted cleanup or fifth but rarely did he play the same position for each game. He would regularly rotate from first base, to catcher, to left field, to third base in consecutive games. A versatile player, he had obviously mastered the intricacies of playing many different positions—something that is exceedingly rare in any sport these days. In his last season, the statistics in the paper showed that his team won 21 games and lost 14, and he led the team in batting with a .415 average.

One piece of memorabilia that managed to survive a disorganized attic box for many years was a 2 X 3 foot poster advertising a game between the Fergus Falls Red Sox and the Minneapolis Millers. Apparently, the Millers were an excellent barnstorming team of paid players in those days, and my father was able to schedule a game with them on September 19, 1936. The poster has pictures of various Miller star players as well as the following statements: "See what My Svare, Sonny Lonstad, Ray Erickson, and Marv Kester can do against League pitchers. The Minneapolis Millers are still known as one of the most colorful baseball teams ever assembled. See them in action at our own park playing against our own boys. You have listened to them over the air, NOW see them all in action. The Red Sox are putting forth a lot of effort to give the local fans an opportunity to see a full League team in action and you should give them your support by attending this biggest sports event in Fergus Falls' history. Admission for adults is 55 cents, children is 25 cents. Tickets are available at The Lantern, Eat-More, Drews Grocery, and Muggs Ice Cream Shop." An article in the *Fergus Falls Daily Journal* proclaimed that "the Red Sox are the best aggregation of baseball players ever turned out in Fergus Falls." Even the mayor got into the act by proclaiming September 19 as Baseball Appreciation Day and urged the citizenry to "give the home team their loyal support in the forthcoming game with the Minneapolis Millers."

With all the "hype," 1200 fans turned out . . . a good crowd in those days—but the Millers proved their class in the exhibition game and trounced the Red Sox 12–0. The headlines in the *Fergus Falls Daily Journal* the next day stated "Great Crowd Sees Millers Trim Locals." This was one of the last entries in my father's scrapbook; it apparently marked the end of his athletic career, as he set out to enter the world with his business training and a salesman's job with Minnesota Mining and Manufacturing (3M).

My father's impressive athletic biography is interesting to me in many ways. Of course, I am proud of his athletic accomplishments but more important, I find it remarkable that he never sought to live out his days on the playing fields through his son. He never badgered me to participate in sports nor did he become overinvolved in my athletic career as it grew.

In short, I think that my experiences with my father were a far cry from what I see and hear today in sports parenting relationships. For example, one is much more likely to hear parents in our present sports culture say things to their kids like: "Did you win?", "How many points did you win by?", "How many points did you score?", "How many hits did you have?", "What position did you play and how long were you on the field?", "Were you aware of the college recruiter in the stands?", "Do you know how much a college athletic scholarship is worth?", "If you want that scholarship, you're going to have to work harder than that", and "Let's forget about a summer vacation this year, you should practice your sport through the summer in order to get better." Similarly, parents today are more likely to verbally abuse officials and coaches as well as second-guess coaching decisions in front of their children and other parents. Everything is fair game and it usually pertains to their son or daughter getting a leg up in the spoils of athletic competition.

Sports participation is more popular than ever, but it seems to be for all the wrong reasons. The focus is not on the process but squarely on the results. Sportsmanship, ethics, team play, fair play, fitness, having fun with friends, and participation are secondary considerations. Winning, athletic scholarships, and professional contracts have become all-consuming for both parents and young athletes. There is no longer anything that even remotely resembles balance. It is all about me and what I can get to advance my own athletic career. And all of it is largely supported by parents who shape this attitude and feed it right from the start. I think that a dose of my father's wisdom would not be such a bad idea in our present sports culture.

3

Less is More

During my middle school years in the southern New Hampshire town of Milford, my nightly routine from November through March was to eat dinner with my family and then escape to our old red barn. Large enough to serve as a scaled-down indoor basketball court, the barn ordinarily housed my father's car as well as a typical assortment of outdoor furniture, tools, and lawn and garden equipment. My father had fashioned two 8' foot high hoops at opposite ends of the barn. For our games, we used a small ball that was about two-thirds the size of a regular basketball. Depending upon who was there, our contests would usually consist of one-on-one or two-on-two games to 40 points; winners would stay in and losers would go out. Fouls and violations were self-assessed and hotly contested games would frequently go into overtime. The first team to go up by 6 points was the winner.

The fun of those spontaneous basketball contests with my friends was something I will never forget. Those memories are as vivid now as they were back then. I specifically remember one best of seven, two-on-two series that we played when I was in the seventh grade. Jon Proctor (two years older than me) and I took on Steve Sears (also two years older than me) and Ken Olen (my age) in a bitterly fought series that went seven games. Jon and I won the seventh and deciding game in overtime when Jon scored an easy layup from a deep outlet pass I threw to him. As victors, we paraded around as though we had just won the NBA championship. Ken and Steve took solace in the fact that there would probably be a return match over the next few days.

Part of the atmosphere for our games was provided by a radio strategically placed close to the court on a corner workbench. Our favorite songs coming out of Boston radio stations like WRKO gave us background music for pregame warm-ups and half-time entertainment. On nights when the Boston Celtics were playing, we would always tune in to WBZ for the play by play of legendary announcer Johnny Most. As he called the games in his famous raspy voice high above the Boston Garden, we listened intently for our favorite players: Bob Cousy, Bill Russell, Bill Sharman, Frank Ramsey, Tom Heinsohn, Satch Sanders, John Havlichek, KC Jones, and Sam Jones. When the games came on the radio, we would pretend that we were the Celtics. Duplicating the plays as we heard them called by Most, we would reenact each possession: Cousy on the fly now up the court . . . he dipsy-doodles to the left . . . into Russell in the post . . . back out to Heinsohn . . . now to KC Jones . . . over to Sharman . . . he shoots from deep downtown . . . it's good!!" For lack of a better term, we called those reenactments "radio basketball." They were as much of a winter and spring ritual as anything we ever did in our young lives.

I especially remember playing games on bitterly cold nights. To my mother's constant irritation, I would usually strip to just a light tee-shirt and shorts because heavier clothes would interfere with my shooting. With occasional surprise visits, she would warn me and my friends that we would get sick if we didn't put our heavier clothing on. We would follow her instructions, only to take sweatshirts and jackets off once she left our domain. This was our place, our refuge, and we weren't about to have anyone else call the shots.

My father never interfered. He never refereed our games nor did he ever give us pointers on skills or rules. His only job was to break up the games if they went too long on a school night.

There were hazards playing in the barn. For example, I will never forget how many times we had to change broken light bulbs that were placed high on ceiling beams. After shattering a dozen bulbs in less than a week and risking injury from broken glass, my father installed protective metal cages around the lights. However, if a ball hit a cage hard enough the filament in the bulb would shatter and the light would go out. As a result, my father purchased several cartons of replacement bulbs so that we would not have to interrupt our games for too long. With a tall ladder, we would climb to the ceiling and carefully remove the wire cage and replace the bulb. It was the job of the team that was losing in the game to do the dirty work of replacing the bulb; the team that was winning took a break by downing some cold soda we stashed adjacent to the side door of the barn.

Oh yes, there were also occasional injuries. Steve Sears was the most physical of all of us. I caught a number of his elbows through the years resulting in split lips, black eyes, and bruises. Jon Proctor was out of commission for a few weeks with a turned ankle and Ken Olen hurt his hand on the rim one evening when he tried to dunk the ball on a fast break. When someone was hurt, there were always replacements. Ted Brown, Steve Proctor, and Loyd McNeil filled in many times and the games would continue uninterrupted.

When I moved to Gardner, Massachusetts in the eighth grade I missed the advantages of having an indoor court. I started a new routine at Greenwood playground where I ventured many summer nights to play pickup games with whoever showed up. Frequently it was with older players and often I was up against kids who were bigger, stronger, quicker, and more talented than me. But I loved the competition and I loved making a contribution to teams where I knew that I would have to work harder to get the ball and defend other players whose skills were better than my own. I still remember my first basket in the new crowd. Eddie Koslowski fed me the ball at the top of the key and I sank a jump shot over the outstretched arms of Ron Lajoie. This was somewhat of a rite of passage; I was not looked upon as the new guy anymore but rather I was proving that I belonged.

When I reflect upon my early athletic experiences, it is remarkable to me how unstructured everything was back then. There were no coaches or parents watching our every move and orchestrating what we did and there were very few summer camps and summer leagues back in my time. Although these options have proliferated in our present sports-obsessed environment, they really provide little in the way of learning experiences and repetition of skills. The focus instead is on the unrelenting pursuit of structured games. In the informal games that I played in my youth and high school days, we took risks and made countless mistakes as we played but that is how we learned. We failed many times but eventually, by trial and error, we learned what would work and what wouldn't work. Above all we learned to be creative—something that is difficult to teach in the game of basketball today.

I am not convinced that kids become better players today by engaging in countless summer camps, organized summer leagues, and AAU basketball. In my day, the options for improving one's basketball skills were few and far between. Summer leagues and camps are not a waste of time, but they usually provide far less unstructured playing time than a young athlete could get from a single evening on a community basketball court. The real success stories that I see today invariably are the kids who make a habit of playing unsupervised games against older and better players on community playgrounds. There simply is no substitute for what can be learned from spontaneous, informal games. Once a staple of a typical youngster's sports experiences, they have all but vanished from our present sports culture.

My community of Bethlehem, New York, is not unlike most suburban areas these days with palatial sports resources. There are basketball hoops in almost every driveway and a town park with several well-lit courts. However, I rarely see anyone playing or practicing in those sports venues as we once did. The reasons are complex but much of it has to do with our desire to create something better for our kids, something more than what we had growing up. Our present sports culture provides all of the advantages that one could possibly imagine, especially if you have the money for summer camps, traveling leagues, and sports academies. But do those experiences necessarily create better basketball players and are kids having as much fun playing games as we once did? Perhaps it is time that we start thinking that less is more. Indeed, maybe our young athletes could use a break today in their structured and overscheduled lives. A return to old red barns and community playgrounds might not be such a bad thing.

4

Passing Through
the Age of Innocence

I was a Wildcat—a Gardner High School Wildcat in the central Massachusetts city situated just northwest of Worcester. Moving to this city in my eighth grade year, I quickly became involved with football and basketball. Though I was strictly average in both sports, I enjoyed my years of interscholastic competition for what they were at that time—low-key athletic diversions that were principally about participation and learning about the values and ethics of the games we played.

Football was king in Gardner. For many years, the Wildcat gridiron teams enjoyed great success, especially under the tutelage of coaches Bob Duncan, Jack Tarpey, Walter Dubzinski, and Marty Anderson. The students at the high school and the Gardner citizenry got behind the players on the team; Saturday afternoon games would attract crowds of 2,000 to 3,000 people on Stone Field behind our school. Night games, which are now such a staple of high school football, were a rarity.

I was a part of those successful varsity teams in my junior and senior seasons. We captured or tied for the North Worcester County Championship in both of those years and lost only three games during that period of time. Our nine-game schedule each year ended with a traditional Thanksgiving Day game against Nashua, New Hampshire. The Turkey Day morning clash, which was the highlight of the season, always brought out the biggest crowd of the year, with many returning alumni in attendance. In those days, the season ended on Thanksgiving Day since there were no state playoffs, superbowls, or all-star games.

The accomplishments of our teams were publicized in the local paper, the *Gardner News*. The coverage usually consisted of a story on Friday previewing the upcoming Saturday game with the results reported in Monday's paper (there was no Sunday paper). The focus of those articles typically was on the team and rarely on individual players. Game reports in larger newspapers with broader circulation did not exist.

Our football teams back then were a real blend of kids from a variety of backgrounds. We were good friends and we played cohesively in the old single-wing offense that was our trademark. This type of offense is built upon a strong running game, simple but highly coordinated blocking schemes, a deceptive spinning fullback on many plays, infrequent passing, and extra blocking from the quarterback position. Our opponents could rarely match us because they usually faced a more traditional T or wing T offense. This gave us an advantage against every opponent.

Our teams also were an example of the whole being much greater than the individual parts. We had no stars and few players were recruited and went on to play in college. In fact, I can't even remember it being discussed that much among us. Aspirations to play on the collegiate or professional level rarely emerged in our discussions and not once do I recall hearing the words "athletic scholarship" mentioned among us or our parents.

As for our parents, they were very supportive of our efforts. During the course of the season, they would host a postgame meal for all the players on Saturday evenings. Also, I don't remember any of our parents squabbling about playing time issues or second-guessing coaching decisions—at least not to our faces. In short, our parents were involved but not too involved to the point where they tried to interfere. Maybe some of this had to do with the fact that there were no parent-run booster groups back then. Such organizations are found everywhere today, often trying to call all the shots, from hiring and firing of coaches to game strategy and playing time issues.

Even though we maintained a winning tradition, our coaches did not achieve this at the expense of providing a fair level of playing time for most everyone on the team. Although I did not become a starter until my senior year, I played in many, if not all, of our games as a junior. Special teams (punting, extra points, kick-offs, receiving teams) were my bread and butter and I felt as though I was a contributor. This can be said of many of my teammates who were not first-stringers. The coaches were good at finding us playing time and making sure that we felt involved. While some kids invariably would leave the football team for one reason or another, I don't recall kids leaving over a lack of playing time.

Football had the attention of everyone in my hometown. This was not true of basketball and consequently the culture surrounding this high school sport had a whole different feel to it. Our teams consisted mainly of football players and the accomplishments of our basketball teams were largely overshadowed by gridiron success. Because of football's winning tradition year in and year out, we frequently were accused of being football players masquerading as a basketball team. Simply put, hoop was considered to be a second-class citizen; it was a game that you played to stay in shape for the next football season.

We were competitive year in and year out but our seasons were mediocre at best, especially when compared to football. Our coach, Joe Bishop, was a fiery competitor but had a soft heart. He carried relatively large rosters (15 or 16 players) and usually tried to play us all in most every game. As a junior, I can't remember a game in which I did not log at least a few minutes of playing time. As a result, like my experience with football, I don't recall kids quitting over a lack of playing time. It just didn't happen.

The game was much less complicated back then. We alternated between a 2–3 zone and man-to-man defense and we rarely pressed. Our motion offense was simple with very few options; our zone offense was designed to look for seams by sending cutters through the defense and posting our big men on the blocks and foul line. We were not a good perimeter shooting team so most of our opponents threw zone defenses at us. The level of sophistication of the game we played was comparable to what most fifth and sixth grade travel basketball teams currently execute today.

Like those who played football, my basketball teammates did not have aspirations to play in college. We knew that our playing days would be over following our senior seasons and there was little talk of athletic scholarships. Our parents were not overinvolved either. They came to games and rooted us on but there was little of the parental angst and intensity that now characterizes interscholastic sporting events.

Our 20-game season concluded after our last regularly scheduled game. There were no playoffs, all-star games, or exceptional senior games. When the season ended in late February, it was time to move on to spring sports, including baseball and track. For those of us who didn't play a spring sport, it was a time to catch up with friends. It certainly was not on our minds to keep playing basketball in the spring, summer, and fall through AAU basketball programs or any of the other highly organized travel basketball leagues that have sprouted up in most communities. These avenues for additional basketball simply did not exist.

I enjoyed playing high school football and basketball at the time. Both the wins and the losses were an important part of growing up and being an athlete. However, what I remember best were the friends I made and the often humorous incidents that came along the way. My teammates included Bob Wojtukiewicz, Jack Siarnacki, Mike Lucier, Ed Jandris, Henry Holmes, John Sutherland, Bob Boucher, Gordon McKellick, Dave Gingras, Bob Dufort, and Ross Blouin to name a few. Though I see them only occasionally, perhaps at a Thanksgiving Day football game or a class reunion, our talk invariably centers around what fun we had rather than the victories and championships. Thus, my experiences were probably not unlike so many who played inter-scholastic sports in the 1960s. It was all so low-key then; it truly was an age of innocence in high school sports.

My high school coaches, like coaches everywhere, wanted to win games. But they also accepted the challenge of guiding young people during a formative period in their lives. They realized that none of us were going to be pro or even collegiate athletes and they maintained a level of respect for what sports at that level should be about. They honored the fact that participation, fun, teamwork and transmitting a love for the game were more important than getting another victory in the win column. I give them credit for subduing their own egos and resisting the all-consuming temptation of winning at all costs. I also acknowledge them for realizing that it only takes a bit of planning to see that everybody on a roster is involved with some minimal level of playing time.

Why can't most scholastic coaches understand that distributing some playing time to all varsity performers is as important today as it was back in my era? I think that much of it has to do with the fact that winning and material gain has become everything. It has polluted our sports landscape at the scholastic level and it now threatens to ruin youth sports as well.

It is remarkable to me how innocent and unsophisticated inter-scholastic athletics were while I was growing up. Things are clearly different now. At both the JV and varsity levels, too many kids ride the bench because winning might be jeopardized. Coaches think that it is too risky to play a less talented kid so they rarely construct a creative plan to get the bottom of their bench into games. As a result, parents become frustrated and the situation in the stands becomes poisonous. Parents grumble and they backstab; they become "playing time police," ready to pounce on the coach if their child has been slighted.

At times, I am more sympathetic to parents than I am to coaches. Having done a fair amount of coaching I know that it doesn't take much in the way of playing time to keep kids involved and their parents happy over the course of a sports season. On the other hand, I also understand that some parents may be viewing an athletic scholarship down the road and anything that impedes progress toward that pot of gold sends them into a tailspin. Although parental scholarship aspirations may be unrealistic in many cases, they often translate into added pressure on the coach to play the best players most of the time.

Not surprisingly, I see too many kids quitting early in their high school athletic careers. Or, if they do make it to the varsity level they invariably quit midway through the season. Why continue to be a part of a team if you are little more than fodder for practices? At one time I bought into the notion that this was just normal attrition and part of the accepted culture of scholastic sports. However, now I am more convinced that much of it is due to the pervasive-win-at all-costs ethic and the scholarship chase that overwhelms sports at every turn.

Just where does that destructive win-at-all-costs ethic come from anyway and why is it so pervasive? Let's face it, interscholastic sports have become the minor leagues of our sports culture. High school athletics were catapulted out of the age of innocence when the decision was made to turn interscholastic sports into a mini version of the pro and collegiate game. With the advent of extensive playing schedules requiring significant travel, and the creation of elaborate state playoffs that are lucrative money-making endeavors for revenue sports like football and basketball, interscholastic sports lost their original purpose long ago.

I'd like to think that we can return to that more innocent time by making significant reforms in sports. However, I am skeptical that this will ever happen when I see how commercial influences are also corrupting the games. High school contests are routinely televised in many parts of the country and even pay per view seems to be finding a niche for those who can't get enough of interscholastic competition. The resulting revenue streams for state high school athletic associations are significant. In fact, in some areas of the country those profits are essential for continuing state playoffs in other nonrevenue sports programs. Sadly, the youth and amateur levels of sports are also following suit with televised playoffs for Little League Baseball and Pop Warner Football.

So, what is the goal now of scholastic sports? Is it fun, fitness, teamwork, and participation or has it turned instead to winning games, making profits, and going after athletic scholarships? Scholastic sports were once pure and uncontaminated. They were considered to be one of the last outposts for amateurism. Now, they have mutated into a dangerous semiprofessional state. I am afraid that the best parts of interscholastic sports are over; they have quickly faded to the point of near extinction.

The goals and ethics of my time, the dark ages of sports, appear to be about as useful and relevant today as horse and buggy transportation on our super highways. Is it possible to save any of this and return interscholastic sports to what they once were, or are we at the final stages of a death watch? Maybe we can reform sports with some concerted changes—a national uprising of sorts. But this could require a cultural revolution comparable to tearing down the Berlin wall and the fall of communism. Until that time, we are locked into a system in which we often bring out the worst in parents, coaches and our young athletes. We must be prepared for more of this unless we make some dramatic reforms in the American system of sports.

5

Throwbacks

A frequently used word in sports these days is "throwback." It often refers to the burgeoning market for jerseys, caps, logos, and other memorabilia from the professional leagues of the 1940s, 1950s and 1960s. The term throwback is also used to describe athletes of an earlier period in time who loved to play sports for the sheer enjoyment of the game, who exemplified the highest level of dedication, dignity, and sportsmanship, and who would run through a wall for their teammates. These were characteristics of an older generation of sports enthusiasts—my generation.

Throwback athletes want to win but they don't care so much about individual success nor are they caught up in the hoopla surrounding sports. They are the guys who are the first to come to practice and the last to leave, they slide headfirst into first base, they practice as hard as they play, they never take a night off, they dive on the court for loose balls, they grab the rebounds and dish out assists, and they do the dirty work as interior linemen. In team sports, their goal is to compete hard and to coordinate their efforts with other players in order to achieve team success. In short, they make everyone else on the team look good because of their unselfish play. Throwbacks are a dying breed in a sports environment that often promotes individual accomplishment over team success. Fortunately, I know a few throwbacks from my town, and two of them grew up in my own household.

My youngest son Mark was a classic throwback athlete. Having sampled many different sports as he grew up, he eventually arrived at basketball and golf as his favorites. He played on the varsity high school golf team beginning in his eighth grade year and played varsity basketball starting in his sophomore season.

In basketball, Mark did all of the dirty work: rebounding, assist making, execution of solid man-to-man defense, and scoring when needed. The well coached and overachieving teams he played on were always very competitive but he was forced to play out of position much of his basketball career. He was only 6' 2" tall and often had to play center or power forward when his true position was off guard or small forward.

Mark accepted the challenge of playing where the team needed him and he always came through. One game in particular stands out in my mind. In the semifinals of the Suburban Council Championship of his senior year, he scored 28 points and had 23 rebounds in a double-overtime game in which his team won. Though he typically averaged around 15 points and 10 rebounds a game, the team needed more from him that evening. Had anyone kept track of assists, I am certain that he probably would have qualified for what is known as a triple-double. Had anyone measured blocked shots, steals, or diving for loose balls, I am sure that he would have also led in those important but unrecognized categories. In short, he put the team on his back that night and did everything he could possibly do to put his team on top.

What is most remarkable to me about my son Mark's high school basketball career is that he performed in such a low-key, unselfish way. Not once did I see him check to see how many points he scored or whether he was featured in the newspaper or during television sports highlights. Never did I see him exhibit unsportsmanlike behavior. Not a single time did I see him question a referee's call or a coach's decision. Not once was he unsupportive of a teammate, regardless of the situation.

My older son John was also a throwback athlete. He sampled a large number of sports during his youth days before arriving at football and track and field in high school.

During his high school football days, John was a two-way performer on the offensive and defensive lines. He played these unglamorous positions in a workmanlike and steady fashion. The teams he played on during that period had success running the ball and it was due in large measure to his performance in the trenches of the game of football. It is a worn-out cliché that this is where football games are won and lost, but nothing could be more accurate. I remember a number of times where he would make an initial block and then make another one down-field in order to spring a back for additional yardage. On defense, he was a good run stopper and also an effective pass rusher. I remember several times when he made an important quarterback sack on the other side of the field after having shed several blockers. His second effort was amazing; he never gave up on a play until the whistle was blown.

Indeed, the success of his teams during that period of the mid-1990s depended upon his dedication to performing his position well.

John never complained about not being in the limelight. He accepted it as part of the normal unassuming role that offensive and defensive linemen play in the ultimate team game in our sports culture. Win or lose, he was satisfied after each game that he had given everything to his team. His even temperament prevented him from becoming too elated with victory or too dejected with defeat. He was the perfect antidote and role model for younger players, many of whom were taken away with themselves or were too swept up in their own accomplishments and egos.

John's unselfish team attitude also spilled over into his high school track and field days. A discus thrower and shot putter, John would make sure that he supported his teammates when his own events weren't being staged. He didn't dwell on his own achievements and then just leave but rather he would root for the rest of his team in other track and field events. This indicated that he truly understood what being a part of a team was all about.

Throwback athletes aren't afraid to play a number of sports during their athletic training. They realize that specializing in one sport at an early age can actually have negative effects on their athletic development. They understand that playing a variety of different sports requiring different skills and different muscle groups can only make them better as elite athletes down the road.

One person who fits the above mold to perfection is a boy I observed in athletics from the time he was a youngster all the way through his college years. Kevin Russell was a good friend of my two boys and he exemplified all of the qualities that you would want to see in a true throwback. Though soccer was his main sport and his first love, he also was a superb basketball and tennis player while in high school. He played all three of these sports with distinction and was always a varsity player that made everyone around him better by virtue of his unselfish and intelligent play. No matter what the occasion, he always came to play. His competitiveness and physical and mental toughness was a joy to watch. In fact, had there not been scheduling conflicts, he also would have excelled at baseball and golf. Skilled at both of these sports in his younger days, he played them recreationally instead of competitively once he got to high school.

I can honestly say that I enjoyed every minute of watching my two boys and their friends playing sports during their development. Although those times ended for me as a parent a few years back, I continue to go to interscholastic sports contests in the area to support the kids of other parents that I know. I savor the moments when I occasionally see throw-back players but their numbers seem to be steadily dwindling. I am overjoyed when I see teams win that don't necessarily have the most talented players but instead have throwback kids who have learned to subdue their own egos and are driven instead by the team ethic. When this occurs, credit must be given in three places: to the kids for under-standing the essence of sports; to coaches who, in spite of the enormous odds against them, have fostered the team ethic and know how to mold an unselfish and hardworking attitude in their players; and to parents for understanding that the sports lives of their kids represent much more than just going after an athletic scholarship or winning games. These things don't just happen automatically; it takes hard work to pre-vent the overpowering tides of our present sports culture from eroding the essence of athletics.

One of my favorite throwback athletes of all time recently retired. John Stockton of the NBA Utah Jazz played 19 seasons with his team and recorded NBA records for assists (15,806) and steals (3,265). In 1996 he was named one of the "50 Greatest Players in NBA History." Stock-ton, who was described by many as being uncomfortable with his super-star status, always avoided the limelight and anything that approached controversy. He was an unemotional leader who never questioned his coach and always led by example. His hustle, court savvy, and complete game were a marvel to watch. Karl Malone, his longtime teammate, had this to say about him: "I used to have a coach who said 'Make your team-mate an All-Star.' That's what he tried to do every night. There will not be another one." In their own way, I think that this is what Mark Svare, John Svare, and Kevin Russell did during their athletic careers. Their intense desire to be team players helped all those around them to be better athletes.

Throwback jerseys are becoming more popular all the time but throwback athletes are vanishing quickly as team sports become more about "me" instead of "we." Just because you wear the jersey, it doesn't mean that you are a team player. If you need proof, go to most any local high school athletic contest and watch how a few athletes dominate the action while everyone else stands around uninvolved. I feel lucky to have experienced some of the last vestiges of throwbacks and I am proud that my kids and some of their friends were certifiable members of that rare club.

Because the negative forces of our present sports culture are so pervasive, we should not expect the declining development of throwback players to reverse itself any time soon. Therefore, in the meantime, we should treasure the few opportunities we have to view young athletes that are really team players and exhibit high levels of sportsmanship and dignity. Get out there and root hard for them because the chances are good that they will someday be referred to as the dinosaurs of sports— extinct and only seen in books on ancient sports history.

Part Two

SERVING OUR YOUTH

The available data indicate that misguided parents and coaches help perpetuate the idea of the "Rocky" story when the reality is that they have almost as good a chance to win the lottery as to guide a child into professional sports. Moreover, this attitude sends an unspoken message that participating in sports is not worth anything unless the participant can parlay that into a paying job.

Chuck Yesalis and Virginia Cowart, *The Steroids Game*

———————

In a world where high school athletes have started bypassing college to jump directly to the pros, the attention paid to youth sports grows ever more astonishing. The Little League World Series is televised live on ABC; Vegas takes bets on the game. The Pop Warner Super Bowl—National championship held every year in Orlando—is broadcast on ESPN. The trickling-down of professionalism from college to high school and now onto the sandlot has fostered ugly consequences. A Little League pitcher in the Bronx employs a fake birth certificate to lead his team to a title. A hockey father in Massachusetts kills a rival father in a fistfight.

Robert Powell, *We Own This Game*

———————

We're taking children and making them professionals. We're stealing their childhood. Childhood was supposed to be a preparation, not a full performance.

Alvin Rosenfield, *The Overscheduled Child*

Kids. What is more precious or important to all of us? As parents, educators, and coaches, we are all working to find ways to prepare youngsters to live in the twenty-first century. Yet, time and again, we witness children being abused in both blatant and subtle ways by the very people who profess to love and care for them.

Fred Engh, *Why Johnny Hates Sports*

6

Forgotten Values of the Game

I played sports as a young person because it was fun and it gave me an opportunity to be around my friends. I also loved the team nature of the games that I played. The feeling of accomplishing something as a group was more satisfying to me than the feeling of achieving a personal goal. I also remember the respect that I had for my coaches, umpires, and officials, as well as my teammates and opponents. And finally, I don't ever remember my parents vocalizing a single negative word about how I played nor do I remember them berating a coach, official, or player. That was a long time ago and things have changed since the 1950s and 1960s.

The core values of sportsmanship, ethics, and teamwork are under siege and are eroding quickly. They are forgotten values of the game and they have taken a back seat in our present sports culture. This conclusion comes from observations of my own immediate sports environment. I have witnessed the following incidents in my area of Upstate New York:

- a Pop Warner Football coach slapping a boy across the face for failing to make a tackle in a game.
- a high school football coach pushing a referee to the ground because he disagreed with a penalty call.
- a scholastic basketball player grabbing the arm of an opposing player, twisting it, and then slamming the player against a concrete wall breaking his other arm.

- a parent running out on a football field just after the completion of a high school game and verbally accosting the head coach for not playing his son.
- a mother of a youth basketball player kicking the opposing coach in the shins after a close game in which her son's team had lost.
- a high school basketball player purposely head butting an opposing player and breaking his nose.
- a high school football coach purposely running up the score against a weaker opponent so as to improve the highlight film for his highly recruited halfback.
- a youth basketball player spitting in the face of an opposing player following the completion of a game.
- a Pop Warner Football coach lying about the age and weight of one of his players so as to enable him to play in a game.
- a youth basketball coach yelling so intensely at one of his fifth grade players that it made him cry and leave the game.
- a high school football player repeatedly talking trash to one of his opponents to the point where he was tossed from the game.
- a Little League parent jumping onto the playing field and verbally accosting an umpire that was 14 years of age.
- a high school basketball coach pouring it on in retaliation for a drubbing at the hands of the same team several years earlier.

Another core value of sports, that of teamwork, also seems to be on its way to extinction. I recently sat through a scholastic basketball game that became more and more difficult to watch as the contest went on. On almost every offensive possession there was one pass and a shot. There was no effort to get everyone involved in the game by executing a number of passes nor was there an attempt to make good screens away from the ball. One or two players dominated the action and neither team executed very good team defense. The level of individualism on both ends of the court far exceeded any semblance of teamwork. Parents and other spectators loudly groaned about the selfish play. The situation deteriorated to a point where players on both teams were squabbling with each other about sharing the ball and sharing the responsibility of playing team defense. Not wanting to watch any more of a game that lacked the core elements of what team sports are all about, I exited the gym several minutes into the second half of the contest.

I wish I could say that this was the first time that I have left a scholastic basketball game before its finish because it did not fit my philosophy of how the sport should be played. However, I am finding it increasingly difficult to attend high school basketball contests when I know the game will be dominated by a few slightly more skilled individuals going about their business while everyone else stands around and watches. It is just not what the game is supposed to be about.

Every year I try to attend the Suburban Council Basketball Championships in our area. Part of the tradition of this game is the recognition of all-stars from around the league during a half-time ceremony at mid-court. As the players are named one by one and awarded plaques for their accomplishments, I have come to expect that the selections will bear little resemblance to the players I would have chosen.

Voted upon by the coaches of the league, the all-stars usually have one common characteristic: they have all scored a lot of points in the league. Beyond that, however, I usually see little evidence in the all-star picks of unselfish play, hustles for loose balls, defensive skills, assist-making, and rebounding—characteristics that usually convert to team success in basketball games and are equally important in a well-rounded player. A number of the selections typically consist of players who launched between 20 and 30 shots a game and who rarely played any defense or only occasionally exhibited team play by giving up the ball for an assist. Not surprisingly, many of these players are members of losing teams. Missing from the team are players who could do it all by scoring, defending, rebounding, and passing the ball to open teammates for easy scoring opportunities. Though these forgotten individuals tend to score fewer points, I select them on my hypothetical all-star squad each year because they are much more effective in helping their teammates simultaneously to win games and enjoy the experience of playing a team game such as basketball.

One need look no further than the NBA to see how far this ugly trend has evolved. With its endless series of clear out and isolation plays, the NBA game no longer resembles James Naismith's team game that we once loved and appreciated for its beauty and simplicity. It has become a game of one-on-ones and every player seems to be able to beat every other player with ease.

The absence of team play and the elevation of individual skills is not limited to basketball or to higher levels of sports participation. Little Leaguers make all-star teams because they can hit homeruns or throw a pitch faster than the next player but rarely do you see the total package of skills including hitting, base running, throwing, positioning, and defense as a part of the selection process. Players no longer play for team goals and championships but rather they play for themselves and the presumed benefits of individual accomplishment.

What drives the trend toward individual accomplishment at the expense of team play is the immense pressure that is placed upon athletes at all ages to specialize and train vigorously for the material benefits of sports. Scholarships and pro contracts have replaced playing the sport for the sheer fun and enjoyment of the game. With this warped value system in place it is hardly surprising that team sports have often become the disorganized free-for-alls that we frequently witness today.

One of my favorite sports books is one that was written by former NBA great and U.S. Senator, Bill Bradley. The book is entitled *Values of the Game* and in it Bradley talks about the core qualities that make a great basketball player: passion for the game, discipline, selflessness, respect, perspective, courage, leadership, responsibility, resilience, and imagination. His description of what it takes to be a championship team is one of the most enlightened ones I have ever read in sports:

> Part of the beauty and mystery of basketball rests in the variety of team requirements. Championships are not won unless a team has forged a high degree of unity, attainable only through the selflessness of each of its players. It is in the moves that the uninitiated often don't see that the sport has its deepest currents: the perfect screen, the purposeful movement away from the ball, the well-executed boxout, the deflected pass. Statistics don't always measure teamwork; holding the person you're guarding scoreless doesn't show up in your stats. But, when you're "taking care of business" you're working to produce a championship team, and "we won" comes to mean more and lasts longer than the ephemeral "I scored." Solidarity becomes an essential part of your professionalism. The society we live in glorifies individualism, what Ross Perot used to champion with the expression "eagles don't flock." Basketball teaches a different lesson: that untrammeled individualism destroys the chance for achieving victory. Players must have sufficient self-knowledge to take the long view—to see that what any one player can do alone will never equal what a team can do together.

Sportsmanship, ethics, and team play at one time represented some of the core values of sports participation. Sadly irrelevant in today's sports culture, they have been replaced with a lack of civility, declining adherence to principled actions, and elevated individualism.

Can we return sports to the values upon which they were originally founded or will they continue to deteriorate at a rapid pace? The jury is still out on that determination. However, my hunch is that a return to those essential values may take a massive reordering of our priorities and a rethinking of how we conduct sports in our present society.

7

On to Disneyworld

For a period of about four years from 1987–1991, my two boys were involved with Pop Warner Football in Bethlehem, New York. During that time, I served the organization in a variety of capacities, from fund-raising to serving as an assistant coach and board member. My kids had a positive experience, learned the basics of the game, and had fun in what could be described as a fairly low-key program.

The normal routine of the season consisted of preseason practice in the month of August with games starting in early September and continuing through the fall. Practices were usually held for 90 minutes a day Monday through Thursday with a game on Saturday or Sunday. The norm was an eight game schedule with playoffs culminating in a super bowl game. For those teams not involved in the playoffs, the season ended with a "fun bowl" game against a team from the area with a similar record. Generally, everything would wrap up the week before Thanksgiving. Importantly, Pop Warner emphasized that every player had to play a set number of plays in each game that was monitored by commissioners from each team. In this way, playing time was almost equalized and every player felt like a part of the team.

Pop Warner Football is a national youth football organization that began in 1929. It presently teaches the game to over 350,000 young kids between the ages of 7 to 16 each year. Each division of play is divided according to age and weight with a special older/lighter category for each division: Mitey-Mite (ages 7–9, 45–85 pounds; older/lighter age 10, 45–65 pounds); Junior Peewee (ages 8–11, 55–95 pounds; older/lighter age 11, 55–75 pounds); Peewee (ages 9–11, 70–110 pounds; older/lighter age 12, 70–90 pounds); Junior Midget (ages 10–12, 80–125 pounds; older/lighter age 13, 80–105 pounds); Midget (ages 11–14, 95–145 pounds; older/lighter age 15, 95–125 pounds). Gradewise, this corresponded to roughly fourth through eighth grade with kids in most areas of the country opting to play at the scholastic level once they are freshmen in high school.

Pop Warner Football recently has instituted some educational requirements that make it stand out in contrast to other youth sports organizations. The program, called Pop Warner Little Scholars, Inc. (PWLS), requires Pop Warner Football participants to perform adequately in the classroom before being permitted to play. Proof of satisfactory progress in school is required and a 2.0/70 percent minimum grade point average is necessary. For this initiative, Pop Warner deserves a great deal of credit since no other youth sports organization presently has an academic requirement as a cutoff for participation.

After having been away from the program for a significant period of time, Pop Warner Football was once again on my radar screen in the fall and winter of 2002. A local midget team from South Troy, New York, won the super bowl in our area just before Thanksgiving. The team then played in the East Coast Regional Championship at Lock Haven University in Pennsylvania and emerged victorious. The National Championship Semifinals and Finals were held in Disney's Wide World of Sports Complex in Lake Buena Vista, Florida, the second week of December. The team won its semifinal game by defeating the Dale City Cowboys from Virginia 14 to 6 and then won the Championship game by defeating the Mexicali Halcones from California 19–7. The two games played in Florida were on a Tuesday and a Friday, therefore necessitating that the players on the team miss most of the school week. Yes, that is right, 11 to14 year old kids (sixth to eighth graders) missed almost a week of school to play in a National Pop Warner Football championship tournament! The football season for these young kids was much longer than most scholastic or collegiate football seasons.

After reading about this in the local newspaper and reflecting upon it, I began to wonder about who was more responsible for allowing something as stupid as this to occur: the parents and coaches for allowing the kids to go or Pop Warner Football itself for structuring a national tournament right smack in the middle of the academic year. Regardless, it makes no sense at all for 11 to 14 year-old kids to be missing that much time from school to take part in a meaningless youth football tournament.

In an extensive write-up about the game (with pictures) in the *Albany Times-Union* newspaper, the coach of the South Troy team, Joe McNall said: "They do what they gotta do to win. That's been their story all year. Take it one game at a time. That's what I preach, and that's what we did." Coach McNall and sportswriter Kristy Shonka made no comments in the article regarding the class time missed because of the playoffs. I guess winning Pop Warner championships and the culture of Disneyworld has a way of making you forget about other more important objectives in life, like education.

Upon returning from their success in Florida, the South Troy team was greeted with a noisy and crowded reception at the Albany International Airport. Local television cameras captured the momentous event and interviewed players and coaches as they exited from their flight. It had all the feel of a victorious NFL team returning from a Superbowl win. Once again, as expected, there were no comments by anyone regarding the time away from classes and how it was managed. Most assuredly, the focus instead was on the "win."

I also thought about the hypocrisy displayed by Pop Warner Football. On the one hand, the organization required a minimum scholastic score for players to participate and on the other hand they snubbed their nose at education by holding a tournament in such a way that kids would have to miss close to a week of school. It is bad enough when collegiate athletes must miss time from classes in order to participate in athletic contests, but when very young Pop Warner Football players are placed in the same predicament it is totally unnecessary and unjustifiable.

Pop Warner Football clearly has changed some of its emphasis since my involvement 10 years ago. Apparently, now it is necessary to have a national championship in order to crown one team as a winner. If the school year happens to get in the way then so what. This is a case of the tail wagging the dog and sports controlling education.

Where are our priorities and haven't we seen this before? College football and basketball players miss classes because of TV arranged weeknight games. The NCAA Final Four basketball tournament locks up players for up to three weeks right in the middle of an academic semester.

Unfortunately, we don't seem to care but we should because it is just another example of how sports are eroding academics. Incidents like the Pop Warner championships send the message loud and clear to parents and kids that education is secondary to competing in sports. This is wrong and only a major reconfiguration and deemphasis of our sports culture will help us to put things back in perspective.

8

Backyard Reform

In 1990, I led a group of parents in my community to create the Bethlehem Basketball Club. Designed to develop basketball skills in fifth through eighth graders, the club emphasized equal playing time and age-appropriate playing rules. Open to all kids, male and female, the club was a "hit" in the community and immediately became a Sunday ritual from November through March.

Once the "house" or intramural league was created, the next logical step seemed to be the creation of a competitive travel team league. In 1991, I co-founded the Capital District Youth Basketball League (CDYBL) with two friends from the Capital Region: Joe D'Agostino from Amsterdam and Vince Bianchi from Niskayuna. Formed for travel basketball teams from the fifth through the eighth grades, the league today consists of 16 communities with a total of 64 teams and over 800 players. Many talented players in the Capital District end up playing in the league during their early formative years. The best high school players in our area are a product of the league and a good number of them have gone on to play in college.

I have stayed involved as president of the CDYBL to make sure that the goals and philosophy of the club would not substantially change. The league was structured to be developmental in nature. Thus, less restrictive playing rules were phased in over a period of years to a point where players, by the eighth grade, were engaging in "real" basketball equivalent to what was seen at the varsity high school level of competition. Several other guidelines were also important such as a participation rule that required everyone on a roster to play in every game, a rule stating that only man to man defenses would be allowed at the fifth and sixth grade levels, and a rule stating that pressing at the fifth and sixth grade levels would be limited to certain times of a game.

In contrast, seventh and eighth graders were allowed to play any type of offense and defense and any type of press at any time during a game.

We were all proud that we had fashioned a mini-version of high school basketball. The schedule included regular season games, preseason tournaments, a Martin Luther King weekend tournament and an end-of-season single elimination playoff tournament modeled after high school sectional play. At this time, I naively thought our league provided a flawless developmental basketball program.

The league functioned well and the kids and parents in the early years had wonderful fun together enjoying the games. Lifelong bonds of friendships were formed with many of the families during these years. Importantly, the vast majority of adults had things in perspective and the right goals in mind. However, as the years went on, the balance began to shift and increasingly there were problems. Coaches and parents began to prioritize winning over playing time and, not surprisingly, their behavior during games was frequently out of bounds and unsportsmanlike. Gradually the fun had been transformed into a very disturbing, negative situation.

An example of this new climate occurred during a close tournament game one season. A coach for one of the league teams verbally abused a referee during the entire game. He was given a technical foul during the contest but his unsportsmanlike and abusive behavior only escalated. When the game ended, the coach charged both referees, got up in their faces in front of the players and parents, and proceeded to rip apart the referees for their perceived poor officiating. The coach was awarded another technical foul at the end of the game, which results in an automatic two-game suspension according to our league rules. At that point, other parents became incensed from both teams and it was apparent that World War III was about to begin. Tournament officials wisely called the police and order was restored. However, considerable damage was done in that an ugly situation involving the important issue of sportsmanship was allowed to envelop referees, players, parents, and coaches. This situation was especially upsetting to me since our league had such an outstanding record of sportsmanship until this point.

Following a routine inquiry, our board informed the president of the club that his coach would have to sit out the next two games and they would have to have another parent take over the team. Two days later our board was informed that the coach refused and was seeking a court injunction to prevent his club from playing any additional games in the league unless he was reinstated immediately.

In spite of the fact that I personally received anonymous hate mail from parents in that community as well as harassing telephone calls from parents and lawyers, our board stuck to its guns and insisted that the coach sit out the required two games. Furthermore, though our board fully agreed with their position, we were under considerable pressure by our officiating group to stay the course and not soften our stance. As it turned out, the threat of the court injunction by the coach caused the club to cancel all of its remaining games in the league and sadly, approximately 60 kids (four teams) in that community had their basketball season terminated earlier than it should have been.

Several weeks later during a contentious three hour league meeting, the club administrators from this community were offered a choice: they could continue in the league if the coach was no longer affiliated with the club, or they could find another league to enter their teams. At one point our board informed the president of the offending club that the actions of their coach were an embarrassment to their club, the league, and most importantly, the kids who play the games. Furthermore, the club president was informed that it would not be tolerated in our league and that the coach had to be terminated in order to head off future problems down the road.

Over the ensuing summer, our board continued to receive pressure from this community to back off. In addition, our referee assignor received hate mail and threats that sought to undermine his status and integrity as a top college and high school referee in the area. Our board continued to hold its ground and prior to our first fall meeting, we were informed by administrators of the community that they had permanently tossed the coach from their program.

Though I breathed a sigh of relief, I was incensed by the fact that this immature adult had threatened to bring our league to a screeching halt. Since this incident, I have asked myself many times how a rational human being could have acted in such an irresponsible manner. The answer to that question is simple. The behavior exhibited by that person is probably inside of us all. More important, however, our current sports culture, with its emphasis on winning and athletic success as opposed to participation, development of skills, and sportsmanship, can make fools of us all.

When I founded the CDYBL some years ago, the last thing on my mind was that I would be fighting off coaches and parents whose lawyers were threatening court injunctions. I didn't really think that it was part of my job description; I preferred to spend most of my time improving things for the kids and making it the best possible experience they could have playing a great sport. I was so infuriated at what had happened I almost threw up my hands at that point and quit the job as president. Had I done that, however, I would have caved in to the negative culture of sports. Instead, I stuck with it and used it as a stimulus for making changes in the league.

We began to focus on our playing rules as a source of the problems we were experiencing. With an overemphasis on winning, our league was promoting the outbursts of out-of-control coaches and parents. Additionally, with winning the primary objective, playing time problems were becoming more of an issue. Increasingly, we were receiving reports that some kids were seeing only a few minutes of playing time in a game.

As a preventative step, we began to mandate that coaches in the league attend a preseason seminar in which we would go over "dos" and "don'ts" of coaching. We focused on explaining the developmental nature of the league and we also emphasized sportsmanship and playing time issues. Also, we spent considerable time on the proper way to interact with referees. The feedback from these preseason meetings was encouraging; we believed that we had set a positive tone for promoting the values and mission of the league. Also, many coaches told us that they found the meeting to be very helpful in planning their upcoming seasons.

In spite of these prevention measures, the ugly situations that we were often forced to deal with got worse each year. On top of these distressing incidents, I noticed that many of the kids really did not have a strong foundation in the fundamentals of the game. Coaches were spending more time on complicated, advanced strategies and little time teaching basic skills. By the time they got to high school, their basketballs fundamentals were deficient and their team ethic was all but absent. As a result, I became so disturbed by these trends, I began to question the structure and mission of the league.

At league meetings I began to vocalize some of my concerns but frequently the debates over playing time rules and defensive and offensive philosophies would get bogged down in the overriding plan of many coaches and that was to play and win as many games and tournaments as possible. Frustrated by these developments, but not having the ammunition to back up my claims that we had built a monster in our own backyards, I began to read as many books on youth sports as I could possibly get my hands on. Many were helpful but only one truly made a difference. A book by former U Penn and NBA player Bob Bigelow entitled *Just Let the Kids Play: How to Stop Other Adults from Ruining Your Child's Fun and Success in Youth Sports* completely changed my outlook on youth basketball. Most important, his book showed that well-intentioned adults like me can make mistakes in youth sports when they structure developmental leagues that turn out in the end to be inappropriate for young kids.

I wrote to Bigelow and subsequently talked with him on the phone many times. We exchanged emails and met in Springfield one day where we talked over lunch for four hours. My intuition had been correct about the needed reforms for the league and Bigelow proceeded to advise me about how I could pull it off.

Armed with more knowledge and a better understanding of what goals are achievable in youth basketball, I wrote a letter in March, 2003 to the 16 community representatives to the league. In the letter, I detailed a proposal that I believed would transform our league into what it should be and that is a developmentally appropriate league for young kids who were still maturing physically, emotionally, and socially. Portions of that letter are excerpted here:

> I believe that the CDYBL is at a crossroads. We have a choice. We can continue things as they are and delude ourselves into thinking that we are doing right by the kids. Or we can take the bull by the horns, make some changes, and end up delivering a much better basketball experience for our players. I want you to think of only one thing as you consider my proposals: Will these changes help CDYBL players to enjoy the game more and develop their skills to a higher level?
>
> *My observations.* We have a great league and in many respects we are light years ahead of other areas of New York State and other parts of the country. We have lots of really dedicated coaches year in and year out, an executive board that cares about the game and the players, club reps who do their jobs diligently, and an unbelievable referee assigner who gets us the best officials for our games. These are the positives and I don't want anyone to lose sight of these things.
>
> At the same time, we have problems that I believe are systemic. In other words, the negative features of our league are a result of our playing rules, our philosophy, and our organizational structure. I believe that these things have to change if we are to

make progress in structuring a league that has as its principal mission the development of basketball skills in young kids.

I watch many scholastic games every year and frequently the vast majority of the players are CDYBL graduates. My observations indicate that basic basketball skills aren't getting substantially better. Dribbling, passing, shooting, rebounding, defense, moving without the ball, setting screens, playing as a team, etc. are no better now than they were when I first started watching hoop in this area 23 years ago. The games are dominated by a few players; as skills have gone down, so has the team nature of the game. In spite of the fact that the teams I have watched have superb long-time coaches, many of the games are hard to watch.

The coaches aren't at fault because they can only deal with what they are given. And, what they frequently have are kids who haven't learned the basic skills at the lower levels. This is due in part to the fact that our CDYBL system promotes a style of coaching that is, at times, antithetical to teaching kids the fundamentals of the game.

There is little question that we have become too concerned with strategy (the winning of a game) and far less concerned about teaching the elements (basic skills) of the game. We have seventh and eighth grade coaches using their limited practice time to teach all kinds of zone presses as well as exotic defenses such as triangle and two zones, match-up zones, and box and ones to defend against players on other teams. Instead, they should be using valuable practice time for the teaching of fundamentals. All of this translates into a pretty poor product by the time our players get to the high school level. In fact, I think I could build a strong case that our scholastic players are no better or perhaps even worse now than they were before the CDYBL started.

Our obsession with playing games and winning is also reflected in the problems that we have when coaches and parents become overinvolved in the competitive aspects of the games. They lose their cool and exhibit all kinds of unsportsmanlike behavior. To make matters worse, coaches begin to shortchange playing time for some players in favor of winning. Even the best coaches in our league can succumb to this ethic since our system breeds it. Just last week I had to deal with yet another case of a coach popping his cork and getting booted from a game. Quite frankly, given the emphasis that we have on regular season games determining seeding for playoffs and then the single elimination tournament, I am surprised that we don't have more problems than we do. The coaches aren't responsible. Rather, a system that emphasizes winning in contrast to skill development is to blame.

I am not singling out our program alone. We are no different from countless programs in other parts of the country when it comes to youth basketball. However, even though the game got its start here in the United States, it is not advancing like it is in other countries, especially in Europe, Australia, and parts of South America. The fundamentals of our players just aren't that good and the team nature of the game has suffered. The highlight film mentality has taken over. Just take a look at Team USA from the World Championships last summer. Some of our best NBA players finished fifth! These were guys that were products of a system in which we ask our kids to play over a hundred games a year between scholastic ball, AAU and travel teams like ours. The focus is on games and not on the fundamentals. It is no surprise to me that European, South American, Australian, and now Chinese players are increasingly turning up on college and NBA rosters. Quite simply, they are better all-around basketball players with better skills and a better team ethic.

I sent all of you an article from a Canadian National team coach in which the point was made that we need to stress practicing of fundamentals and back off on games. The analogy was made between teaching a math class or a science class and the amount of class teaching that must be done before you have a test. In basketball, the classroom teaching is the practice session and the test is the game. We have way too many games and far too few practices. As the article stated: "If you were teaching a math class or a science class would you teach 2 days a week and give the class a test 4 days a week? Of course you wouldn't—because the students would not have the base academic fundamentals to pass the test. You would be setting them up for failure!" But this is precisely what we do in our league. We set up our players for failure down the road. If we think that we are going to develop better basketball players in this way—by emphasizing games (tests) over practices (classroom teaching)—then we are seriously deluding ourselves. One thing I can tell you is that the other countries, the ones that are becoming highly successful at the international level, don't do things like we do.

I was in Australia at this time last year and I saw firsthand how they do things. They practice fundamentals a lot and it is paying off. Just look at how foreign teams are beating up on us now in international competition. The reason that they are so far ahead of us now is because of their unrelenting pursuit of fundamentals in practices. Games at the youth level are not a focus. As the article states that I sent to you: "We need to play fewer games and practice more. Let's get back to basics: 2 foot stops; pivots; footwork; lay-ups; passing; cutting (back-door; ball cut; basket cut); shooting and lots of it; spacing; triangles. 40 or 50 games don't make kids better; 40 or 50 jump shots, cuts and passes do!"

I say all of this as a person who once bought into the notion hook, line and sinker that if you played a lot of games your players would get better. I was the founder of the Albany City Rocks basketball organization and coached in that program for six years. I wish I had those days back. I know now that all the games we played, all of the weekends in which we played countless games in pool play all over the country, probably didn't help a lot of my players in the development of their skills. Many would have been better off had they practiced taking 200, 2 foot stop, jump shots every day in their driveway. AAU has some value for older kids; it helps them to be seen in meat market tournaments and perhaps get recruited. However, because of sophisticated recruiting services these days, a good player is going to be "discovered" and recruited well before spring, summer, and fall AAU basketball. Again, even for older kids—sophomores and juniors—I don't see much value in the endless number of spring, summer, and fall basketball games that are played. The time would be better spent on strength and agility training and especially the development of basic basketball skills.

I think that we have the potential to be a model basketball program, but it will take some significant changes and we have to think outside the box instead of follow the way things have been done in the past. We can't just say that "this is how it has been done in the past by everybody else" or that "this is how it is done at the varsity level of competition" and pass this off as solid reasoning for continuing a system that is fundamentally flawed. Some of my proposals will be controversial and a bit hard for some to swallow but please remember what I said earlier, think about the kids and their ability to get better in the truly fabulous game that we call basketball.

My recommendations. I have a list of changes—concrete proposals—that I want to be discussed and voted on at our upcoming meeting. Some are symbolic while others are philosophical. They are summarized with commentary below.

1. *We need to change our mission statement.* We need to get rid of the statement in our guidelines that we are a "feeder" program. We should replace this with a statement that says we are a league principally interested in participation and improving basketball skills. The perception now is that kids are anointed at the fifth grade level and they will be the ones playing on the varsity because their dads are coaching them. Let's have a statement that truly reflects what we should be and that is a league that wants to teach the kids the fundamental skills of the game.

2. *We need to insist on man-to-man half court defense and man-to-man full court presses at all levels.* The league must go strictly to man to man at all levels. No zones should be played at any time. Also, no double teaming unless it is in the paint. The greatest basketball minds in the world (Coach K, Bobby Knight, John Wooden, Red Auerbach) have advocated this approach. They have all said that kids should not even be playing zones until they are in high school. Zones inhibit offensive skill development especially in kids that are not physically capable of making a skip pass or even a good chest pass. Zones also inhibit the development of man-to-man defensive skills which provide the basis for the execution of all defenses—even zones—as kids get older.

    We also need to insist on man-to-man presses at all levels. Because our current rules allow pressing of any kind, many games deteriorate rapidly when they are used. When trapping occurs, kids frequently aren't physically equipped to beat it by executing long and difficult passes. The contests become mayhem and we teach nothing about the fundamentals of the game—in fact, we inhibit fundamentals of the game. We need to outlaw any kind of zone press or double teaming. Players have to stick with their man in a press. They can "run and jump" which is vastly different than trapping and double teaming but they cannot double team on or off the ball.

    Quite frankly, I think that the only reason we have permitted half court zones and zone presses in the past is for a coach's ego in the winning of games. Let's take this out of the equation by freeing coaches to spend their game time and practices on the fundamentals instead of spending endless time strategizing on how to execute or attack a half court zone or a full court zone press.

Some will say that this is not true basketball and that seventh and eighth graders should be able to do whatever they want. I don't agree with this at all. We don't allow 7th and 8th graders to drive cars and we don't teach them advanced calculus. The reason we do not is that they are not ready for it. Even seventh and eighth graders, due to their relative physical immaturity, are not ready for zone presses and half court zone defenses.

3. *We need to insist on a minimum playing time rule.* As you know, right now we have a statement in our rules that says that every kid must play in every game but the amount of playing time is up to the coach. This needs to change. I see many cases year after year in which kids get a couple of minutes in a game and that is it. It gets worse as the season goes along and the pressure builds for seedings, winning tournaments, and then winning the single elimination playoffs. Strategizing and winning becomes the focus and player development goes out the window. Our present system breeds this kind of behavior in our coaches.

Kids can't learn the game and they can't enjoy it unless they play and they must play more than they are now. We can't just focus on the kids who are the best players at this level by ignoring playing time. Kids develop at different rates. The kid who isn't a star now may be one in high school. I have seen this time and again and I have experienced it myself. I will never forget one boy who I cut every year as a sixth, seventh, and eighth grader; he ended up making the varsity as a junior and was a key performer when Bethlehem went to Glenns Falls in sectionals a few years back. He developed late—he couldn't get out of his own way when he was in middle school and many wrote him off as I did. He ended up having a good high school and college career.

So, what do we do? I think that the answers are easy. At all levels, we mandate a playing time requirement of meaningful minutes. I define that as at least 12 minutes a game for every game. Most teams have loads of assistant coaches. Our plan should be to have one assistant coach on each team monitor playing time for their own team. The club reps must supervise things and if there are problems then the coach is reprimanded by his club rep. If it continues to a second time, then the coach is tossed from the league.

To accomplish this, we need to increase the available minutes in games by increasing our quarters to 8 minutes (instead of 7). Eight minute quarters are used virtually everywhere. So, this gives a total of 160 possible minutes in a game (5 players on the court at any one time, 8-minute quarters = 160 available minutes) and if you have a 10- or 12-man roster, you should be able to easily accomplish 12 minutes for everybody. At the same time, we should reduce the amount of time between quarters and halves in order to keep on schedule. If we don't have zones, then coaches should no longer need the time they once had to strategize about attacking them/executing them during time-outs and quarter/half breaks.

4. *We need to get rid of all tournaments; we need to replace the single elimination playoffs with an end of year modified jamboree.* We will have a 16-team league next year which means a reasonable 15-game regular season schedule. We will be able to start a bit later and finish a bit earlier. At the end of the year, we will have a modified jamboree at each grade level for East Conference (8 teams) and West Conference (8 teams). Here is how it can be done: Based upon standings, take the top 4 teams in each conference and have them play a round robin (each team gets 3 games) and take the bottom 4 teams of each conference and have them play a round robin (each team gets 3 games). Do this for each grade level. It is 24 games per grade level for a total of 96 games. Presently we play a total of 64 games for our playoffs but only a few teams get most of the playing time. If we go to the pool play modified jamboree format, everybody gets playing time instead of just a few teams advancing and getting the bulk of the games. I would also advocate throwing in a tee-shirt for everybody as well as a pizza party to the extent that we can afford it.

The teaching jamboree at the beginning of the year is one of the best things ever done for our league. It is wonderful and we should keep doing it if we can. I am strongly opposed to tour-naments prior to or over the course of the season, however. Yes, they make money for some clubs but they should not be justi-fied on that basis. You can make money during the end of year jamboree if you host games and you can charge at the door for regular season games if you need to.

The New York State Public School Athletic Association says that a 20-game regular season schedule is enough for fresh-man, JV, and varsity. Modified teams play even fewer games. The most qualified educators in our state and in the country are looking after the health of our kids and what is appropriate and what is not when it comes to athletics. I think that we need to listen to them when it comes to CDYBL athletes. The season of most varsity teams ends after the first round of sectional play so their schedules are only 21 games. So, it is not rational that we play so many games especially when we know that more games do not add up to making better players. I would advocate that coaches use their free time—time they would have used for tournaments and more games—to get people in for clinics for their teams and/or devoting time to the practice of fundamen-tals. You can also partner up with other school districts during vacation times or long weekends and host mini-camps or clin-ics. Your scholastic coaches could serve as instructors with the focus on skills and drills. The time you devote to doing this will be time well spent. It certainly will be better than competing for another tee-shirt or trophy in a tournament.

5. *We need to encourage the development of in-house recreational pro-grams.* Many of our CDYBL programs have solid in-house recre-ational programs in which everybody plays equally and kids learn the fundamentals. However, not every community has this and there are serious problems for those who do not. When the focus in a community is completely on travel basketball, then the pressure to play on such teams becomes enormous. Not sur-prisingly, the focus in these communities is on playing games and winning to the detriment of player development. At the same time, kids are labeled at an early age as either "having it" or "not having it" and a clear message is sent to them in the fourth or fifth grade to go elsewhere and try something else. The problem is, many of them don't have any other place to go

because there is no recreational basketball outlet. I believe that this can be a disaster for many of our communities since they potentially lose out on some very good basketball players.

Having an in-house league takes the pressure off and it also develops players for your program. I have seen countless examples in the past of kids improving their skills after having been cut from a travel team. Many of them improve to such an extent that they ultimately make a travel or scholastic team. Putting together a recreational program is work but the benefits are tremendous. You end up keeping kids interested that otherwise might have quit. And, because of differing maturation rates, these kids ultimately could be your stars down the road. If you give up on them at an early age then everybody in your program potentially loses.

Please share the contents of this letter with your coaches and assistant coaches. Don't hesitate to show it to your athletic directors and your varsity coaches. Discuss with them the points I have made and gauge their feelings regarding my recommendations. All members of our community basketball programs have a significant stake in the future of the league and you should listen carefully to their opinions prior to our meeting.

I know that this has been long winded, but I wanted to make sure that I justified to my basketball colleagues how much I think we need to make changes and why the changes need to be done in a timely fashion. I love the game of basketball and I love the CDYBL for what it has given me in the friends I have made. I am also proud of the fact that we have provided opportunities for young kids to learn the best game on earth. Now we need to take it to the next level and make it better. I am hopeful that you will join with me in accomplishing this goal.

I sent this letter out as an email attachment and it apparently was forwarded far and wide. I heard from many parents and coaches in the CDYBL but I also heard from varsity high school, college, and AAU coaches. For the most part the responses were supportive although there was a small minority of people who still did not really "get it."

Our league meeting several weeks later proved to be productive and gratifying. I found wide agreement and support for my proposals and we approved the major reforms that I advanced in my letter. This was highly satisfying and for the first time, I felt as though we were on the right track in terms of providing a program for the kids in which there would be the right blend of competition, skill development, and fun. The road will be filled with bumps here and there, I am sure. But knowing that we are now focused on more important objectives has calmed my fears for the future.

These events proved to be important ones in my personal journey to reform sports. I realized that before you can start talking about changing sports on a national level, you first must get your own backyard in order. I have tried to do that through my involvement in local and regional programs and, admittedly, it is not easy to do. It involves making the case for change, staying patient and committed, keeping your eye on the ultimate goal, and, most important, getting a coalition of backers to provide support. As tough as it can be, the rewards for our young athletes can be tremendous.

Sports reform will not take place unless it starts in thousands of local communities such as my own in the Capital District of New York. But, it is the personal responsibility of those who shepherd the next generation of athletes to look within themselves and ask, "Are we doing the best that we possibly can for our young athletes?" When I asked that question of myself, I realized that the answer was a resounding "no." Telling the truth about sports first requires that you look at yourself in the mirror. This is what I did and I am much better off for having done it.

9

The Professionalization of Peter

I attend many different sport events over the course of a year and one thing that I especially like to do is to spend time talking with athletes of all different ages. Many of these exchanges have been revealing since they often provide a glimpse into the goals and aspirations of the next generation of athletes. Some of my most memorable conversations have occurred with younger athletes who are still learning about the world and trying to figure out where they fit into the general scheme of life.

An interesting and all too typical conversation took place a number of years ago while I was watching some basketball games at a local youth tournament. The players were 9 and 10 years of age (fifth graders) and the tournament consisted of select teams from 16 different communities in the area. As I sat and watched I was impressed by the high level of play for kids that were so young. The players really knew what they were doing; they executed some simple offenses very well and played pretty good man-to-man defense.

One young boy who caught my eye was a player I'll call Peter. He played the point guard position and was particularly impressive that day. Having the "court sense" of a much older player, he clearly was the floor captain of the team. Not only did he make good decisions by distributing the ball to others when he should, but he had a nice shooting touch for a youngster. I made it a point to talk with him once his game was over.

"You had a pretty good game out there today," I said.

"Thanks," he replied with a sheepish smile on his young face.

"What do you like best about playing basketball?" I inquired.

"It's fun and I like playing with my friends, " he remarked without hesitation. This was soon followed by a disturbing statement from the mouth of one so young. He remarked, "My dad thinks I can get a college athletic scholarship when I am older."

Later that day at the concession stand, his father said to a group of parents, "I think we're looking at a scholarship down the road and I want to position him for it in every way I can. He's been playing travel team since the third grade and he just gets better with each game. That's why I held him back in school as a first grader. That's what everybody does these days to give their kid an advantage when competing for a scholarship."

I kept my eye on Peter through the years as he moved from the youth level to the scholastic ranks. It seemed that his life was filled with basketball and more basketball so that by the time he was in the sixth grade he had fully committed to the sport. He played the game year round from an early age and stopped his other sports and extracurricular activities so that he could more fully concentrate on just one. Additionally, Peter's parents did everything necessary to position their son for further basketball development. This included personal strength trainers, nutritionists, and skill coaches. There was no let up; it was basketball 24/7.

He played on a select AAU basketball team during the spring, summer, and fall and would travel far and wide to play games in regional and national tournaments. I remember his father telling me how expensive and time-consuming it was to do all the traveling, but it was always followed by a statement like: "I know that it will be an investment that will be well worth it in the end because I know that he will have a college scholarship at some point. I won't have to pay a dime for his education."

As time moved on, I noticed that Peter transferred several times to different public and private schools during his middle school and high school years. The moves were never done for academic or social reasons but instead it always revolved around basketball. The word was out that his father was orchestrating the transfers to ensure that his son would be playing at schools where he would get the most playing time at the point guard position, where his father believed that he was best suited. Word had also gotten back to me that Peter's father had become very meddlesome, constantly calling coaches and berating them if he disagreed with how they utilized his son in games.

Much to my dismay, I also learned that teachers at certain schools were giving Peter a needed "boost" here and there when he needed it. Peter struggled in the classroom but always seemed to be the beneficiary of a passing grade to keep him eligible for the court. Summer school also seemed to be a regular fixture in his life. Promoted each year to the next grade, his academic skills significantly lagged behind those of his classmates.

Peter was basically a compliant kid who wouldn't hurt a fly, but as his success in basketball grew he began to enjoy his favored status and at times abused it. This was fostered by some coaches who realized that they couldn't really win unless Peter was on the court. One story that got back to me regarding Peter during his playing days in high school was a report that he arrived late for a game one evening, missed warm-ups, and sat on the end of the bench eating a McDonalds hamburger and fries for his dinner. Instead of benching Peter for the entire game and perhaps giving him a suspension, Peter's coach put him into the game after he finished eating and allowed him to play for the rest of the game!

The pressure placed upon Peter to excel in basketball seemed to escalate with each passing year. Because he spent more and more time on practices, games, traveling, summer camps, and clinics, his grades suffered. Peter was not dumb; it was just that he often did not have enough time to spend on his studies. His parents, who by now were totally swept up in his athletic success, rarely spent the necessary time to promote any kind of educational goals or values. At the same time, local newspapers began to give considerable attention to Peter's athletic success and started to chronicle his career in more depth. This attention not only went to Peter's head but it also affected his parents, who routinely told others that their son would be the next heavily recruited athlete in the area.

Because Peter was not strong academically, he ended up farther behind the eight ball with each transfer. He graduated by the skin of his teeth but needed a year of prep school to help him prepare academically for college. The prep school where he ended up also had a very strong basketball program that was known for getting its players recruited by top Division I coaches. The coaches and administrators of the prep school were very good at landing athletic scholarships for their athletes. In contrast, the academic rigor at the school was hardly challenging; the athletes did little more than major in "staying eligible."

Peter managed to get by academically at prep school but he was not recruited heavily by any major college. He ended up with a scholarship at a low-level Division I program where he rarely played during his freshman season. His coursework, which was arranged by academic tutors within the athletic department, could not be called challenging. Though he managed to stay eligible it was only because he was funneled toward a phony major and toward courses where faculty were known to go easy on athletes.

During his sophomore year, Peter seldom played and then quit about one-fourth the way through the season. By then, Peter had lost interest in basketball, but because he was not prepared for academic life he soon dropped out of school.

Peter is working now and from what I understand he is adapting to a more normal life without basketball. Perhaps he will try to finish his education by taking classes in some evening college programs. His father, who had engineered his son's success in basketball beginning at an early age, was shattered that his dream had not been fulfilled. In contrast to his son's seemingly rapid adjustment, it has taken him more time to adjust to life without basketball. Their father-son relationship, though initially strained by the separation from basketball, should survive and hopefully will enter a new level of maturity.

As a research psychologist for most of my adult life, I have always avoided making conclusions based upon a limited amount of information. I have been taught to collect data from many subjects and to analyze that information carefully. But, Peter's experience with sports is disappointingly similar to others I have witnessed or heard about through the years.

Increasingly, coaches and parents have attempted to professionalize athletes at earlier and earlier ages. This takes the form of intensive (and expensive!) year round training, often to the exclusion of educational objectives and other activities that are equally if not more important for well-rounded development. As a result, sports at all levels have become very serious business. It is not about fun, teamwork, sportsmanship, hard work, and affiliation and camaraderie with other athletes. It is instead a pressurized world of competition with the acquisition of material gain the ultimate goal.

Peter was a good kid with a great deal of potential to be both a good athlete and a good student. His focus on one part of his life (basketball) to the exclusion of another (his mind) compromised his development as a person. While he fell short of his athletic objectives, he may someday fulfill some other goals that are far more important to his successful functioning in our society. Continuing his education will help him become an important contributing member of his community.

Peter's story is yet another reminder that our current athletic culture is fractured and has been turned upside down. Sadly, it is no longer rewarding enough to play sports for the intrinsic satisfaction derived from the activity itself. Instead, there is an ulterior motive that is often related to boosting one's status or acquiring monetary rewards (e.g., college scholarships and, for a precious few, professional contracts). Those motives are learned, and most often they are promoted by adults (parents and coaches) who often feel that all human activities must be materially rewarded in some way or they are not worth pursuing.

Who is to blame for Peter's rough road through our present athletic jungle? Clearly, Peter and his family bear much of the responsibility for many ill-advised decisions. However, a society that rewards and fosters a sports culture far more than an educational culture is partly to blame. In many ways, Peter never had a chance. He was a victim of a sports environment that is out of control and chewing up young athletes faster than our society can replace them.

10

The Athletic Scholarship Chase

In the fall of 1996 at Central Connecticut State College, I coached a select team of basketball players from the Capital District of Albany, New York, in a weekend tournament during the so-called NCAA live period. This tournament, like so many others during the spring, summer, and fall, brings top scholastic-aged basketball players together where they are viewed by college coaches from across the country. Supported by Adidas, the tournament was the usual three game pool play, shootout format. Winners of pool play advance to single elimination competition the next day and losers lick their wounds and go home following their third game on Saturday.

My team, the Albany City Rocks, consisted of some of the most talented high school juniors and seniors in the area. While my players were very good athletes, I also made sure that they were performing adequately in the classroom. In my mind, it wasn't worth it for kids to be spending so much time playing basketball if they weren't also doing well in what really counts, and that is academics. I also didn't want the kids to be traveling too far or playing too much basketball. So, I confined most of our tournament play to sites within six hours of Albany. I also backed off on our schedule and only played in the spring and a few dates in the fall. The kids supported almost all of their own travel and I would always manage to scrape up a few extra dollars from sponsors and donations to help out those who could not foot the bill.

We usually held our own against top-flight competition but we always struggled against the very best teams out of Boston, New York City, and Washington. Our opponent in the first game of our pool play was the Boston Amateur Basketball Club (BABC), a team that is noted for very athletic players who are regularly recruited by top Division I college teams in the country. The team was coached by the maverick

Leo Papile, who is currently the director of player personnel for the Boston Celtics. I was prepared for an up-tempo, above the rim game.

Our game on court 1 of the main gym seemed to attract a fair amount of attention. Prior to its start, I noticed in the crowd high-profile college coaches like Jim Calhoun (UConn), Mike Jarvis (George Washington and later St. Johns), Jim Boeheim (Syracuse), and Steve Lappas (Villanova and now UMass). Just before the tip, there were around 50 or 60 college coaches, all sporting their school colors with warmup jackets and golf shirts. I was certain that very few of the coaches present were there to see my players; the blue-chippers from BABC were the main attraction.

We scored on the opening tip and BABC then proceeded to run off 30 straight points, 16 of which came on thundering slam dunks. The rout was on and there was little we could do to stem the tide against the full court pressure and athleticism of the BABC team. Although we made it more of a game in the second half, it was only because Papile played most of his weaker players, many of whom were only freshman. Final score: BABC 94, Albany City Rocks 48.

As we walked off the court with our tails between our legs, I distinctly remember one of my players saying, "Coach, I learned something in this game. I learned that I should direct more of my energies into studying real hard in school!" I smiled and was happy that he realized where he stood regarding his future in Division I college basketball. I remarked, "That's probably not a bad idea."

Several Division III coaches approached me after the game to talk about some of my players, all of whom were relatively smart kids in good academic standing. Meanwhile, Papile was holding court with the Division I coaches as they fawned over his players and competed for his time.

Later that day I talked with Papile a bit about his players and the BABC program. "We've been on the road since late March," he said, "and we've been everywhere—Vegas, San Diego, Indianapolis—you name it, we've gone to it. I don't know how many games we've played but it has to be close to a hundred. My players are mostly from greater Boston and many are from broken homes. I'm like a parent to many of them. Sneaker money and donations help us to do all the traveling."

Papile's story was not unlike many others I had heard or read about over the years. Like many AAU coaches, Papile's primary credential for his job as head honcho of BABC was his ability to cajole and pick up the best players in the inner-city Boston area. Premier AAU programs like BABC, Mickey Walker's All Stars, the New Bedford Buddies, the New

York Gauchos, and Riverside Church have a formula that seems to work in today's sports culture: acquire the best players, attract sneaker money, then parade the talent around to all the coaches in the spring, summer, and fall tournaments.

The college coaches love it because all they have to do is go to the "meat market" tournaments, watch them play, and pick who they want to recruit. The AAU coaches love it because it gives them power over the lives of young kids and the potential to attract even more sneaker money down the road if they land their players in top college programs. The sneaker companies love it because it gives them an opportunity to identify the next Michael Jordan and affix their company logo to him before anyone else does. I hate it because it includes all of the worst aspects of sports: exploitation, abuse, greed, and all too frequently unrealized and broken dreams for young athletes.

As I sat in the stands watching other games that day, I thought about what was down the road for my players and Papile's BABC players, all of whom were African Americans. With graduation rates of Division I African American college basketball players at an all-time low, I couldn't help but think that many of his players probably would have benefited more by spending their time in learning centers as opposed to being out on the road all the time trying to attract the attention of college coaches. I also thought about where many of them would end up and how few of them would actually get their college degrees or even go to college for a period of time. I thought about the awful system that is now in place which rewards the exploitation and unethical behavior of everyone involved—players, coaches, parents, sneaker companies, and colleges.

Later that day, I struck up a conversation with the college basketball commentator and former Seton Hall basketball coach, Bill Raftery. His son was playing for a New Jersey AAU team and, being a long-time fan of his style, wit, and tell-it-like-it-is manner, I introduced myself. I told him a bit about my background in sports and education and revealed my uneasiness about what was happening at almost all levels of sports these days. "Bill, I just don't see much hope for sports with all of these crazy things happening that are serving to undermine the essence of athletics" I lamented. "I just don't know where all of this is going."

Raftery filled me in on some recent horror stories he had heard regarding recruiting and then looked at me with those twinkling eyes of his and tried to console me. "Many of us are concerned," he said, "but it is people like you who need to stay involved so that we can get the bad apples out."

I was flattered by Raftery's compliment and I guess I took it as a cue to do something about the deplorable state of sports in our country today.

I tried to keep track of Papile's BABC players from that year. A few received scholarships from some major Division I basketball programs but ended up leaving after brief stints. Most of them I never saw or heard from again. Some reports indicated that others ended up in junior college programs. While I can't be certain, my guess is that the vast majority are walking the streets of Boston at this very moment with nothing to show for being paraded across the country during their springs, summers, and falls.

Every player that I coached on my Albany City Rocks team from 1996 advanced through college and earned a degree. A good number of them played collegiate basketball and some even had athletic scholarships. Others had academic scholarships but did not continue playing basketball. I believe that all of them will be productive citizens in our society. I am not so sure if the same can be said of Papile's BABC players.

My involvement in AAU allowed me to witness just how the college basketball recruiting game is done these days. It combines equal dosages of coaches' greed and sports apparel money and plays upon a young person's desire to obtain an athletic scholarship and potentially a professional contract. This powerful mixture is so corrupting that it lures many young kids into a dream that cannot possibly be realized given the long odds of success. The current system is especially exploitive of African-Americans; they are constantly brainwashed by our current sports culture to believe that the only way out of the ghetto is through athletics and not education. In spite of the fact that the road to the NBA and NFL is littered with unsuccessful stories, the carrot for many young athletes continues to be the quest for a full scholarship ride in a Division I sports program. True reform in our country's current sports landscape will not occur until we begin to get the message across that academic scholarships outnumber athletic scholarships by an order of about 70 to 1 and the only dependable road to long term career success is through education. When that day arrives, we can begin to salvage the next generation of young athletes and turn the tide against a sports culture that presently sends mixed messages about the role of education in human development.

Part Three

BE TRUE TO YOUR SCHOOL

Sport does not build character, at least not in the way many Americans assume that it does. Overall, sport does not promote substantial educational or socioeconomic attainment. High school sport does not reduce delinquency or racial prejudice. Moreover, during the course of an individual's life, high school sport does not promote social success or health. In short, there is no statistically measurable positive long-term benefit for those who played high school sports when compared with those who did not participate.

Andrew Miracle and Roger Rees,
Lessons of the Locker Room

———————

School-sponsored sports, especially in our high schools serve a small number of students, distract from valuable teacher time, and waste money and time that could be better spent on other resources more relevant to teaching, the central mission of schools. Eliminating school-sponsored sports from our educational system would be one of the most powerful ways we have for addressing misplaced priorities.

Etta Kravolec, *Schools that Do Too Much*

———————

While the health benefits that accrue to athletes are well documented, they remain a vague afterthought to coaches and athletic administrators . . . our sports programs are elitist and exclusionary, neither designed nor conducted with the health benefits of participants in mind. If we were interested in deriving the greatest health return on dollars spent on athletics, more resources would be spent on broad-based, participatory, intramural, club, and physical education programs than on the current programs designed to cater to a small population of elite athletes. If community and education leaders were committed to using athletic participation as a tool to improve public health, school systems would be strengthening, rather than weakening, physical education requirements and appropriating increasingly scarce public education dollars to these programs rather than to the football or basketball teams.

John Gerdy, *Sports in School*, 2000

———————

They are stronger and more skilled, but year round commitment to a single sport and far-flung travel for more and better competition are isolating our best young athletes from their communities and changing the all-around athletic experience that has been at the heart of American sports for generations.

Alexander Wolff, *Sports Illustrated*

———————

11

Jock Culture 101

Fonda-Fultonville, New York, is a small, blue-collar community of about 5,000 people located just west of Albany along the Mohawk River. The high school sports program competes in the Class C small school division of New York State. Under long-time football coach, Alex Mancini, the school has an impressive history of winning teams and success in regional and state championship play.

Back in 1996 I closely followed a story that came out of this community when it was reported in the *Albany Times-Union* Newspaper that eight football players, most of them starters, were suspended from the team for building and planting twelve potentially lethal bottle bombs that were capable of causing serious injury. Luckily no one was injured, but the incident caused quite a stir at the time because it pitted athletics against both legal and community standards.

The players and their parents had signed a code of conduct statement at the beginning of the season in which the consequences of illegal behavior were clearly spelled out. Any infraction would result in suspension from the team. Because the players were charged with third-degree criminal possession of a weapon, which is a felony crime, they were automatically suspended for the last two games of the season. However, with the team sporting an impressive 7–1 record and the state playoffs just around the corner, Coach Mancini petitioned the Fonda-Fultonville school board to lift the suspensions to enable the eight accused players to return to the playing field.

The meeting to determine the players' fate was held before a packed audience and the board president, Jason Downing, was vilified when he suggested that the two-game suspension imposed by Coach Mancini was too lenient. The public commentary during the meeting included frequent taunts and open hostility as numerous people spoke in support of reinstatement of the athletes. Assistant football coach

Craig Phillips was loudly cheered when he said, "The kids made a stupid mistake over one weekend. Think of the times you have driven with booze on you. How many times have you jacked a deer? How many times have you tried drugs? And you know, America is a great place, and I think everybody should have a second chance in life."

Likewise, Coach Mancini believed that the players had suffered overwhelmingly because their names and photographs were published in the local newspaper. He was vigorously cheered when he said, "The punishment borders on the punitive. No one could describe their pain. For them to come back would be rehabilitative." On the other hand the board president, Jason Downing, was called "a disgrace," "hatemonger," "vindictive," and "classless" for his insistence that the football players should continue to sit out.

Many parents, students, and teachers went before the board and argued strongly that the players should be permitted back on the field if it was Coach Mancini's decision to allow them to return. They believed that such a decision had nothing to do with football itself but rather it had everything to do with putting the decision in the hands of the coach and no one else. According to newspaper reports, only two people dissented and agreed with the school board president's position that the punishment was too lenient. They were roundly booed.

In an amazing turnaround, the board relented to the pressure, lifted the suspensions, and allowed the athletes to compete in the playoffs. This decision was met with a public outcry in the Capital District Area. Numerous editorial columns and letters appeared in local newspapers, many of which found the actions of the Fonda-Fultonville school board and the people of the community to be a travesty. An *Albany Times-Union* editorial concluded, "In a matter of a few short weeks, eight young persons charged with a felony have been converted in the eyes of many into almost victims themselves, persons at any rate in need of the therapeutic and rehabilitative regimen of the gridiron. And so, it was decided, they will suit up for the next game. The community response to this alleged offense reveals much about this particular school district, and maybe much about the rest of America as well."

More recently, another interesting case of misbehaving athletes and community reactions emerged in a suburban Capital District community. Averill Park, New York, is a rapidly growing town about 20 minutes northwest of the Albany-Troy corridor. In the fall of 2001, the Averill Park School District was rocked by allegations of hazing on the football team. In the incident, a 14-year-old freshman accused teammates of dragging their genitals across his face in a hazing ritual that is referred to as "tea-bagging."

The parents of the victim initially went to teachers to complain but nothing was done, so they then told police of their allegations. As a result, three varsity football players were arrested and charged with misdemeanor harassment, endangering the welfare of a child and unlawful imprisonment. Additionally, two teachers were charged with misdemeanor counts of witness tampering after police alleged that they tried to cover up the incident by not immediately reporting it to the police and by trying to get the victim and other individuals to change their story.

As the story unfolded over the next few months in the community, long time athletic director Lou Cioffi accused the school district of failing to respond to previous warnings and incidents of hazing. He told administrators that "unhealthy and harmful" behavior was taking place in the locker rooms and nothing was done. He further alleged that the football program was run in a "cultlike" fashion and that the administration ignored it for years. Though he received significant support from coaches and teachers in the district, Cioffi was removed from his position as full-time athletic director but was allowed to remain in the school in another capacity.

Several months later, Cioffi lodged a $4 million lawsuit against the district, arguing that he was unjustly fired as a consequence of the hazing incident. The charges against the teachers were dropped but those against the students involved in the hazing are still pending.

Most important, the victim of the hazing transferred to another school. The family sued the school district for $4.5 million, claiming that officials of the school (superintendent and assistant superintendent, athletic director, head and assistant football coaches, and the school principal) failed to act on their boy's complaint of hazing. Both lawsuits are still pending.

In the aftermath of the hazing incident in Averill Park, members of the community have become very concerned about the abuse that students have received at athletic contests against neighboring schools as well as in various community businesses. For example, tea bags have been thrown out on the court at basketball games and adults and students have been ridiculed at stores when their connection to Averill Park was detected. Averill Park school board president Tom McGreevy expressed those concerns: "I worry when comments are made to our kids, and coaches from other schools turn a blind eye to it. I worry when kids go to business establishments and take harassment from people working there."

In our current sports culture, we are bombarded almost daily by media reports of out-of-control college and professional athletes involved in crimes against women, paternity suits, drug and alcohol addiction, and violent criminal behavior. Is there any doubt that the origin of much of this outrageous behavior is in part the by-product of the indulgence, pampering, and exalted status that jocks have received since their early years on the scholastic playing fields?

Some have concluded that there is a dangerous and pervasive "jock culture" that permeates athletics at almost all levels of organized sport in this country. The origin of that culture may reside in a sense of entitlement and being "above the law" that occurs among many of our athletes beginning at an early age. Clearly, when coaches, administrators, parents, and entire communities bend the rules and/or overlook them entirely, then collectively they plant the seeds for what follows in the years to come. The incidents in Fonda-Fultonville and Averill Park are symptomatic of a sports culture that frequently extends privileges to athletes because of their presumed role model status. If we are to prevent the negative consequences of our present jock culture, we must be prepared to make major changes in how we treat athletes and how we organize sports in this country.

12

Scholastic Recruiting Wars

Several years ago I received a telephone call from an individual in the Capital District regarding a spring basketball recruiting camp that was being held for eighth graders in the area. The stated purpose of the camp, as expressed by the caller on the other end, was to "expose promising young basketball players in the area to local varsity high school coaches." The caller further described the 2-day camp as a "method for private high school coaches to recruit and possibly offer scholarships to some of the players." Oh yes, the caller also mentioned that there would be "discussion of available academic programs at the participating private schools."

As president of the Capital District Youth Basketball League (CDYBL), the largest boys' youth basketball league in the area, I was contacted for the sole purpose of providing names, telephone numbers, and email addresses of youth coaches who might want to send players to this mini-camp (my translation: meat market). My reaction was that of sadness and disgust, and I made no bones about my feelings to the organizer. The caller in turn berated me for closing the door on opportunities that might be available to gifted players at this time in their life. Needless to say, our discussion did not last very long as it was clear that our philosophies represented two contrasting viewpoints that were as different as night and day.

Having been around sports in one form or another for quite some time and being familiar with what can go on with the recruitment of young athletes at this level, I was not surprised that I would receive such a telephone call; I was only shocked at how blatant and out in the open things had become.

One only has to watch the widely acclaimed documentary movie of a few years ago *Hoop Dreams* to understand how far we have really fallen into the sleazy abyss of the recruiting wars for blue chip scholastic athletes. The movie chronicled the recruitment of young inner-city basketball players by private schools in the Chicago area.

Sadly, such tactics are becoming commonplace to the point where players as young as grade school age (fourth and fifth graders) are now being recruited by private schools in many metropolitan areas for the sole purpose of beefing up scholastic basketball programs. Promises of increased playing time and winning records, increased exposure, tuition scholarships, personal tutoring and cash payments (bonuses) in some extreme cases are becoming more and more prevalent as the stakes for having a winning program become higher and the motivation to obtain college athletic scholarships gets greater.

Basketball, even at the scholastic level, has become big business, with some highly successful high school programs and their coaches receiving sneaker contracts much as their predecessors in the college and professional ranks have done before them. In some areas of the country, the survival of private school athletic programs and steady enrollments depends, in part, upon recruiting top athletes and winning on the playing fields. If your teams can string some good years together, you can expect more students to come your way, better athletes, more sneaker money support, and more prestige. A run of bad years can potentially result in just the opposite with fewer resources and possible extinction down the road.

Those who see nothing wrong with the escalating practice of recruiting young athletes will tell you that it is an opportunity for such individuals to excel and potentially attract an athletic scholarship down the road. This perception, however, is a notoriously inaccurate one both nationwide and locally. When it comes to the Capital District Area, for example, where the competitive level of scholastic basketball is considered to be quite good, very few athletes each year obtain basketball scholarships at Division I and II schools (Division III schools are not allowed to give athletic scholarships, only need-based financial aid).

While the decision by recruited youngsters to attend a particular school for academic or religious reasons can be a wise choice depending upon individual circumstances, it cannot be said that such decisions automatically ensure greater opportunities for basketball success and scholarships down the road. In fact because of the explosive growth and widespread popularity of basketball (it is the leading participation sport among youths in the United States), the probability of obtaining a basketball scholarship is quite small.

It can also be said that transferring sometimes causes significant academic hardship, especially for a student who is marginal to begin with. I have seen some athletes in this area transfer as many as three times over the course of a scholastic career. With each move, there are different educational and behavioral expectations in the new school environment. This can lead to a fractured trail of academic and social failure that benefits no one. It can leave a young athlete with a high school diploma that is not worth the paper it is written on.

Perhaps the most disturbing aspect of the recruiting of young athletes however, is the brazen abuse and misuse of power by some adults that are in a position of authority. Coaches are fueled by their own egos and desire to win at all costs; parents are swept up in the distorted references to their kids as "franchise players" and MVPs; kids, with their vulnerable egos and developing self-concepts, are caught in the frenzy and often get sucked into believing that they are in fact the next Michael Jordan. Clearly, there is little question that the blame for this rising form of exploitation in our country must be squarely put upon the shoulders of the adults in charge.

And if we think that this is a problem limited to just a few private schools and just to the sport of basketball we should all think twice. In the Albany Capital District Area, there are a number of situations every year in which athletes transfer from adjacent school districts, other parts of New York State, or even other countries for the sole purpose of playing a particular sport in a noted high school athletic program. The men's soccer team at nearby Shenendehowa High School in Clifton Park, New York frequently shows up in national rankings in *USA Today*. It has produced a long line of local, regional and state championships. Curiously, the 1996 U.S. Olympic soccer team carried two athletes on its roster who played together during their high school years at Shenendehowa. With the probability of this coincidence somewhere between slim and none, one might reasonably ask whether or not both individuals grew up in the Capital District Area? At least one of the players came from outside the area and, for those who are not naïve about the realities of enticing scholastic athletes to come on board to build dominant teams, the logical inference is that some form of recruiting may have taken place.

The New York State Public High School Athletic Association (NYSPHSAA) has sought to discourage the transfer of students for athletic reasons. This has been done through the establishment of residency requirements and a penalty in which transfers must sit for the first four games of the season following their school change. However, it is all too apparent that some parents, coaches, and administrators routinely find ingenious ways to bypass these rules and there is regular movement of players in this area on a yearly basis. One only needs to maintain an address within the school district in order to qualify as a bona fide student and often such addresses are with aunts, uncles, older sisters and brothers, or even cousins. Unless they have been tipped off by someone else, administrators frequently do not check addresses to verify if a student is actually living at a particular location. In certain schools that are lax in their accountability procedures, it is always interesting to see who will be on their athletic rosters from year to year and just who they have picked up by way of the transparent and easily circumvented transfer process.

NYSPHSAA presently has no specific regulations prohibiting the recruitment of players by coaches, except those pertaining to foreign exchange students. The most recent NYSPHSAA manual states that "there shall be no evidence that a student, school, or other interested party has influenced the assignment of the foreign exchange student to the school." Though recruiting of players within the United States is not addressed in the manual, Assistant Director of NYSPHSAA Walter Eaton, states that "we rely upon the NYSPHSAA basic Code of Ethics to cover this area and we depend upon the common sense, ethics, and morals of coaches and administrators in local school districts for enforcement. When a school, public or private, applies to NYSPHSAA for membership, they must agree to abide by our code of ethics." He further stated that "in the case of recruiting, enforcement of the ethics code can only occur when parents decide to blow the whistle if their child is being recruited and formally charge a coach with an ethical violation."

The effectiveness of this deterrent seems weak, however, since making such an accusation would then probably involve lengthy legal proceedings, especially if the accused coach denied the charges and went after the parent with his own defamation lawsuit. With these possible scenarios and the prospects of expensive litigation on both sides, it is easy to see why recruiting continues to take place at the scholastic level. Clearly, when there are no specific rules and no significant penalties for recruiting, unethical coaches with uncontrollable egos will look for any edge that will allow them to be more successful at winning. While the problem oftentimes may be limited to only a few schools and their coaches, it does not take long before others follow suit in order to keep up with a school in the adjacent district.

The handbook of the New York State Public High School Athletic Association clearly states its ethics code: "It is the duty of all concerned with high school athletics to emphasize the proper ideals of sportsmanship, ethical conduct and fair play." This statement sounds pretty good but in reality those espoused ideals are eroding with each passing year. Maybe it's time to think of a new way of organizing sports for our young athletes. Perhaps we should think about getting sports out of our schools altogether and handing them over to private clubs as it is done in Europe and Australia. Our schools have enough to think about in the academic arena without also having to contend with issues like the unethical recruiting and transferring of athletes.

I spoke with a local high school coach who once lost one of his key players over the summer to a private school in the area. He knew that the coach had placed unrelenting pressure upon the young athlete to change schools with all kinds of promises but there simply was nothing he could do to prevent it from occurring without coming across as self-serving in his own way. These situations crop up all the time in the scholastic recruiting wars. As a result, good coaches are confronted with ethical dilemmas that challenge their sense of fair play. Most do not give in to the pressure but some do by retaliating in their own way.

The question is: why do we allow recruiting and transferring of scholastic athletes in the first place? The answer is simple: because we are more interested in fulfilling the win-at-all-costs egos of coaches and parents as opposed to caring about the health, welfare and academic progress of young athletes. Until the time comes when adults in a position of authority can make better decisions and rein in their own egos, we can fully expect the unethical recruitment and transferring of young athletes to continue unabated at the scholastic level. This form of abuse and exploitation, though it is more subtle than what we read about at the collegiate level, has the potential to be every bit as damaging to the long-term development of our youths.

13

Suburban Council Rules

Most mornings during his summer school vacation period, special education teacher Jesse Braverman would spend his time pitching batting practice to anyone who showed up at the Bethlehem Middle School baseball field in Delmar, New York. From Little Leaguers to college kids home for the summer, everyone got a chance to hone their batting and fielding skills in informal pickup games where there were no rules except to have some fun. Braverman volunteered his time with no compensation for a number of years, and countless Bethlehem youths benefited from what was affectionately called Jesse-ball. It was a throwback to an earlier time when athletics was far less competitive and much less serious.

Braverman, a self-professed baseball junkie, also coached the varsity baseball team at Bethlehem Central High School as well as the local Mickey Mantle baseball team for age 15 and under players. He won numerous championships with both teams and was generally considered to be one of the finest baseball coaches in the entire Upstate New York Area. However, his dual coaching posts were challenged a few years ago when he was informed by school administrators that he could no longer coach both teams. A rule set in place by the Suburban Council, an association of 10 public schools of which Bethlehem is a member, prevents scholastic coaches from off-season coaching when more than half the participants are also on the school team.

The rule, which was probably well-intentioned, was enacted to relieve youths from any kind of undue pressure to participate on their coaches summer teams in order to secure a position on scholastic teams.

84

It was also enacted to prevent one school from getting a leg up or competitive advantage over another school during the off season. The same rule was originally a part of the New York State Public High School Athletic Association (NYSPHSAA) code but was quickly dropped because it was unenforceable and because it unnecessarily restricted volunteer efforts of coaches especially in rural areas where such individuals are at a premium.

The Suburban Council opted to retain the code in its bylaws and took action against Braverman. This was done in spite of the fact that other infractions in surrounding school districts were ignored and there were no complaints from any players or parents that they were somehow being coerced by Braverman to play on his Mickey Mantle team. The Bethlehem Central School District supported the Suburban Council decision and requested that Braverman leave his Mickey Mantle coaching position or face termination from his scholastic coaching position.

Braverman challenged the rule and fought a court battle to overturn the Suburban Council code so as to restore his right to coach both baseball teams. He was committed to the kids in the community and believed that he never directly coerced a player to be a part of his team. He strongly believed that his right to due process was compromised and, more important, his Fourteenth Amendment rights of free association were violated. A $1.75 million dollar judgment was filed before the courts in which Braverman sued the Suburban Council and the Bethlehem Central School District for violating his civil rights. At one point, he stated that he would use every penny of the money to build a new first-class baseball stadium for the community if he won.

As the case unraveled over a two-year period, there was heated commentary on both sides of the issue. Also, many in the community were disappointed by the fact that the conflict could not be resolved before lawyers entered the scene. School board meetings were increasingly devoted to sorting through the issues and many in the community became restless over the fact that so much time and money (via lawyers' fees) was being spent to resolve an essentially nonacademic issue.

Initially there was a groundswell of public support for Braverman's position and a great deal of negative commentary regarding the position of school district officials and the Suburban Council. However, as the issue was played out in the local newspapers and in the court of public opinion, there was a small but vocal minority who contended that Braverman should not hold both positions and that he did indirectly coerce players to play on his summer Mickey Mantle team. Importantly, some of the coach's critics wrote letters to the local newspaper claiming that a win at all costs attitude on Braverman's part often meant that many players through the years hardly played or were only given "garbage time" when a game was clearly won or lost. These accusations, which some viewed as "sour grapes," may have been inaccurate representations of what actually transpired on the baseball diamond between Braverman and his players. However, the fact that a small minority voiced concerns about the proper place of winning in our current youth sports culture was at times refreshing. In fact, some concluded that an open discourse on this topic could be just as important as debates regarding the propriety of a coach's desire to shepherd both a scholastic team and a summer team with ostensibly the same players.

Braverman eventually lost his court case and the Bethlehem Central School Board forced him to step down from his varsity baseball coaching position. Apparently, a resolution could not be agreed upon that was acceptable to all parties. Braverman chose to coach his summer Mickey Mantle team and therefore was no longer allowed to coach his scholastic varsity team. As a result, the school district lost a good baseball coach and many potential young athletes lost out on an opportunity to benefit from a truly gifted and dedicated baseball mind.

Was the decision a correct one? Technically, in this community, it probably was the right thing to do and the school board correctly determined that there was a conflict regarding Baverman's dual coaching duties. However, in this day and age of our highly competitive scholastic sports culture, hardly anyone outside of Bethlehem, New York, really cares about the possible ethical issues raised by a scholastic coach guiding his same players in the off season. Why? Because it is done all the time in most parts of our country where players at the scholastic level are expected to keep playing their sport throughout the year. Indeed, outside of the Suburban Council in Upstate New York, there is no rule against it and it simply is not an issue.

The rule, which is obsolete and selectively enforced, could have been the necessary justification to get rid of a coach. A more enlightened and optimistic view, however, is that Braverman may have been the victim of a community's desire to return to some sense of sanity regarding what sports should be about at the scholastic and youth levels. Thus, instead of rubber stamping our current landscape, which has deified winning and competition at an early age, the action of the school board and the community signaled a desire to return to a sports culture of 50 years ago. Right or wrong, the action taken against an exceptional baseball coach can be viewed as an anomalous event in a country that is otherwise obsessed with sports for all the wrong reasons.

Though Braverman's situation may seem like a minor, community sports issue, it really epitomizes many of the things that are wrong with scholastic athletics in our current sports-crazed culture. There is an overemphasis on competition and winning, which breeds an atmosphere of distrust and suspicion regarding rules and regulations. This results in countless hours spent by administrators creating additional rules to level the playing field and make sure that coaches are doing everything by the books.

As evidenced by the Braverman case in my community of Bethlehem, New York, apparently some people are beginning to get concerned about what really ails our modern youth sports culture. It is tragic that the real substance of scholastic athletics is largely being ignored across our country by those who are in the best position to do something significant about it. There is not enough serious discussion among state education officials, athletic councils, athletic directors, principals, school superintendents, and school boards regarding the many important issues that dramatically affect scholastic athletes and our sports landscape.

For example, meaningful discussions about the age at which scholastic sports should emphasize winning versus participation are critically needed. Likewise, we desperately need remedies for issues like declining sportsmanship, increasingly physical and often dirty play, the alarming rise in athletic injuries, the often unsafe and inadequate athletic facilities in many schools, the increased usage of performance-enhancing drugs by very young scholastic athletes, the unethical recruiting and transferring of players, and the increasing expectation that athletes begin to specialize in a sport at an early age and devote almost their entire waking existence to it.

Other important issues include the lack of available intramural athletic programs for middle school and high school students, the escalation of out-of-control coaches and parents at athletic contests, the infiltration of sports apparel money into the support of high school athletic programs, increasingly long sports seasons because of state tournament play, the double standard that often exists for scholastic athletes in communities and the corresponding rise in a negative jock culture, the continuing Title IX problems that exist in some areas of the country, the lowering of academic standards by many schools to enable athletes to participate, the inability to get enough competently trained and certified coaches and trainers to supervise scholastic teams, and the whole problem of the increasingly difficult job of funding interscholastic sports.

The list of important problems goes on and on. Many of them are an outgrowth of the epidemic that we call winning and competition while others have to do with the organizational and managerial problems associated with the explosion of sports in our society. If they were brought to the forefront as they should be, serious discussions in every community would take place regarding possible solutions and reforms. Instead, educational leaders in many communities and in state athletic associations have all but given up. The usual response is to enact layers of rules to equalize competition. Such rules are usually created out of a basic sense of distrust and are largely unenforceable. In view of this misguided emphasis, the major issues impacting the quality of a scholastic athlete's sports experience have been given lip service or, even worse, are totally ignored.

At the same time, we must recognize that we live in an age in which we increasingly are asking our public schools to do more and more for our young people. They have become training grounds for chemistry, math, English, history, biology, physics, economics, sociology, psychology, health, computer technology, music, drama, theater, and yes, athletics. These efforts are supplemented by an array of counselors, social workers, special education teachers, psychologists, and administrators of every specialty imaginable. Our schools have become mini cities with all of the services one might reasonably see in an average metropolis.

How much can schools really be expected to do? How much should they do? Are some things more important than others? Should some things fall by the wayside because they are costly and benefit only a few people? In short, why do we even have things such as interscholastic athletics when increasingly they take up more and more of our school budgets and more and more of our school committee time and effort to resolve "important" issues?

More important, however, the educational relevance of interscholastic athletics is being questioned by many people. Some say that it really only benefits a few students, and that it is increasingly about winning and not participation and learning the values of the game. Critics also claim that if athletics are so good for everyone, then why do we deemphasize physical education, fitness classes, and intramural activities? Schools are trying to be all things to all people and in doing so they invariably please no one.

We have been diverted from the true mission of our public schools and that is education. The product, the learning by our students, has been diluted. Maybe it's time to think of another way of doing things that might benefit more people or, better yet, perhaps it's time to start over again and seriously evaluate whether or not we should have an expensive system of interscholastic sports supported by our financially strapped public schools. It's just a thought, but one you think about when you see a town waste close to two years on a noneducational issue concerning a coach and a rule.

14

The Endless Season

The suburban community of Bethlehem, New York, is inhabited by 31,000 people, many of whom work in state government in the Albany Capital District Area. Known for its excellent public school system, the town is geographically located just outside the Albany City limits. As a result, it is no surprise that the town consistently attracts many families who desire to be close to Albany and who want the best possible education for their kids. This is where my wife and I put our roots down a number of years ago and it is a decision that we have never regretted.

Both of our boys attended Bethlehem Central High School (BCHS) and received a well-rounded academic and athletic experience. Competing in the Suburban Council, the school's sports teams always did well and won their fair share of games and championships along the way. Like many communities, football has strong support and traditional Friday night games are relatively well attended. While never a powerhouse, the Bethlehem Central Eagles have always been competitive but not dominant in their league.

The long-time head coach of the Bethlehem football program was John Sodergren. Leading from the sidelines for 29 years, the past 20 as head coach, Sodergren never had advanced to the playoffs and never had won a sectional superbowl. However, everything seemed to come together for the Bethlehem football team in the 2001 season.

Going into the sectional superbowl game, Bethlehem was 8–1 and faced a perennially strong Troy High team that was 7–3. Before a crowd of close to 4,000 people, Bethlehem crushed Troy 34–6. Their running and passing attack couldn't be stopped and their defense made big play after big play to thwart their opposition. Following the game, Sodergren was clearly thrilled with the result. "It's all about respect," he said.

"We've been talking to the kids all week long about Bethlehem football history and what a victory in this game would mean. I realize what we accomplished tonight. I still don't think the players realize it." At this point, Bethlehem now had a shot at the state championship and a trip to the Carrier Dome in Syracuse.

Until 1993, there was no playoff system for scholastic football in the State of New York. The season ended in each of the 11 sections with a superbowl game held in early November. The brainchild of veteran Shenendehowa football coach Brent Steurwald, the major impetus seemed to be the fact that other states like Pennsylvania, Texas, and Florida had state championships that were extremely popular and well-attended. Also, other scholastic sports in New York State had championships so the thinking was why not football too.

It took some time for Steurwald to steer his idea through the entire state. Some sections didn't like it because it necessitated starting the playing of regular season games before Labor Day. Other sections believed that it unnecessarily extended the season through to the beginning of December and overlapped with the start of winter sports seasons by as much as three weeks. These issues, as well as the challenge of keeping athletes interested, energized, and focused for practices over such a long season suggested to some that it just wasn't worth it.

In spite of these problems, all sections of the state eventually came on board and the decision was made to have title games for all five classes (AA, A, B, C, and D) in late November/early December at the Carrier Dome in Syracuse. Sectional, regional, and semifinal games are held in the three-week period in November following the sectional superbowl championship game.

Now firmly entrenched in the state, the playoff system is not without its difficulties. Every year, newspaper reports chronicle the problems that pop up when schools keep advancing. Athletes must practice in the cold and often unpredictable weather, travel long distances for games and, for those simultaneously participating in a winter sport like basketball or wrestling, miss practices and games. In addition to athletes being stretched to the limits, football coaches who also do a winter sport must double up on supervising their practices. In spite of these problems, the attendance each year keeps getting larger and the revenues grow.

In a regional game the following Saturday evening in Kingston, Bethlehem defeated Newburgh Free Academy of Section IV 32–6. With a large and boisterous contingent from the town supporting the team, the BCHS Eagles totally dominated their opponent on the ground and in the air. Coach Sodergren was beaming following the game. "This is a great thrill for our players, the fans, the coaching staff, and me," he said.

But in the semifinal game the following weekend against North Rockland of Section I, things did not go so well. In front of a capacity crowd in Kingston, the undefeated suburban New York City team proved why they were ranked number 1 in the state as they smashed Bethlehem 27–7 with a powerful running game that couldn't be stopped. The North Rockland team was simply bigger, stronger, and quicker. Sodergren remarked following the game, "We scrambled on offense but we couldn't make the big play. I was pleased with the preparation by our coaches and our players. They (North Rockland) were just a better team tonight. This is a tough way for our 26 seniors to end their careers. But, unless you win a state title, it's going to end like this."

Several months following the state championship run and a record breaking 10–2 season, veteran head coach John Sodergren retired. Finishing on top, Sodergren received praise from a number of people, including Bethlehem Athletic Director Chuck Abba: "He's always been a straightforward, smart, well-organized guy," he said. "For my money I think of him as old school, a rock solid, salt-of-the-earth guy . . . He's a wonderful person, teacher, and coach."

In the spring and summer, I had the chance to talk to a few parents whose kids had played on Sodergren's last team that year. All were thrilled for the coach that after a long career he was finally able to enjoy a championship season in his farewell to football. Most said that the experience was a demanding one but it was great for their kids. However, there was a small group that questioned the importance of the long season and whether or not a state championship should even be held. One person typified the comments of this small minority when he said the following: "My son was burned out following the sectional title game. If the season had ended there it would have been perfect. Instead, it put him behind the eight ball with his studying, college applications, and campus visits. It also delayed him from starting the winter sports season with everyone else. A state tournament serves no purpose except to satisfy a coach's ego. It certainly doesn't do the kids much good. The season seemed endless."

I was sympathetic to this parent's dissatisfaction but unfortunately he only had half the story about why there are New York State interscholastic football and basketball tournaments. The other major reason, in addition to satisfying a coach's desire to be called king of the hill, is that the revenues from these lengthy but well-attended tournaments are huge and they are used to support state tournament play for non-revenue high school sports like track and field, volleyball, field hockey, and golf. Does this sound familiar? Clearly, like their college counter-parts, educators at the scholastic level of sports have also been corrupted by commercial interests.

Interscholastic athletics can be a mixed bag. When everything is kept in perspective and our educational leaders run things properly, they can be positive experiences. However, I am not completely con-vinced that a state championship for any sport is such a good idea, not when it continues for so long and can become disruptive to the primary educational function of our public schools.

Our state athletic associations and our schools are trying to mimic what they see in our colleges. The ridiculously long Final Four Cham-pionship in collegiate basketball and the Bowl Championship Series for football unnecessarily takes students from the classroom for extended periods of time.

I have two important questions. First, has the educational sound-ness of state athletic championships ever been seriously discussed? Sec-ond, whose interests are really being served when we create a state scholastic football championship? I think I know the answer to both questions. I believe that commercial interests are being served as well as our sports culture's demand (read: high school athletic directors' and coaches' insistence) that we determine "champions" in everything we do. So, the desire to earn a buck and the egos of our coaches trumps sound academic policy and education loses again.

CREATIVE ATTEMPTS TO GET THE SAME MEDIA BUZZ AS THE SPORTS PROGRAM

15

Your High School
Sports Hall of Fame

In the summer of 2001, I was asked to be a member of an exploratory committee charged with studying the possibility of a high school sports hall of fame. The committee was formed within the Bethlehem Central High School Athletics Association Booster Club, an organization to which I had belonged during my two sons' involvement in high school sports from about 1990 to1998. It was nice to be considered for the committee but I didn't give a yes or no answer right away. I needed time to think about the whole concept and I wanted to do a little investigative work on my own.

Sports halls of fame can be found in many high schools in every part of our country. Most are located in very visible spots, such as a main corridor or in a lobby adjacent to a gymnasium. They typically include pictures, memorabilia, and trophies. My own informal study here in the Capital District of New York showed that many high schools have one— some more elaborate than others—and most schools seem to devote some resources to their establishment.

For the most part, sports halls of fame seem to be the joint responsibility of the athletic department and athletic booster groups. The Schenectady City School District established an athletic hall of fame in 1998 and presently has 16 inductees. The hall of fame is found at the Pat Riley Sports Center at Schenectady High School and presently contains 20 members. Each inductee is honored with a bronze hall of fame plaque and there is a trophy case decorated with hall of fame photos and memorabilia.

An important question is why we even choose to have high school sports halls of fame in the first place. This is not tough to answer because it inevitably comes back to priorities. I guess the goal is to immortalize

95

former athletes whose accomplishments on the scholastic playing field were so extraordinary that generations to come needed a permanent reminder. But there is an irony here. If high schools are principally about education, why not have an *academic* hall of fame in which we include the names and pictures of class valedictorians and salutatorians, national merit scholars, and students that have obtained perfect scores on SAT exams? Or better yet, why not have an *alumni* hall of fame honoring famous graduates who have gone on to distinguish themselves in science, government, law, education, business, the arts, and yes, even athletics? If we want our kids to emulate what's really important—and that is the value of education—why do we restrict high school halls of fame to outstanding athletes?

My questions took on added meaning recently when I journeyed to my high school in Gardner, Massachusetts. Hoping to find a more enlightened perspective on the issue of high school sports halls of fame at my alma mater, I was quickly disappointed when I saw what had transpired since I graduated in 1967. Yes, my beloved Gardner High School has its own sports hall of fame with a special area devoted to those enshrined. At the current time, there are 120 inductees into the hall of fame. Each hall of famer has a plate the size of a car license affixed to the wall with the inductee's name, year of graduation, graduation photo, and the listing of sports accomplishments. I also learned that the hall of fame has an elaborate induction ceremony and banquet each year.

Like any sports loving community, Gardner has had its share of outstanding athletes through the years, but it is football that has always attracted much of the attention in this community of 18,000 people. In fact, members of the football booster group recently erected a sign near the football field that has the names of those backs who have gained over 1,000 yards in a season. My congratulations to those who made the list, but is this really necessary?

At the same time, I saw nothing visible in the school to recognize students that graduated with superior academic accomplishments. Nor did I see anything to acknowledge famous alumni that have become nationally or internationally recognized for their accomplishments.

For example, Gardner High School graduate Diane Dumanowski was an acclaimed staff writer for the internationally recognized *Boston Globe* and co-authored the award-winning and ground-breaking book, *Our Stolen Future*.

Alumna Hadassah Freilich Lieberman, wife of Senator Joseph Lieberman from Connecticut, worked for the prestigious National

Research Council in Washington and has committed her time and energy as a spokesperson and volunteer for a number of internationally recognized philanthropic organizations.

Kenneth Briggs, also a graduate of Gardner High School, has written extensively on religion while serving on the staff of both *Newsday* and the *New York Times*. His book entitled *Holy Siege* is considered to be a classic on Catholic life in America.

Gardner High graduate Mark Gearan held the post of deputy chief of staff and director of communications and strategic planning in the Clinton White House, later became director of the Peace Corps, and is now serving as president of Hobart and William Smith Colleges.

These are people that our young students should know more about and perhaps emulate as they receive their education at Gardner High School. Shouldn't their pictures and accomplishments occupy a very visible place in the halls of my alma mater? Doesn't Gardner High School want its students to know that individuals other than athletes have distinguished themselves? My former high school should not be chastised too vigorously, however, since I failed to find the presence of a more encompassing hall of fame in any high school that I have ever walked through. Perhaps I missed it or perhaps it was located in a remote part of the building. Chances are, however, there just wasn't one at all.

Sports halls of fame seem to be popping up in many different locations these days. Just recently it was announced in the *Albany Times-Union* that the Capital District Sports Hall of Fame had been established by long-time newspaper writer Gene Levy. In its first class, the hall inducted 34 members, including NFL Hall of Famer Ernie Stautner, NBA player and coach Pat Riley, LPGA golfer Dottie Pepper, NBA player Luther "Ticky" Burden, Olympic gold medallist Jeff Blatnick, and legendary boxing coach Cus D'Amato. While I am not sure that there is truly a need for a sports hall of fame in the Albany area, all of the inductees are certainly worthy in view of their athletic and/or coaching accomplishments.

Enshrining at least one of the individuals, Ticky Burden, is somewhat dubious in view of his criminal record. In 1980, Burden was arrested and later convicted of serving as the mastermind of a bank robbery in Nassau County. The conviction was overturned four years later by an appellate judge because police failed to obtain a warrant to search Burden's home following the robbery. He eventually pleaded guilty to possession of stolen money—a lesser offense—and was released from jail. Though Burden seems to have turned his life around, the Capital

District Sports Hall of Fame might want to rethink its criteria for future inductees. The mixed message that is sent by Ticky Burden's induction is not the kind I would want any kids to read about and then emulate.

In recent announcements in newspapers throughout the state, the New York State Public High School Athletic Association has put out a call for nominations to its inaugural hall of fame class. The plan is to have inductees honored at their annual convention and banquet. It will recognize athletes, coaches, officials, and administrators. The nominees have to be at least 35 years of age and have exemplified sportsmanship and ethical conduct during their careers, as well as having made significant contributions to interscholastic athletics in the State of New York. The idea to create a statewide high school hall of fame grew from the one that presently exists for the National Federation of State High Schools (NFSHS). The creation of a state hall of fame assumes, but certainly does not require, that the nominations come from those that have already been enshrined in a local high school sports hall of fame. With this in mind, I am certain that high school sports halls of fame will proliferate and become even more important as time goes on.

After my investigation of high school sports halls of fame, I contacted the exploratory committee in town and let them know that I was not keen on the idea. I mentioned that a better idea would be the creation of a more encompassing alumni hall of fame that would recognize the accomplishments of graduates who had gone on to distinguish themselves nationally or internationally in any field, not just athletics. At present, I don't know what direction the committee is going in but I am hopeful that my comments may have had some effect in dissuading them from their original goal.

While the recognition of athletes in high school sports halls of fame is not a bad thing, I am left to wonder where the balance is. Ours is a culture that values athletic accomplishments a lot and educational achievements only a little. Parents and kids look to these visible signs of accomplishment all the time and the signal that is clearly sent in our present culture is that if you can dunk a basketball or hit a home run or catch a touchdown pass you are certain to get permanently recognized and rewarded for it in one way or another. But, if you hit the honor roll year after year or become a national merit scholarship winner or graduate first or second in your high school class, your recognition might, if you're lucky, include a brief write-up in the local newspapers.

My youngest son Mark graduated from high school in 1998. In a class of 319 students he qualified for the National Honor Society along with about 25 of his high school classmates. The brief 45-minute induction was held during the spring in a small, cramped classroom toward the back of the school. There was a collection of proud parents present as well as the faculty advisors for the ceremony. There was no banquet or more extended celebration that might have included more of the school's faculty as well as administrators. There were no outside speakers that perhaps could have included a distinguished local scientist, lawyer, engineer, educator, artist, or other accomplished professional. There was no picture of the inductees nor was there a write-up in the local newspaper. Moreover, there was no picture or listing of honor roll students in his class yearbook. In short, there was little fanfare for the event and an important accomplishment was concealed, almost hidden to all but a few parents who knew that it had occurred. A defining academic moment for some hardworking students was relegated to the status of an afterthought. Moreover, it was all but invisible to the community at large. An opportunity to recognize what is really important in our society was totally missed.

There is no balance in our present sports-obsessed culture. In the battle between academics versus athletics, it is not even close . . . sports have won in a rout.

16

School Budget Blues

I have been fortunate to live in a school district in Upstate New York where public education is taken seriously and valued by residents of the community. Bethlehem Central School District regularly meets or exceeds standards set by the New York State Regents. With an annual budget of about $53 million a year, the district educates about 5,000 students yearly, employs 744 instructional personnel and staff, and is spread out over 7 buildings. The facilities include an early learning center, 5 elementary schools, a middle school, and a high school.

The Bethlehem Central School District enjoys an outstanding reputation that is well deserved. In 1998, for example, Bethlehem Central High School was nationally recognized by *Newsweek* magazine as one of the top 100 public schools in the nation. A very high percentage of graduates go on to college each year, often to some of the best institutions of higher learning in the country. Accomplishments like these have led even the most critical observers to conclude that the instructional staff and administration are exceptionally talented and dedicated. As a result, real estate values in the community are very good and the Bethlehem area is viewed as an extremely desirable place to raise a family because of its excellent schools.

Year in and year out budgets are proposed and passed with high acceptance from local voters. The school district, like so many others, develops a school budget by seeking input from all elements of the community through budget workshops that are hosted by the school board and administration. Because the community places such a high emphasis upon academic excellence, budget sessions go smoothly and well-thought-out justifications are usually advanced for new and continuing budget items. Funding for extracurricular activities, including sports, seldom is debated for long even when new items, such as the adding of a sport, are presented for discussion.

The budgetary process in Bethlehem stands in stark contrast to that in other communities, where cantankerous discussions result in contingency budgets because of voter disapproval. Sometimes this results in deep athletic budget cuts to make up for the shortfall. Under this scenario, outside fund-raising becomes a way of life and user fees are established for each sport. I have seen this time and again in communities in this region and elsewhere and it is not a pleasant circumstance especially when a family has several kids playing expensive sports like football, lacrosse, and ice hockey. User fees result in a two-tiered class system—the haves and the have-nots—and it divides communities like a knife. In some areas it also results in lost opportunities for kids whose families can't afford to come up with the extra cash that it takes to play if you make a team.

Athletic school budgets are being scrutinized more these days especially as the economy worsens and state aid decreases. In my community of Bethlehem, interscholastic sports funding (physical education and health are separate and part of instructional budgets) is rarely questioned but perhaps it should be. The 2002 budget showed expenses of $434,000 ($290,000 for salaries, $99,000 for contractual expenses, $45,000 for materials and supplies). This represents less than one percent of the total $53 million budget. The conclusion by many is that interscholastic sports are relatively cheap and, because so many are participating, it is a small price to pay for keeping kids off the streets and active with sports. Both conclusions are grossly exaggerated and in some cases outright myths.

Bethlehem Central School District, like many suburban school districts, supports a wide array of athletic offerings including football, ice hockey, gymnastics, golf, wrestling, field hockey, and boys' and girls' lacrosse, swimming, cross country, volleyball, soccer, basketball, indoor and outdoor track, tennis, bowling, and baseball. A number of these sports such as football, basketball, baseball, and soccer include modified, freshman, JV, and varsity teams. In 1998, the year my youngest son graduated, 1,072 students were rostered on the various sports teams out of approximately 1,800 students from grades 7 to 12 that were eligible. This means that 60 percent of the student body was involved in sports. However, because many play two or even three sports, a more realistic figure is that a much smaller percentage of students, perhaps only about 20–30 percent, actually participate.

Some argue that interscholastic sports are cheap—less than one percent of the budget—but this is a deceptive figure as well. In truth, most school budgets for interscholastic sports do not include the price tag for insurance, employee benefits, debt service, maintenance of gyms and fields, as well as transportation and other operational expenses. These figures are never broken out into their contribution to athletics but if they were, some believe that the total athletic budget would be closer to 10 percent of the actual school budget. In the case of Bethlehem Central High School that would be somewhere in the neighborhood of $5 million a year devoted just to interscholastic athletics.

Bethlehem Central School District in the year 2003 wrestled with the possibility of deep budget cuts because of lowered school aid resulting from the post 9/11 downturn in the New York economy. Though there was talk that as many as 17 teacher positions might have to be cut along with some programs, local school taxes were hiked and money was budgeted to restore staffing to acceptable levels. The budget was passed by district voters in the spring in spite of continued worries about increases in local school taxes. Interestingly, throughout the discussion of the school budget, there was no mention of cutting sports or going to a user fee system. In fact, I heard some in the community talk about adding sports such as crew, women's ice hockey, and cross country and downhill skiing.

In the fall of 2003, the school district passed a $93 millin bond issue to add instructional and athletic space for the rapidly rising enrollment in the community. As part of the plan, two expensive new gymnasiums were included for the high school and middle school. The bond issue, which was one of the largest in the history of upstate New York, passed by a very narrow margin. Once again, other than perfunctory discussions regarding the addition of the new athletic facilities in the development of the bond issue, there was no serious discussion given to whether or not the new athletic facilities were truly justifiable from an instructional/educational perspective.

The question remains as to whether or not my school district as well as others in our country can continue to sustain dramatic tax hikes for the support of school-based athletics. For at least two reasons, we need to start thinking outside the box on this issue. First, we have a costly system of interscholastic sports in place that serves only a small fraction of students. Second, with the exception of a few scholastic athletes, our young people have become less active and more obese in part because physical education and fitness classes have been dramatically deemphasized in our schools.

With the above facts in mind, it is difficult to imagine that we can continue to invest so heavily in so few when the educational priorities of learning and lifelong fitness and health are not being met in many of our nation's schools. Has anyone thought that there may be a better system in which we no longer ask our public schools to foot the bill for sports and we instead ask the community to do so by way of sports organizations, clubs, and private businesses? Europe and Australia do it all the time and as a result they do not have to deal with compromised education of their young people. My question is, why can't we do the same thing in the United States?

To my knowledge, it was never etched in stone or mandated by anyone that we support interscholastic athletics through our schools. The value of school-based sports as mainstream education is a myth; it grew from an outdated historical tradition that is no longer relevant in our sports culture today. We have tried to be all things to all people and in doing so we have sacrificed the core mission of our public schools and that is to educate our young people. In a day and age when we need to refocus our attention on core academic priorities as well as health and fitness for all, competitive sports in our schools is a luxury that has long outlived any educational relevance that it once may have had.

Our students' ability to develop lifelong habits of health and fitness and to compete successfully in an increasingly sophisticated, technology-driven world should not be held hostage to an expensive sports entertainment sideshow that benefits only a few. Clearly, the time has come to make some long overdue changes in the educational priorities of our public schools.

I recently looked at my oldest son's 1998 senior yearbook. Of the 224 pages, 52 (23 percent) were devoted to interscholastic sports. Perhaps it is not a fair comparison, but my senior yearbook from the class of 1967 in Gardner, Massachusetts, shows that the page count for interscholastic athletics was 15 out of 119 pages (about 13 percent). Does this tell you something about the increasingly prominent role that sports occupies in our public schools today?

Part Four

SPORTS CASUALTIES

The fact is that the appetite for steroids and other performance enhancing drugs has been created predominantly by a societal fixation on winning and physical appearance. This behavior is learned. Children play games for fun, at least as long as they can before adults intervene to tell them that winning is what's important. One of the strongest reasons we should not give up the struggle to make sports contests fair and to encourage young athletes to be good sportsman is because their ethical conduct on the playing field lays a foundation for later ethical conduct in life. Life is a team sport. Competitiveness and a fierce desire to win are qualities that have made this nation great. But before we allow our children to compete, we must first establish in them a moral and ethical foundation so they have boundaries they will not cross in pursuit of victory.

Chuck Yesalis and Virginia Cowart,
The Steroids Game

The number one fallacy is that injuries are inherent; that they are going to happen no matter what you do. The vast majority of injuries are completely preventable.

David Janda, *The Awakening of a Surgeon*

Lesson 1: Point spreads are the currency of American sports, and not just for guys who look like they should be in the Sopranos. For college kids, betting generates much of the energy you see in arenas and stadiums.

Lesson 2: If you can't get a bet down on any college campus in America, you aren't trying. Bookies are everywhere. And most of them are students.

Lesson 3: An awful lot of student bettors are convinced that games are getting fixed by student athletes in their midst.

Tim Layden CNN-SI Commentary

It is an anomaly that our society is in the middle of what can be described as a fitness boom and yet our youth have never been less fit. In fact, there is a crisis in fitness among American's children.

Andrew Miracle and Roger Rees,
Lessons of the Locker Room

17

Fitness Failures

There is a fundamental paradox about our present sports culture that is difficult to understand: competitive sports in our country have grown and elite athletes have become better, but the health and fitness of the average young American has never been worse. Here are some interesting statistics that speak to the issue:

- Nearly half of American youths ages 12 to 21 years are not vigorously active on a regular basis.
- About 14 percent of young people report no recent physical activity.
- Participation in all types of physical activity dramatically declines as age or grade in school increases.
- Only 19 percent of all high school students are physically active for 20 minutes or more, five days a week, in physical education classes.
- Illinois is the only state that requires physical education and only 26 percent of U. S. high schools offer daily physical education.
- Forty percent of high school students are never enrolled in a gym class and for high school seniors the percentage is 75 percent.
- Colorado, Mississippi, and South Dakota have no physical education requirement of any kind.
- Only seven states require elementary schools to have certified physical education instructors, meaning that oftentimes classroom teachers have the principal responsibility of teaching physical education classes.
- A recent Gallup poll showed that 54 percent of adults believed that public school curricula should be improved but only 2 percent

mentioned health related and physical education classes as the focus of change.

As our society has become less physically fit and active, millions of Americans suffer from illnesses that probably could be prevented or at least significantly improved if they engaged in regular physical activity:

- 13.5 million people have coronary heart disease.
- 1.5 million people suffer a heart attack in a given year.
- 8 million people have adult-onset (non-insulin-dependent) diabetes.
- 95,000 people are newly diagnosed with colon cancer each year.
- 250,000 people suffer from hip fractures each year.
- 50 million people have high blood pressure.
- Over 60 million people are overweight, with childhood obesity becoming an epidemic.

As we upgrade athletic fields and gymnasiums in our colleges and universities, high schools, and community athletic clubs, those facilities increasingly are being used for the training of elite athletes. In the meantime, the average young American benefits very little from the palatial sports complexes that have become such a fabric of scholastic, intercollegiate, and community life. Therefore, in spite of the well-known benefits of life-long fitness training, we have become a nation more concerned with watching a few elite athletes than participating in sports for the exercise and health benefits they potentially provide for the vast majority.

I needed some answers for this disturbing trend so I talked to a master physical education teacher who has received state and national accolades for his role as a physical educator. Pete Hogan, a recently retired physical educator in the Bethlehem Central School District in Upstate New York, has won numerous prestigious awards in his field. For example, he was named Physical Education Teacher of the Year in New York State and was also a finalist for the National Association of Sport and Physical Education national teacher of the year award. Hogan also has been involved with writing curriculum for the New York State Education Department and is considered one of the leading innovators of physical education and fitness in the country. He graciously spent considerable time responding to some questions that I posed regarding physical education and fitness. Edited below are Pete Hogan's answers to several of my questions.

Q. *Based upon your experience, are we in the midst of a crisis in fitness in this country? If you do believe that we are in a crisis, then just why has it evolved this way and what (who) is to blame? Why don't we commit more resources to it, especially in view of the fact that it costs our nation billions of dollars when unfit kids turn into adults with costly health-related problems?*

A. Perhaps epidemic is a more accurate word to describe the current fitness/health dilemma. Everywhere you look there is evidence to support the notion that our children are the least fit, most nutritionally deficient generation. Poor nutrition as a result of contemporary lifestyles is certainly a significant factor that contributes to the potential health consequences of heart disease and diabetes. Research has clearly shown that young children have very high cholesterol levels. Heart disease remains the number 1 killer in America and diabetes is increasing at an alarming rate. We know these truths, yet the lines at fast food establishments are always full and portions far exceed normal limits. The rise in youth obesity is quite evident. The potential for the ever-increasing unhealthy, overweight, out-of-shape generation of children to bankrupt the health-care system of the future is catastrophic.

At the same time, there have never been more opportunities for improving personal health and fitness. In addition, there is more accurate and helpful nutritional information than ever before that could literally extend longevity and impact quality of life issues for consumers. Curiously, eating habits are very similar to physical activity habits. Lifestyle choices are ingrained very early in life and although not impossible to modify, habits are hard to break. Just as one should select fish over beef, they should also participate in Nordic rather than alpine skiing. We know, however, that is not usually the case.

I believe this whole question points to issues of lifestyle choice and culture. By the way, it is ironic that there has been an increase in fitness activity for adult populations and yet children of these role models are only perfunctorily involved with fitness. Developing fitness is not as much fun as shooting baskets or hitting a ball. It is one of those delayed gratification aspects of life that seem to be destined for the patience and perseverance of later years. On the other hand, most team sports and some individual sports offer participants instant gratification in terms of social or emotional value, but not a lot of long-term fitness rewards.

There is a critical misunderstanding by the general public regarding the illusion (or delusion) that lifetime fitness activities and popular traditional sports are interdependent and offer similar health benefits. This misconception leaves many team-oriented disciples wondering how they got so out of shape after their active playing days have ended.

On one hand, a child's first contact with organized sports and physical movement involves activities that do not promote and develop lifestyle fitness concepts. Yes, some credit can be mentioned for motivating children to engage in physical activities by participating in these games, but unfortunately, that is where the merit ends. There is an old saying that goes "people who grow up playing team sports end up to be people who watch team sports." *A physically active lifestyle is not a spectator sport.*

The sports common to young American children are enjoyable (for the most part), but not without their drawbacks. Let's take a look at the traditional "big three." For example, there are very few, if any aerobic benefits to Little League Baseball or baseball at any level. Pop Warner Football is actually less cardiorespiratory-oriented than baseball. Basketball is conceivably better than the first two—if you end up on the starting five or six.

Now, let's look at a few modern-day additions to youth sport opportunities. Youth soccer is the best in terms of health-related fitness so far, but still not sustained enough to produce any long-term health benefits. Hockey and lacrosse are very good cardiorespiratory conditioners but are more specialized than other sport opportunities. The list could go on and on and with each refined addition, we see more specialization. With a greater degree of specialization comes more specific equipment, facility, coaching, and participation requirements.

So the recreational sandlot activities that were almost a daily part of our formative years are nearly nonexistent now. There was a time when all you needed to play was an object and a group of kids. Everything is so specialized and adult organized now that extemporaneous play is no longer the rule, but rather the exception. Organized practice, uniforms, equipment, referees, and adult misguided control have replaced the healthy practice of daily neighborhood, backyard activity.

If you take a good look at the activities mentioned, there aren't a lot of health-related fitness benefits involved. Remember the components of health-related fitness are cardiorespiratory, flexibility, muscular endurance, muscular strength, and body composition. There are many performance or skill-related fitness factors in the activities mentioned. Skill-related fitness relates to skills of motor performance generally associated with sports or athletics rather than personal health. Skill-related fitness involves balance, agility, speed, power, coordination, and reaction time.

With the current two periods per week, thirty to forty-minute elementary physical education time schedule, it is not realistic to believe that a school-based physical education program can attain, maintain, or improve cardiovasacular fitness. In 1998, the National Association for Sport and Physical Education (NASPE) recommended that elementary school-aged children should accumulate 30 to 60 minutes of age and developmentally appropriate physical activity on all or most days of the week. It is difficult to achieve minimum fitness levels when the scheduled class time is considerably less than the guidelines being suggested.

What can be accomplished is a comprehensive, interdisciplinary health education approach to the instruction of traditional physical education that can demonstrate and promote the benefits of a physically active lifestyle. If we, as educators, pay close attention to personalizing the learning experience by facilitating what a physically active lifestyle does for personal health and well-being during childhood and adolescence, we will have a major impact on the lifestyle choices that our students make when they become adults.

In 1987, the American Academy of Pediatrics (AAP) stated that physical education programs should be emphasizing lifetime activities and sports like cycling, swimming, and tennis. At the same time, the AAP recommended that schools should be decreasing the amount of time spent on skills for team sports such as football, basketball, and baseball. Furthermore, it was strongly recommended that school-based physical fitness activities should promote a lifelong habit of aerobic exercise.

Some of the sports that would decidedly make a difference in personal health are cross country skiing, long distance running, endurance bicycling, hiking, and sustained swimming. The majority of the youth population does not engage in these types of high-output, personal fitness activities simply because Americans have socialized and nurtured a different physical activity culture. The American sports culture is based on highly-organized team sports that make a very positive contribution to our social culture, but do very little for our personal health and well-being. While I believe that team sports are an integral and valued part of the American culture, there needs to be a better balance of lifetime health-related activities. That's where a change in the traditional physical education program is needed.

Including more health in physical education programs can positively influence the personal health and well-being of our students. That goal alone should be the driving force in physical education. Increasing more health education is necessary if physical education intends to keep pace with the twenty-first-century needs of consumers. Personal health will remain a key factor in valuing and evaluating the need for school-based physical education. (Let's not forget that it is our current students who will be making decisions on school budget issues in the future.)

If physical education remains content to continue strictly as a sport or skill model, community sports programs (which have already become a very powerful interest group in many school systems) will begin to question program redundancy. There was a time when the skills learned in physical education class served as a necessary precursor to higher level athletic participation. Today, that is the exception, not the rule. By modifying the physical education model to include the interdisciplinary aspects of health education, there is greater cause for justifying its existence and even upgrading its educational impact.

In summary, the health implications of contemporary society are extremely complex, and difficult to change. Education is one of the keys to improving the health of the American people. In particular, physical education can have an important and lasting impact on developing healthy lifestyles, but not in its present sports model framework. If the nation turns to education to empower students with the knowledge and values to make healthy lifestyle choices concerning AIDS education, sex education, or even driver education then a comprehensive health-related physical education curriculum based on lifetime sports not team sports would develop the knowledge and values necessary for a healthy, active lifestyle.

Q. *Regarding New York State mandates for physical education, do you believe that they are too lenient? Do you believe that elementary through high school aged kids are not getting enough physical education time over the course of a normal week?*

A. I have always felt that state mandates were like the proverbial stop sign that everyone in the neighborhood disregards because they (1) do not respect the rule(s), (2) they consider the rule(s) a nuisance and find ways to get around them, and (3) they know they can get away with it. And if, by chance, they get caught (either at the stop sign or not following the mandates), they rarely suffer any consequences that would impress them enough to change their attitude. In addition, the mechanics of compliance or should I say noncompliance make it relatively easy for school districts to submit an alternate plan and evade the responsibility of providing a quality physical education program. Throw in a heavy helping of politics and you have mandates that are about as good as a Florida swampland deal. Finally, the support staff to enforce the regulations numbered six (or more) in the Physical Education Bureau years ago and there is only one left today.

As far as your question goes, I believe the "mandates" are a joke if they are not valued by the districts and enforced by the State Education Department (SED). The word "mandate" means to "command" or "entrust." In the case of the word "mandatory," it means "required." That is simply not the case. If the mandates are "commanded" or "required" by SED and "entrusted" to the leadership of local schools, then why are there so many school districts not complying? The answer is simple. Physical education is not valued enough to warrant mandatory status and districts can get away with not meeting the regulations. In light of the recent higher standards created by the Regents and Commissioner of Education, schools are always looking for more time in the day to insert additional academic resources so they can meet these new standards. Obviously, there is only so much time available in a student's day. Districts have been increasingly chipping away at physical education, art, and music time to provide additional academic services to students in need of extra help. By no means do I justify or condone this practice, but the priority of "reading, writing, and arithmetic" has always taken precedence over physical education.

The current New York State requirements for physical education state the following:

- All students in K–12 must attend and participate in a physical education program.
- All pupils in grades K–3 shall attend and participate in physical education on a daily basis.
- All pupils in grades 4–6 shall attend and participate in physical education not less than three times per week.
- All pupils in grades 7–12 shall attend and participate in physical education for not less than three times per week in one semester, and not less than two times per week in the other semester.
- The time requirement per calendar week is 120 minutes exclusive of any time that may be required for dressing and showering.

There is also a clause which says that an equivalent program may be provided if approved by the commissioner of higher education. That simply means that there is no real mandate because an alternative plan can be submitted to the commissioner. Districts are required to submit an alternative plan if they cannot meet the mandates. However, with 714 school districts in New York State and one individual in the Physical Education Bureau of SED, alternate plans are rarely if ever reviewed. In the 33 years I taught elementary physical education, not one single child from any elementary school in the districts where I was employed attended physical education according to the 120 minutes per week mandate.

Now for the practical application of all this regulation baloney. I suppose that if there weren't Commissioner's Regulations, many subject areas (including physical education) would be far less than they are or perhaps nonexistent. Having said that, I've always believed the elementary pupils never receive enough physical education. Some junior high school or middle schools are close to the time minimum and the same may be said for high schools. In the case of our own middle school, the daily physical education program is more a product of scheduling than it is of commitment to New York State mandates.

There is another perspective to the question of "more is better." Quite frankly, more is not always better. In fact, more of the same poor quality physical education taught by an unmotivated and incompetent teacher is not a good idea at all. For every one highly effective and master teacher of physical education, there are an equal number (or more) of incompetent people who do not measure up. These people are the "gym" teachers who still believe in dodge ball, relay races, running laps for punishment, and picking sides. It is these individuals who continue to degrade the profession and counter the tremendous work of dedicated professionals. That is a major reason why physical education is not viewed as an essential piece of the overall education program. In addition, ask school board members about the physical education experience they had in school. They will tell you about redundancy, long lines of meaningless drills that promoted boredom instead of fitness, and traditional curriculum that became old by the time they got to high school. Then gym was when the coach rolled out a few basketballs and the kids played pick-up games all semester.

Those very same board members decide which programs will be funded, decreased, expanded or eliminated. The negative physical education experience acquired from being in a poor scholastic program that many people currently in positions of authority and power have had is very difficult to change. If physical education offered more than the "same old, same old," perhaps more value would be placed on it and therefore more financial support raising its position and effectiveness in the hierarchy of the curriculum.

Q. Some say that we expect too much from our schools these days. For example, extracurricular activities (theater, music, drama, and interscholastic sports) increasingly seem to take away from basic academic and fitness for all curriculums. Have these activities become an expensive sideshow? Perhaps we need to curtail them in order to make sure that we devote the proper time and attention to the essentials of education (e.g., core academic and fitness curriculum).

A. I believe the more diverse the curriculum, the better the outcome in terms of student growth, development and progress. If part of the process of education is restricted or limited in some form, the end result will always be less than expected. It would be like trying to teach a somersault to a gymnastics student without first learning the "tuck" body position. In addition, if a physical education curriculum concentrates only on team sports, then the knowledge, skills, and values of lifetime sports will be neglected. If only fitness education is offered, other essential areas of a well-rounded curriculum will be absent from the educational process and the product will not be complete.

I am not convinced that the quantity of interscholastic and extracurricular choices needs to address every individual's interests. In other words, just because some students share a common interest and enthusiasm for rock climbing doesn't necessarily mean the board of education should allocate money to build, maintain, and operate a climbing wall in a school facility. Unfortunately, the lack of prudence, restraint, and control of past practices have placed many viable and educationally sound programs on the same cutting board as unessential interest group "frills."

The time to evaluate the merit of nonessential add-ons is before they get implemented, not after they have been operating. Therein lies the rub. A committee of so-called experts must be able to make the tough decisions when it comes to adding curriculum—denying access when they feel that the proposal is not essential and creating space and financial support when needed. The difficulty now is that school budgets are burdened with costly extras. The challenge is for someone to decide what is kept and what is not. For example, how does a group justify cutting the jazz band while keeping lacrosse?

Interest groups seem to have an increasingly greater influence on many budgetary decisions of school districts. While I don't disagree with the political process, educational decisions should be left in the hands of educators and the people responsible for the educational leadership of a school system. Those decisions should never be made or even influenced by special interest groups. We both know that is not the reality of current trends. The board of education must be involved in these critical choices and more often than not, that group's decision making process is adversely affected by politics. The bottom line is that when interest groups are successful in influencing institutional leadership and implementing their personal agendas, many things change and not always for the better.

Q. *The basic message that one hears over and over again is that many ill-nesses could be prevented or at least significantly improved if people engaged in regular physical activity. Why is it that this message apparently is not getting through? Are those habits just not emphasized enough early in life? What can be done about it so that the pattern of physical inactivity can be reversed? Is this something we need to work on even more with our young people at a very early time in their life?*

A. Our culture is not lifetime-sport oriented. Our children grow up with a steady diet of team sports, some of which are very poor fitness choices. Yes, they are fun and require proficient motor skill development, but at some point people no longer participate because they have gone as far as their skills can take them or the organizational support structure disappears. By the way, the performance pyramid has been lowered so far in youth sports that kids are being cut by the time they finish middle school. Can you imagine that! By the age of 13 or 14 most of the children who entered team sports at 5 or 6 are finished. And what do they have to show for it? A few trinkets and trophies (everybody gets them) and hopefully some good times, but not much in the way of physical fitness or a nurtured interest in a lifetime activity that will translate easily into their adult years.

Let me share an example of what happens in our sport culture with one of my favorite team activities, basketball. It is a great game requiring an immense amount of diverse skills, but it is not a great fitness choice for the general public. Let me try to capture the sport of American basketball as I see it. Children start by shooting a smaller, lighter basketball at graduated-height baskets. They progress to some drills (dribbling, passing, shooting), but since drills are so boring, scrimmage games quickly take over. Scrimmage games help everyone learn the sport, but when competition enters the picture too early in the developmental stages, the goals and objectives of active participation are displaced by the concept of winning. Incidentally, I believe that competition actually does more for developing the "blue chip" player while "weeding out" most others. There is more beneficial physical activity in drills (if there are enough basketballs) rather than games. But playing the game is the predominant reason for participating in the sport even if the less skilled players don't warrant a lot of court time. We both know the reason for that. The team could lose if the best players are not in the game. But that's okay, because it's the team that really matters (right?) and besides, at least they're on the bench while the other 90 percent of the kids that tried out were cut. Years go by and the highly skilled players move up the pyramid while the majority of players are relegated to a "HORSE" game in the driveway of their home. At long last there are 12 (?) players on the high school team, five to seven who play enough minutes to gain some cardio-vascular benefits. The rest of the "wannabes" are in the bleachers watching or later on in life sit in a sports bar rooting for their favorite team. This scenario is repeated year after year with every new generation of potential players on courts, fields, and diamonds all over America. Ours is just not a society that promotes and develops an interest in fitness-centered lifetime activities.

Q. *Over the past 10 to 20 years, our culture has become more concerned with elevating academic standards. Thus, more money was targeted toward perceived weaknesses (math and reading performance) as well as developing advanced placement classes. Unfortunately, money and other resources (sometimes classroom space) were taken away from physical education. Some therefore feel that physical education has become marginalized because of an elevated emphasis on academics. At the same time, competitive interscholastic sports were considered sacred and actually expanded during this time period. Based upon your experience, do you think that there is some truth to the possibility that physical education has been marginalized and it has been caused in part by strengthened academic standards and increased emphasis on interscholastic sports?*

A. I do believe that quality physical education has been compromised by a "curriculum crunch." At times throughout the school year, conflicts arise when functions are scheduled in the physical education classroom—the gymnasium. It happened to me more times than I care to remember. Someone else always seems to have a greater need than the physical education teacher does for using the gymnasium. As a personal aside, I commonly referred to my gymnasium as my classroom. Other people called it the "all-purpose room" or the "auditorium." Whenever there was a discussion about another group using the "auditorium" (and displacing physical education classes), I responded by insisting that I have the right to teach in my "classroom" just like any other classroom teacher. Anything less would be considered a breach of my contract and grounds for a grievance. Thank goodness I was never really tested on that assertion. I'm not sure if my interpretation would have been supported. In the end, I did compromise many times for schoolwide programs and other functions, but at least I was consulted before the room was scheduled.

The reason I bring this up is that there has always been a double standard when it comes to uses of the gymnasium other than physical education. Each year I probably lost close to 15 days of accumulative instruction time due to not having my teaching station. Classroom teachers would not allow their instruction to be disrupted so often by having to give up their classroom and find somewhere else to teach. Realistically, I know that my classroom served many purposes, but it was more the attitude of colleagues, administrators, and the general public that physical education (in its rightful setting) was expendable at any time. That attitude clearly shows how little physical education is genuinely respected and valued.

However, those occasions present more of a nuisance factor than a serious change in the structure and function of a course of study. When academic standards are raised and the scope and sequence of learning expanded, something has to give. There are only so many hours in the day when subjects can be taught. If new or revised courses are added to an already overloaded curriculum, instructional time and scheduling to meet the new requirements becomes a critical issue. Physical education is usually one of the recurrent and unwilling recipients of program interruptions, cancellations, and reductions.

If there is anything I've learned over the duration of my career it's that there is (like it or not) a curriculum hierarchy. At the upper end are the absolute necessities of learning—reading, math, language arts, and science. That's fine with me. However, there is something to be said for the concept of a healthy mind and a healthy body so that would support the idea of a physical education program. There are also cultural and fine arts considerations that suggest programs in art, music and drama.

From that point on, the position of subject importance is directly related to several variables. These factors may include but are not limited to local and/or state requirements or mandates, community interest and influence, school geographic location, climate, student interest and demand, economic and employment considerations, and staff competency.

Regarding staff competency, I believe inferior and complacent teachers (bordering on incompetent) share some of the responsibility for the demise of physical education. Furthermore, a stagnant, outdated, and redundant curriculum model contributes to the gradual decline of and respect for the content of a physical education program.

It is disquieting to realize that teachers who remain steadfast to the ways of the past continue to think they are doing exactly what they are supposed to be doing, when in fact, they are acting like coaches who treat their players the way they were treated when they played. Some are still using tactics (assigning laps for punishment) and teaching exercises (hurdler's stretch) that have been discontinued 25 years ago. It's not all that different from teachers who teach the same thing in the same way for their entire career.

Nevertheless, the consumers (students) of such physical education programs are bored and tired of redundant content and unmotivated to participate at a level that would be of any physical benefit. All of a sudden something new happens. New directions become available for engaging, stimulating, and exciting lifetime activities (i.e., adventure education) which expand the curriculum and empower students to become active and involved. However, the "old school" either stonewalls the ideas or refuses to participate at all. I wonder what would happen to a math teacher who refused to incorporate new math concepts or a science teacher who didn't keep up with technology? The same could be said for history, language arts, or any other discipline. As professionals, teachers have an obligation to keep apprised of current knowledge and practices in their respective fields. Why then has physical education remained so lethargic?

I also firmly believe that setting higher standards and requiring more rigorous coursework in reading, math, language arts, and science are valid and appropriate for the majority of the student population. There are some segments of the student population that will not benefit from more demanding and inflexible standards. Also, the increased emphasis on cognitive tests that measure student performance has become a "double edged sword." There are many arguments for and against testing as a necessary evil, but the bottom line is accountability and I have no problem with that. It is puzzling to me that interscholastic athletic teams appear to be the "sacred cow" during budget time. I've never quite figured that out. How some subject areas have to cut back on books and learning tools while teams get new uniforms has always been difficult to figure. There have been a few times when I can remember local budgets being voted down several times leading to a contingency budget that didn't include interscholastic sports teams. However, that has been the rare exception rather than the rule. There was even a time when our family experienced a "pay for play" situation.

It never ceases to amaze me how library propositions get defeated and sports proposals pass. Perhaps the public sees interscholastic sports as physical education. We already know that a percentage of physical education people do. If this is the case physical educators should take note and immediately begin to make the necessary changes in programs that separate the two. If nothing is done, there remains the probability that the redundancy issue will gain momentum. If the scenarios comes to fruition, physical education will be headed to a much different outcome.

Q. *Some have noted that physical education and fitness-based curriculum in our colleges and universities are virtually nonexistent. I know that your experience has been in our public schools, but based upon what you know, what do you think of the demise of physical education and fitness classes in higher education?*

A. Yes, I have heard of colleges and universities that have discontinued the physical education graduation requirement. However, it would seem to me (if elementary, middle, and high school physical education were doing their job effectively) by the time a consumer (student) reaches college or college age, he or she would have the knowledge, skill, and desire to be physically active. That is an outcome of any quality physical education program. After 12 years of scholastic physical education, high school graduates should be knowledgeable enough to lead a physically active lifestyle without further "requirements."

Having said that, when colleges discontinue the physical education requirement, can scholastic institutions be far behind? There is something to be said for holding on to the physical education requirements simply because institutions of higher learning are supposed to know the right things to do, such as valuing the importance of physical activity. Retaining the physical education prerequisites demonstrates a model of academic leadership for other institutions to emulate. By requiring its students to earn a designated amount of credits in physical education as a graduation requirement, colleges send an important message about physical health. Just as English 100 is required for all first-year students so should Physical Education 100.

It really is not difficult to plan a sequence of coursework to include independent study in order to meet a physical education obligation. A quality program would actually enhance the college experience. The challenge would be to find a staff versatile enough to offer a wide variety of courses so students could expand their physical horizons.

The proverbial bottom line is the almighty dollar. College tuitions are excessive and the obvious question arises as to the priority of tuition dollars spent on meeting a physical education requirement or spending that money on additional coursework that would prepare someone more thoroughly for the job market. As a physical education teacher I would support the physical education requirement. As a parent paying the bills, I might think differently.

Q. *Some have argued that we should remove competitive interscholastic sports from our schools and hand them over to outside sports clubs. This is the European or Australian model that has been adopted in every other country except the United states. If we did this, it would then allow us to devote scarce resources to physical education and fitness for all. What do you think of this? Could it ever happen in the United States?*

A. My initial response to this question is while I realize that financial resources favor athletics over physical education, I honestly do not think that future funding would increase if athletics were privatized and removed from the jurisdiction of schools. As a matter of fact, I would be more than a little concerned that the general public (as well as boards of education) would continue the incorrect affiliation between athletics and physical education and wonder why physical education was needed if schools no longer had the athletic program. It's one of those, "be careful what you wish for" things.

As far as the thought about such a situation happening in America, I believe it already is happening in some form for a few highly technical athletic interests. Gymnastics comes to mind right away and ice hockey has always had its own advanced system of junior leagues for talented players. I'll admit, those examples are not exactly the same as what you describe in your question, but some of the same elements are embedded. The difference is right now, a high school gymnast or hockey player often has the choice of playing on the high school team or going private. I am sure there are instances where there is no school-sponsored sport, but I'm not aware of that many high school sport teams that have actually been displaced by private enterprise.

I have to confess I am guilty of more than a little "old fashionedness" and traditional feelings — none of which makes a lot of practical sense. That's the way it is, however, right or wrong, there is something to be said for the value of school spirit and pride that school teams bring to a school. Over the years I was involved in high school and college athletics. There was a great sense of self-worth and personal contribution that my teammates and I brought to our alma maters. The rewards of athletic participation offered more than climbing the social ladder (although I'll admit the dating choices improved as athletic stature increased). However, those social dividends were mostly short-lived. As I reflect on my athletic career, I think of the pride of chenille athletic letters, letter sweaters, pep rallies, athletic banquets, and a host of other occasions where being a part of a team brought honor and respect to my school and myself. In retrospect, it gave me an opportunity, that I otherwise would not have: to make a positive contribution to the life of a school. I shudder to think what schools would be without the excitement and enthusiasm of athletics.

I have to say that I do believe athletics is much bigger than it should be or needs to be. I also firmly believe that the "purity" of amateur high school athletics has suffered from the "trickle down" effects of college athletics gone mad. I also understand that the media has done more to hype the perceived importance of sport and contribute to the misplaced values of athletics. That is also a family issue as well. However, that is another complex question for another time.

Sometimes I wish people would keep a more healthy perspective on the values of athletics, but I also know that to be very naïve. In my opinion, the whole system is way out of whack. In the community where I live (Clifton Park), you wouldn't believe the pressure to have your child (whether he or she likes it or not) begin a sport at age 5 or 6 and continue in that sport year-round (with few, if any, other interests allowed), for the next 8 to 10 years in order to be able to have a 50 percent chance to play on the high school team. No kid needs that kind of pressure for that length of time. The mismanagement of youth sports has always been one of my biggest concerns. As a parent, I had an up-close and personal view because of all the clinics, camps, and leagues our boys were pressured to join. As a teacher, I was constantly seeing the fallout of sports parents who thought their child was Division I, full scholarship material at age 8—and always at the expense of others.

Pete Hogan gave me a lot to think about. Most important, he convinced me that the young people of our nation have become fitness failures and it is easy to see why. We invest heavily in youth, scholastic, and intercollegiate sports. In a sense, competitive sports in our schools have become little more than a costly sideshow. And, because of the cultural tradition of interscholastic sports and the apparent inability of our physical educators to sell the average person on the distinction between physical education and lifetime fitness versus athletics, we are mired in a culture that leaves many on the sidelines as spectators instead of participants. Clearly, tradition drives much of our thinking about sports in our schools. But some traditions in our society have become so obsolete and counterproductive that they have lost any relevance to more important missions. It is time to rethink sports in our schools in light of the crisis in health and fitness and invest our limited resources more wisely.

Should our schools continue to be the principal mechanism for developing more outstanding quarterbacks, halfbacks, wideouts, point guards, shooting guards, pitchers, and catchers? Should we continue to foster the athletic abilities of an elite minority to the detriment of the health and fitness of the majority? And, for some sports like basketball and football that are especially costly, should we continue "business as usual" even though these sports principally serve an entertainment function (in contrast to health and fitness function) for our schools and communities? In short, have our schools become nothing more than sports factories with education a distant second priority? Lastly, if a cost/benefit analysis was done on the advantages of investing more in health and fitness classes in our schools and less on interscholastic sports, what would we see in terms of reduced costs to our society in the present epidemics of heart disease, obesity, colon cancer, diabetes, and high blood pressure?

Though these are difficult questions for communities to ask of themselves, we must begin to address them. Hanging in the balance is another generation of fitness failures who will be more than satisfied to carry on a sedentary lifestyle once they enter their teens and early 20s. We do not need more stadium seats and more multimillion-dollar sports complexes so that we can be entertained nor do we need a continuing emphasis upon interscholastic and intercollegiate sports to the detriment of a fitness curriculum for everyone. Instead what we need is a basic change in educational philosophy, with more resources devoted to health and fitness and perhaps less to interscholastic and intercollegiate sports. If this is achieved, we can change our present sports culture from one that emphasizes watching to one that stresses participating. If we are interested in the long-term health of our nation's people, then choosing the right path for the future is a no-brainer. More important, with healthcare costs skyrocketing at an exponential rate in most segments of our society, can we really afford not to make this fundamental change? Once again, our sports culture needs a major overhaul if we are to confront the challenges of an unfit society.

18

ACL Epidemic

One of my most indelible images of collegiate women's sports was watching University of Connecticut's Shea Ralph tear her anterior cruciate ligament (ACL) for the third time in her career in a 2001 nationally televised game. The MVP of the Women's Final Four in the previous year and consensus all-American, Ralph was the epitome of skill, passion for the game, and guts. After twisting her knee, she crumpled to the floor of Gampel Pavilion in the Big East Championship and her season was done.

Though Ralph was drafted by the Utah Starzz of the Women's National Basketball Association (WNBA), she never played a game because she damaged her knee again before the season started. Finished as an athlete at the age of 24, she is now employed by the Hartford public school system as an assistant for student activities. She also is an assistant coach with the Springfield Spirit of the National Women's Basketball Association (NWBA).

For a player of her accomplishment, it seems like cruel and unusual punishment to have a career terminated so early by injury. But she has wisely decided to put long-term recovery ahead of short-term professional glory. The risk of future injury is quite high and she knows that she would just be asking for trouble down the road.

Her story made an impression on me because in my town of Bethlehem, New York there is an epidemic of sorts in ACL injuries among women athletes. I can point to a number of superb young female athletes who have had the same misfortune as Shea Ralph. Their stories help to put a face on a sports injury that seems to grow in numbers with each passing year.

- *Lilly Corrigan* was one of the best all-around female athletes to ever attend Bethlehem Central High School. From 1995 to 1999

128

she played soccer, basketball and lacrosse. Playing on varsity teams from her sophomore year on, Lilly routinely was one of the best female athletes in the entire Capital District Area. In her junior year of basketball, she suffered a partial tear of her ACL. Lilly did not have surgery but instead vigorously rehabbed the knee, only to suffer a complete tear while playing club soccer in the spring. Following surgery to rebuild her ACL, Lilly once again rehabbed diligently and played all three sports in her senior year of high school. At Harvard University she played soccer during her freshman year but once again tore her ACL and did not return to the team. For the second time she endured ACL reconstruction and lengthy rehabilitation. Lilly tried playing lacrosse in her sophomore year but, because of periodic discomfort in her knee, she left the team after their spring trip and did not return. She played club rugby and graduated in the spring of 2003 from Harvard.

- *Ericka St. Lucia* was an outstanding three-sport athlete at Bethlehem Central High School where she played field hockey, basketball, and lacrosse from 1994 to1998. In May of her senior year she damaged her ACL in a lacrosse game but finished out the season by wearing a supportive knee brace. Ericka continued to wear a brace through her freshman year at Manhattan College, where she successfully competed on the lacrosse team. She had ACL reconstructive surgery in the summer, successfully rehabbed her knee through the fall, and played lacrosse for the next three seasons. Ericka graduated from Manhattan in the spring of 2002.

- *Kate Smith* was one of the most competitive female athletes to have ever attended Bethlehem Central High School. As a high school soccer and basketball player from 1994 to 1998 she was a key member of several championship teams and won league honors for her stellar play in both sports. Kate attended Union College, where she continued to play both sports at a high level; she led her teams to several successful seasons in conference and regional NCAA contests. In her junior year of college basketball, Kate tore her ACL. Following surgery and extensive rehabilitation, she was able to return for both sports in her senior season. For basketball, Kate was voted to the conference all-star squad and finished as the second leading scorer in the history of Union women's basketball. For soccer, Kate was named as conference rookie of the year and was also named to numerous all-star teams. Kate graduated from Union in the spring of 2002.

The ACL injuries suffered by Lilly, Kate, and Ericka were all of the classic variety. That is to say, in each case there was no physical contact. The ligament tear occurred when one foot was planted and there was a change in direction. In each case, surgery and significant rehabilitation were required. Moreover, there is no guarantee about what may lie ahead for these women in the future. The long-term consequences of knee surgery are to increase the vulnerability of the joint and elevate the risk of early arthritic conditions.

The ACL epidemic among female athletes in my town prompted me to spend time talking with Dr. John Czajka, an expert orthopedic surgeon and sports medicine specialist in Albany. Czajka routinely does many ACL reconstructions every year in his practice and knows as much about the devastation wreaked by the injury as anyone. After talking with him, I learned that women athletes are roughly 6 to 10 times more likely to have ACL injuries than males. The injuries tend to occur in jumping and pivoting sports like basketball, soccer, and volleyball. Also, there are four principal theories as to why females are so much more vulnerable to this type of injury. First, the anatomical theory suggests that because women have wider hips and a lower center of gravity than men, they put additional pressure on the knee. Also, the female knee is built differently than the male knee. A notch where the ligament is attached in the knee is much narrower in females than males, thus preventing flexibility. Second, the hormonal theory argues that estrogen secretion in females, especially at the time of ovulation, makes their ligaments looser and hence more likely to tear. Some data suggest that around 70 percent of ACL injuries occur during ovulation. Third, the muscle mass theory states that because a woman's quadriceps and hamstring muscles are not the size of a man's, there is less protection when a woman's knee is injured. Fourth, the style of play theory suggests that female athletes tend to play sports in a more upright fashion with their knees extended instead of flexed. This puts additional pressure on the joint and increases the vulnerability of the knee to injury.

Research examining prevention is in its infancy but some sports medicine specialists are advocating quadriceps and hamstring muscle strengthening as well as explosive jumping drill training. In the case of the latter, it is thought that learning how to jump and land in the flexed knee position can reduce susceptibility to ACL injury. The development of good prevention training programs would seem to be a high priority and some doctors and trainers are suggesting that they should be started as early as elementary school. Some recent reports suggest that prevention training can reduce the frequency of ACL injuries by as much as 88 percent. According to Czajka, however, the adoption of such programs is inconsistent and highly variable, especially for young athletes, and the initial reports suggesting such dramatic improvement are preliminary and overly optimistic. What many agree on, however, is that more spending on research is critically needed to address the problem.

The NCAA recently signed lucrative new long-term contracts to televise the men's and women's Final Four basketball tournament. On the men's side, the contract with CBS calls for $6 billion over an 11-year period. The women's contract with ESPN calls for $200 million over 11 years. Though the NCAA's coffers are fat thanks to TV money, they spend precious little of it on addressing issues like sports injuries. With our nation spending $250 million annually on ACL surgery and rehabilitation it seems ironic that NCAA spending on sports science research is a paltry $70,000. I asked John Czajka what he thought of these figures and he quickly responded: "It is absolutely indefensible that the NCAA should spend so little on research when ACL injuries have reached such epidemic proportions in women."

A reasonable person simply could not conclude that our sports culture does right by our female athletes, especially when a wealthy sports governing body looks the other way and more or less says that this is the price women must pay for competing. It is also reasonable to conclude that if the same injury rate plagued men's sports the way it does women's, there would be a lot more being said and done about ACL injuries. Our sports culture needs an attitude change before more young women athletes are devoured by a system that increasingly exploits them for their talent. Lilly Corrigan, Ericka St. Lucia, and Kate Smith suffered ACL injuries in the prime of their sports lives. Do you think that these women athletes and their families would have liked to have seen the NCAA spend a little bit more on sports science research? I can't speak for them, but my conclusion is that our sports governing bodies regularly put their own interests ahead of our athletes; I don't need to see one more ACL injury in another top female athlete to confirm it for me either.

19

Peaking at 15

Like many in the Capital District of Upstate New York in 1993, I was astonished to read about the athletic exploits of Saratoga High School cross-country runner Erin Davis. Beginning in just the eighth grade, Davis competed on the varsity team with enormous success. She won the Section II cross-country championship in the second-fastest time ever recorded at the Saratoga Spa State Park and then won the state public high school title by 24.7 seconds. In the Federation meet, which combines all public and private schools in New York, she again won, with her closest competitor finishing 34 seconds behind her.

While these accomplishments were impressive, the best was yet to come. Davis and her teammates competed in Birmingham, Alabama, at a national meet called the Vulcan Classic. With more than 200 top high school runners from around the country competing, Davis finished first. To put icing on the cake, her high school team also finished first. The next year, as a high school freshman, Davis won the prestigious Foot Locker Cross-Country National Championship in San Diego. At the tender age of 15, Erin Davis was a national champion with everything in front of her. She was profiled in the *New York Times* and collegiate and Olympic stardom seemed to be just around the corner.

Davis continued to excel at the high school level, where she won four consecutive Federation cross-country titles and was named runner of the decade for the 1990s by the New York State Sportswriters Association. She returned to the national finals two more times and finished fourth as a sophomore in 1994 and seventh as a senior in 1996.

Based upon her superb high school cross-country performances, Davis accepted a full scholarship to attend Penn State. However, in college, she never met the high expectations that were placed upon her. Beset by numerous setbacks including a lower back injury, knee problems from the physical pounding delivered by training, a change in the coaching staff, and burnout, her collegiate running career was well below average. She failed to make all-American status in any year that she competed and missed part or all of a number of seasons.

Some medical experts have concluded that young girls that over-train are especially vulnerable to injury because their bodies mature differently than boys' and they are not capable of handling the kind of physical pounding that they must endure with frequent running. While experts conclude that moderate running is acceptable for young girls, intense training as they go through puberty has very serious risks because bones and muscles have not fully developed. Some research also indicates that participating in a single sport all year round for more than 15 hours a week produces a greater probability for serious injury. These risk factors may have been operating in the case of Erin Davis and could explain in part her declining performance and interest in running competitively.

In an interview in 2002, Erin Davis discussed her career in running with *fast-women.com*, a web site devoted to road runners. Many of her comments are interesting since they reveal the difficulties of becoming a top runner at a very early age and what can happen when things begin to go wrong. Portions of that interview are excerpted here.

Q. *How would you say your college running went, in general?*

A. It started off decently. I won my first two collegiate races my freshman year. That was a great feeling. Soon after, I hurt my lower back. It was my first major injury. It took a whole year to fully heal. The lifestyle and training was so different in college than what I was used to in high school. My life and training was so very structured in high school. [Saratoga Springs high school coaches Linda and Art Kranick] were top-level coaches and I was very confident in them. I was not used to change. I ran very well my sophomore cross country season. Then I had injuries off and on throughout the rest of college. Running became a job, it was frustrating. I tried my best each race and tried to contribute to the team as much as I could, but it just wasn't the same. I didn't feel the same drive and determination as I did in high school. I felt lost and would miss my high school coaches when I felt driven to run fast again. Or, I would wish I could just experience college like a normal student during times I was not feeling the drive to train and compete like a Division I athlete.

Q. *How was your overall experience at Penn State?*

A. It had its ups and downs, with running and school. The social life was great. [It's a] large university, there are so many people from so many different backgrounds. I made a lot of great friends that I will never forget. I would have liked to have had a year to experience it as a normal student and focus on what I might have really wanted to do with my future. My only goal while I was there, besides running at my best effort, was to graduate. I went to college not knowing what I wanted to really study. I studied recreation and park management in hopes of working at a major resort. Here I am today wanting to work in sales and continue ski instructing.

Q. *There are a handful of very young girls in this country running very well at a young age. What kind of advice would you give them, having gone through this yourself?*

A. Remember, it's a sport. Run for yourself, not others. Even when running on a team, there are other ways to contribute if you aren't having a good day. Some of my favorite teammates were not always the best runners, some never even competed. They brought encouragement and team spirit to the team. I tried to keep running as fun and enjoyable as possible. Feeling overwhelmed and stressed out at a young age is a huge red flag, a caution sign. Burnout is no fun.

Q. *This may tie in with the last question, but is there anything you wish you had done differently during your competitive running career?*

A. Like what I said, I wish when I was having bad days (even months) of running, that I would not have let burnout get to me. I learned how to relax and readjust my goals during the times I was injured. Sometimes, an injury is a much-needed break. I wish I would have stayed in touch with my high school coaches and tied their training skills and advice with my college coach's. I believe I would have stayed more focused and motivated to run well if I had done that.

Q. *How big of a part do you envision running having in your life in the future? What other kinds of things do you see yourself focusing on and what kinds of dreams/goals do you have?*

A. For now I'll just take it one year at a time. I have people wanting to coach me to get back in the running scene again, but I'm not ready yet. I don't even know if I'll ever want to train for competition again, but who knows, my moods these days change like the weather. My dreams will let me know if and when I'm ready to race again.

Erin Davis seems to have survived the ups and downs of being a top athlete and can talk about it in a mature fashion. However, there is little doubt that she was in part the product of an obsessive sports culture that places enormous emphasis on achieving success at an early age.

She received her high school training from cross-country gurus Linda and Art Kranick. Both teachers at Saratoga High School, the Kranicks developed a long line of cross-country champions. They coached their teams to many New York State Championships and their 1993, 1995, 1996, and 1997 teams were national champions. Their 1994 and 1998 teams finished the year ranked as no. 2 in the country. For these accomplishments, the husband and wife team were chosen U.S. Coaches of the Year in 1998 for high school girls track and field by *National Scholastic Track Digest.*

While recognized as cross-country coaches who could produce winning teams and national champions, the Kranicks were not without their critics. In 1994 several parents whose children were coached by the Kranicks voiced concerns to the Saratoga board of education with accusations of overtraining, dispensing vitamins such as B-12, and mental abuse. In particular, the husband and wife team were accused of suggesting strict diets, discouraging active social lives, and advocating running seven days a week, year round. The parents also asked the board to dismiss the coaches.

When the board of education reviewed the complaints, they found that no rules had been broken nor regulations or statutes violated. They further ruled that the Kranicks should not be dismissed. The parents then appealed to the state education commissioner Thomas Sobol and asked that he intervene to review the case. The appeal was dismissed by Commissioner Sobol but he ordered the Kranicks to comply with a Saratoga Springs School District policy that prohibits the distribution of vitamins to students.

One set of parents however was not satisfied and sent a letter to the school board as well as the media and coaches throughout the country. In the letter they accused the Kranicks of engaging in diet control, over-training, and obsessive cultlike isolation of the runners from other students and activities. In response to these widely circulated statements, the Kranicks then sued the parents for $27 million in a defamation lawsuit. The lawsuit, which dragged on for close to four years through state supreme court and later appellate court, was eventually settled out of court for the sum of $67,500.

Though the Kranicks appeared to be the ultimate winners, the fact that the ugly situation was played out in public did little to enhance the tarnished culture of competitive cross-country running at the high school level. Increasingly, the tactics of youth, amateur, and high school athletic coaches are being called into question, especially when over-training and burnout casualties are on the rise at this level of sports. It is difficult to determine whether or not the Kranicks were right or wrong in their training tactics, especially when their methods are probably no different than those used by many other coaches at the high school level. But some have speculated that their training techniques may be more appropriate for collegiate or elite amateur athletes than for middle school and high school runners. If this is true, it reflects the ever increasing tendency to professionalize athletes at earlier and earlier ages, even though the physical, social, and psychological risks may be considerable.

Our sports culture, which emphasizes immediate gain and an almost cavalier disregard for long-term health, frequently chews up many of our athletes at an early age. Young girls who compete in figure skating, gymnastics, and cross-country running are especially vulnerable to overtraining, burnout, eating disorders like anorexia, and a host of emotional and social problems that can leave lifetime physical and psychological scars. This is the product of intense specialization at an early age. Many, like myself, wonder whether or not it is all worth it when you consider athletes like Erin Davis who peak at 15 and are burned out from their sport in their early 20s.

Just who is responsible for the increasing trend toward early specialization? There is enough blame to go around to many different quarters. Clearly, a sports culture that exploits athletes at an early age must be held accountable. Also, young athletes often place way too much pressure on themselves to achieve success at an early age. Finally, coaches and parents become obsessed with achieving greatness for young athletes without giving adequate attention to the inherent risks in specialized, intense training at an early age. Sadly, young athletes all too often become an economic investment that must pay off in wins, scholarships, and professional contracts if they are to be justified.

Do we really need to hear more stories like those of Erin Davis to convince ourselves that something is wrong with our sports culture? No one can persuade me that it is good for athletes to peak at 15 years of age and then grow physically and mentally tired of their sport in their early 20s. If this is considered normal and the price one must pay for being a top athlete in our present culture, then we must prepare ourselves for many more casualties due to burnout, overtraining, and physical injury down the road.

Some recent remarks from Erin Davis are very revealing. When asked about her college running days she said in the *Albany Times-Union* "Actually, I hated college running." More important she added: "Everybody envisions themselves running in the Olympics. I just didn't realize later on down the road that I would have so much wear and tear on my body that running wasn't that fun anymore."

Sports are supposed to be for fun but instead they have become way too serious, especially for our young athletes. Just ask Erin Davis.

20

Signing Day

From 1997 to 2002, I witnessed a media spectacle in the coverage of two heavily recruited scholastic athletes from my area of the Capital District of Albany, New York. The extensive newspaper and television reporting on these two blue-chippers heightened my awareness that we are exploiting young athletes, sensationalizing their accomplishments, and professionalizing their status before many of them have even reached puberty. Their stories are a lesson in the excesses of media coverage at the local sports level.

Staff writer Dan Howley of the *Albany Times-Union* newspaper was present when blue-chip high school football player Josh Beekman from Amsterdam, New York, finally made his college selection. His description of the events that day in February 2002 ("A Big Eagle in Making: Amsterdam Star Beekman to Play for Boston College") paints an all-too-common picture of the circus-like media atmosphere that surrounds the recruitment and signing of young scholastic athletes today.

The anticipation thickened as the clock neared 3 pm. The lobby at Amsterdam High School was crowded. There was a lot of whispering and guessing. Television cameras were in place and microphones sat on an empty podium.

Josh Beekman, the school's 6 foot 2, 320 pound offensive lineman, had scheduled a news conference to reveal whether he would play football for Boston College or Michigan State. When he made his appearance, he was wearing an olive suit and tie and was followed in single file by his coach and parents. The entourage made its way through the milling crowd under a hail of applause and cheers, much like a heavyweight fighter making his way to the ring.

At the microphone, he kept up the suspense, reaching into a paper bag and pulling out and then discarding T-shirts from Notre Dame and Rutgers, then holding up shirts side-by-side from Boston College and Michigan State.

He finally tossed aside the Michigan State shirt and draped the one from Boston College across his chest.

It was out. He would play for the Eagles. The gathering of about 200 students, teachers, friends, and family roared its approval.

On the local evening news that night, Josh Beekman's signing day was featured by all four of the local channels. Amsterdam New York's most famous athlete was enjoying the notoriety and fame of the moment and those supporters around him from his coach to his parents gushed with pride in interviews. Beekman was one of the most sought after athletes to ever come out of the Albany Capital District Area and his athletic resume was impressive. He was the only player ever to be named to the *Albany Times-Union* All Area Football Team for four consecutive years. In his senior season (2001) he was named *Albany Times-Union* Co-Player of the Year and earned all-American honors from *PrepStar* and all-Northeast honors from *SuperPrep*. He was intensely recruited by just about every major Division I college in the country.

Beekman came onto the radar screen of the local media as early as the eighth grade, when he first started playing on the Amsterdam varsity football team. Local newspapers devoted lots of ink to him as he progressed through his scholastic years. Not surprisingly, the gluttonous media of the Albany Capital District Area took every opportunity to inform the public of all that there was to know about Beekman and his family.

Article after article appeared in local newspapers chronicling his athletic development and no stone was left unturned. Newspaper readers and viewers of local television sports programs learned, among other things, that he wore the same number as his father before him, that he could bench press 430 pounds and run a 5.3 second 40 yard dash, and that he was also a fine basketball player but dropped the sport so he could concentrate on lifting weights, etc. etc. Likewise, on-line recruiting services reported on his every move while he was searching for the right college match. An Internet search at the time revealed over 50 recruiting reports on Beekman, including interviews and detailed reports on such things as what he liked about certain schools and their programs, how comfortable he felt on his visit, how he performed at their summer football camps, his outlook on his senior season of football, and what position he intended to play in college. The coverage of Beekman was exhaustive and way over the top for a young athlete.

The amount of media attention directed toward Josh Beekman was clearly excessive, but it paled in comparison to the local newspaper and television coverage of basketball player Craig Forth. I first saw Forth play when he was in the sixth grade. Even then I knew that the eventual 7 footer from East Greenbush, New York, would be something special. All he needed was a little bit of time to grow into his body.

Brought up to the varsity by the end of his eighth grade season, Forth quickly became the most dominating player in the area. Although his high school teams were mediocre at best, Forth's personal accomplishments were impressive. He established school records for career scoring, rebounding, and blocked shots. He earned Suburban Council honors twice and was a league all-star four times. He was the envy of every major Division I basketball program in the country and attracted a legion of high-profile college coaches for every summer AAU game that he played. *The Sporting News* ranked Forth as the fifth-best senior center in the country, and another recruiting service listed him as the 24th best senior in the nation at any position.

The focus on Forth by the local sports media was the most intense that I have ever seen for a scholastic athlete in this area. Television highlights on the four local television programs were dominated by Forth footage during the scholastic basketball season. Interviews with Forth following the games were not unlike those seen for college and professional athletes. The local newspapers covered just about every aspect of his life during the time that he was in middle school and high school.

As the recruiting wars intensified for Forth's services in his junior and senior years, it was not unusual to see several stories a week, thus enabling the sports community to keep abreast of the latest information on his decision-making process. A search in the *Albany Times-Union* newspaper alone revealed that from 1997 to 2001, 206 articles were written on some part of Craig Forth's basketball career. In at least one-third of those articles, Forth was the main or sole focus of the story. Coupled with large pictures of Forth, the titles of the articles alone and their large bold print on the cover of the sports pages were meant to attract readers right away: "High Impact Expectations Growing by the Day for

Columbia 7-Footer Craig Forth," "Scouts Flocking to Forth," "Fine Year for Forth," "Forth Struggles to be Dominant," "Forth's Dad Dismisses Transfer Rumors," "A Forth to be Reckoned With," "Center of Gravity Inner Strength Makes Forth a Powerful Force," "Columbia Gets No Fifth From Forth," and "Forth Faces Finest."

After Craig Forth signed with Syracuse during the early signing period, staff writer Mark Singelais of the *Albany Times-Union* wrote the following article entitled "Syracuse Better by One Forth: Columbia 7-Footer Chooses Orangemen Over Boston College." The article typifies the kind of newspaper coverage given to young athletes on signing day, one of the biggest days of a young athlete's life.

Columbia High center Craig Forth said he chose Syracuse University partly because of its success in developing big men into NBA players.

Look at Rony Seikaly, Derrick Coleman and John Wallace, to name a few.

But even if he doesn't follow in that tradition, Forth said, at least he'll have an education that will give him a career to fall back on.

Forth, a 7 foot, 240 pound senior, made an oral commitment Wednesday to the Orangemen, ending the most heated recruiting battle for a Section II basketball player since Shaker High's Sam Perkins chose North Carolina 20 years ago.

"I wanted to get it over with because every time I turned around, someone was calling me," he said.

Forth chose the Orangemen over Boston College. He raved about Syracuse's elementary and special education programs, and said he wants to become an elementary school teacher.

"I'll be extremely marketable after college if the NBA doesn't want me," Forth said. "Syracuse offers special ed. and elementary ed. combined, so after four years I'll be certified in both."

Forth said he was leaning toward Syracuse even before head coach Jim Boeheim and assistant Mike Hopkins visited his home last Thursday, the first day allowed by NCAA recruiting rules.

After BC coach Al Skinner visited on Monday, Forth talked late into the night with Columbia High coach Jim Obermayer and his staff, and Jim Hart, Forth's AAU coach with the Albany City Rocks.

"I think (the difference) was how comfortable I felt on the campus and with the coaches," said Forth, who made several unofficial (unpaid) visits to both campuses.

Forth said he also was swayed by the fact that Syracuse has been to the NCAA Tournament 20 times in Boeheim's 24 seasons as head coach, with two appearances in the national final.

BC, meanwhile, is 31–56 in three seasons under Skinner, and Forth expressed some discomfort that he would have been viewed as the program's savior.

"As far as (Syracuse's) level of basketball is concerned, I feel they're at the top of the line," Forth said. "We could have something great if we get the players we need and everyone's committed to doing what we need to do."

The sheer amount of media coverage devoted to Craig Forth and Josh Beekman every year during their scholastic careers probably left many to conclude that there just wasn't much else of value to report on in the Capital District Area. To the contrary, however, there were probably many interesting and informative stories that never got covered— some sports-related and some not—but the choice was made to give the community a blow by blow account of Forth's and Beekman's athletic accomplishments and the recruiting competition for their services. Such stories are surprisingly easy to do, require little creativity because they have been done so many times before, and usually add little to the reader's understanding of a sport or the seedy process through which young athletes often must go to make themselves competitive for a scholarship. The blame for this excessive coverage and exploitation falls squarely upon parents, coaches, school systems, and the media because collectively they allow it to continue almost unchecked in our present sports culture.

The fact that both star athletes were extensively covered by the local media during their scholastic playing days is certainly not unusual. It happens all over the country with blue-chip high school athletes that are being recruited by colleges and universities. After all, local television and community newspapers need something to talk and write about as they strive to satisfy the appetites of those who watch the shows and buy the newspapers. However, the bottom line is that they are selling entertainment and even local high school and youth sports is valuable entertainment these days. Clearly, local newspapers are reaching down to younger readers all the time in order to enhance profits and expand their demographics. It is regrettable that hyping young athletes seems to be an important part of the mix in appealing to a wider readership.

What is most sickening about the process, however, is that it has professionalized young athletes to a point where there is little difference between the media coverage of local high school athletes and professional players. Moreover, the coverage is so unbalanced and overdone that it gives the impression that athletics are much more valuable pursuits than other career paths which arguably are more valuable in the long run to the developing individual and society at large.

Clearly, it is doubtful that we will see anytime soon a daily "Education" page in our local newspapers that is strictly devoted to the learning accomplishments and college decisions of talented students as they compete for academic scholarships. However, is it too much to ask that we cover the educational accomplishments of our young students a bit more vigorously and simultaneously tone down the coverage of our young athletes' exploits? Balance is the key and right now there is no balance in the coverage of academic and athletic accomplishments.

When Josh Beekman and Craig Forth finally signed to play at their respective colleges, they probably breathed a sigh of relief realizing that they could now move on to other things in their lives. The coverage no doubt was intrusive for their families but the sad fact is that there is always another local star athlete around the corner to take their place in the media whirlwind that finds us covering the exploits of young athletes at earlier and earlier ages.

My conclusion is that local media have an insatiable desire to place young athletes on stage, professionalize them, and then exploit them in order to sell more papers and increase television viewership. Our present out-of-control sports culture promotes this kind of exploitation; it will not stop until important reforms are made in our existing system of sports.

21

Collegiate Gamblers Anonymous

You never know who you will strike up a conversation with when you're stuck in an airport waiting for a flight that has been delayed for several hours. Such was the case recently when I came across two recent college graduates who were returning from some vacation time down south. With the Final Four college basketball tournament in full swing, and the topic of NCAA "braketology" and sports gambling heavy in the air, one thing led to another and they agreed to tell me about their own experiences on their respective college campuses.

Excerpted below are some of their answers to questions I posed in a spur of the moment interview that took some surprising twists and turns as we waited for our flights. I've guaranteed their anonymity so I'll just call them Steve and Mike and leave it at that. Steve attended a relatively large state university while Mike attended a small liberal arts college. That being said, I have a feeling that they could have come from just about any institution of higher learning in the United States where many students tend to major in gambling on collegiate basketball and football games. Sadly, it has become a full-time occupation (read addiction) for some.

Q. *Can you describe what the sports gambling scene was like at your respective schools?*

Mike: The sports gambling scene at my school was not huge. Being a small school, I feel that it could have been too great of a risk for someone to try and be a major bookie on campus. Throughout my four years at the school I did hear of a few on-campus bookies from time to time but never actually bet through one. I do know that at large schools close to me, these bookies operate at a much more professional level.

Steve: Gambling was all over my school. The main two sports were football and basketball (both college and pro). There would also be a fair amount of action on major boxing matches and playoff baseball. During the football season, almost all male conversations would start with "How did you do today?", meaning how did you do gambling. People were especially interested in how I did because at one point I was booking myself. People were always interested in how people did in general and could gauge that on how I did. You could definitely say that gambling was a major part of college life for the average male at my school.

Q. *Was it easy to bet on games?*

Mike: Finding a place to bet on games was never a problem.

Steve: It was incredibly easy. There was never a time when there were not at least three major bookies at my school. Plus, guys would always make random bets with each other when they had been drinking.

Q. *Was it easy to lodge a bet with a bookie?*

Mike: Betting on a game with a bookie during my college days was easy. Never did I bet with a bookie on my campus, however, I did bet through one student I knew who used a bookie from another school.

Steve: Yes, never a problem.

Q. *Are there student bookies right on campus, perhaps in your own dorm?*

Mike: There were small bookies on campus but at no time could I ever have identified any one person as an on-campus bookie. Anything I knew was hearsay.

Steve: Yes, like I said earlier, I myself was a bookie at one point. Even when I wasn't, I never had a problem finding one to place a bet.

Q. *Was the amount of money involved in sports gambling on your campus pretty substantial? Can you give me some estimates?*

Mike: The amounts of bets that I saw people bet on college games ranged from $30 to $300. I would say on average students would bet $50 a game, on both college football and basketball.

Steve: There was a wide range of bets. The lowest around $25 per game, the highest in the upwards of $800 per game. Broke students somehow always found a way to bet, and pay. The more expensive bets were made by restaurant owners and other professionals.

Q. *Were lots of students involved in sports gambling on your campus?*

Mike: Some groups of students more than others. In class I would hear students talking about gambling the night before from time to time. In the group of eight students that I lived with in my senior year, two would bet frequently, multiple times a week, or many games on a college football Saturday, two or three never and the rest were occasional betters, more of the type who would bet on bowl games or other big games that they planned on watching.

Steve: Yes, probably 65 percent of my male friends.

Q. *Did your respective schools place much pressure on students to limit gambling activity?*

Mike: My school had talks with their student athletes and a seminar I believe about sports gambling, but nothing for the average student.

Steve: None at all. My school paid so much attention on cutting back on drinking, that other things like gambling and drugs just slid by.

Q. *When you first arrived on campus was there a lot being said to new students about the dangers of gambling?*

Mike: I don't remember anything being said when I arrived on campus about gambling. So, if it were, it was nothing major or serious.

Steve: Nothing that I recall.

Q. *Were there severe penalties on campus for being detected for gambling? Do you know of anyone on campus that was punished for sports gambling?*

Mike: I have no idea. I did not know of anyone who got caught gambling.

Steve: If anyone was to get into trouble, I would imagine the police would be involved. I don't know of anyone getting caught.

Q. *Did you know of anyone that got in over their head to the point where they were scrambling to make good on loans and perhaps engaging in illegal activity (like stealing) in order to "pay up"?*

Mike: I knew one student my freshman year who got in a little over his head. He lost $300+ on a college basketball game after already being down a certain amount. I remember that he was nervous about the situation, but he was not a close friend and I do not know how he handled it. I believe he paid the guy off over a few weeks, but I do remember him trying to figure out how he was going to come up with the money.

Steve: Absolutely. Almost everyone at one point or another had to "scramble" at one point. Many kids sold their books, or stole books and then sold them back. Some kids stole money from their jobs.

Q. *On your respective campuses, were students using the Internet to place their bets at off-shore sites?*

Mike: Many people used the Internet sites for gambling knowledge. Only one student I knew actually used it for gambling purposes. If there had not been bookie access, I believe this avenue would have been explored more.

Steve: Yeah, but not a lot. The draw there was that you could place very small bets (like $5 bets). The smallest bet a bookie will take is usually $25, and the only reason he will take that is because the juice is 20 percent as opposed to 10 percent. The other positive about those sites is that you can also bet almost anything. The problem for college students though is that you need to front the money, so they didn't like mailing in the money ahead of time.

Q. *If there was a federal law passed prohibiting the publication of betting lines for collegiate sports and prohibiting betting on collegiate sports, do you think that students would still find ways to do it?*

Mike: Yes, but at a smaller scale. If bookies had to create their own lines, it would make it tough for the bookies to be as successful and therefore less would be in business. I believe that gambling would still go on and once another source for lines became established and reliable, the action would be back to normal.

Steve: Hard to say. Probably a little because the lines wouldn't be so readily available, and the sportscasters wouldn't mention spreads of lines during games. However, two things would keep it going to real gamblers. One is that a federal law would not stop off-shore sites from creating lines. Second, most people that have been around gambling for a while are pretty good at creating their own lines. I could go through a full Sunday lineup and be within a half point from almost every game. Also, a federal law would prohibit sports gambling in Las Vegas, and I don't see that happening.

Q. *Based upon what you have seen and heard on your campus, do you believe that the fixing of college football and basketball games probably occurs at a level higher than what many people believe?*

Mike: Yes. I believe that there are so many college games, and so many student athletes in financial trouble, that many probably take money to throw a game. I believe that it is totally naïve to think otherwise.

Steve: Not really. First of all, most players in a position to point shave probably have a good chance to make it in the pros and it isn't worth the risk. Also, I think it would be incredibly hard to point shave in football. It would be hard to shave points and not lose. I definitely could be wrong though.

Q. *Do you think that it would be very easy for a student gambler and a college athlete on a campus to get together and fix a game?*

Mike: I believe that fixing a game would probably be done more so through a larger money source. I'm sure corruption occurs between student-athletes and a student gambler, but I feel that if an outside source that had more money than a college student came into play that the athlete would be much more likely. I also feel that many athletes accumulate debts and are forced into throwing games instead of facing more serious repercussions.

Steve: I guess if there is a will, there is a way. It is very likely that a very good college player has a good friend that is a bookie. In fact, I know of one in particular that plays on a major team right now that has a bookie as one of his best friends. I just think that most athletes take their game too seriously now. There is too much money on the flipside to risk it all now.

Q. *Do you know of an athlete on your campus that was approached by anyone to throw a game?*

Mike: No, not at my school.

Steve: Not on my campus.

Q. *One recent study shows that 23 percent of students gambled at least once a week and that 6 to 8 percent are "problem" gamblers. Based upon what you have seen, do you think that these numbers are pretty much on target?*

Mike: Yes, from my knowledge I would agree with those numbers.

Steve: I think that 23 percent is a little high, if it is considering females. That means that half of guys gamble at least once a week. I don't know about that. As far as the 6 to 8 percent, that seems accurate . . . maybe even low.

Q. *Do you think that the authorities on many college campuses are much more interested in binge drinking, drugs, and date rape as opposed to sports gambling?*

Mike: Yes, I feel that the administration feels that these other events can cause more of a black eye for an institution and therefore they focus on them.

Steve: Absolutely, but they probably should be. Gambling can definitely become a problem, but should take a backseat to those other three, especially in college.

Q. *Based upon what you have seen at your respective schools, do you think that many college athletes bet on sports? Do you think that they bet on their own games?*

Mike: I have nothing to base an answer on.

Steve: My answer depends upon what you mean by athlete. Do I think that players on Duke and UNC gamble? Probably not that much. Do I think that athletes at my school do? Absolutely.

Q. *Do you think that betting at an early age—let's say middle school and high school—promotes betting when a person enters their college years and beyond?*

Mike: Yes. Betting at young ages definitely plays a part in whether you decide to bet once you have hit college. Many students have formed personal feelings toward how they deal with money by this age. Some feel that gambling is too huge of a risk, and are very careful with their money. Other people are always willing to take the easy way to making money. It is tempting to a college student to try and make a quick $50 watching a football game. If you gamble frequently at a young age, you are much more likely to do so once you live on your own.

Steve: I would think so, just like most addictions.

The interview above was a casual, impromptu conversation with two savvy college kids who really knew the ropes of college sports gambling. It should not be construed as a randomly drawn scientific sample that is necessarily representative of all college students. Putting aside those limitations, the discussion proved to be on the one hand enlightening for the forthrightness of their opinions, and on the other hand extremely bothersome for the implications of what they said.

Sports gambling on our college campuses is pervasive; I really don't need a systematic study of the issue for me to conclude that it is a problem for a significant and growing number of students every year. Likewise, I am also not naïve enough to conclude that gambling poses no threat of any kind to the integrity of collegiate sports. Yet, with the exception of some minor prevention work on campus for athletes, we do little if anything to educate and warn regular students about the potential pitfalls of gambling activity.

Have we just given up? Is legislation to make gambling illegal too difficult to accomplish because of vested interests? How many more cases of point shaving and fixing of games will we need before we make some major changes to address the problem? Do we really care about the interests of athletes and nonathletes when we just brush the problems aside and concentrate more consistently on seemingly more important questions like "Will college football ever have a playoff system like other sports at the Division I level?"

If we really don't care enough to do anything, then we should expect a steady increase in the number of problem student gamblers, and we should consider inviting Gamblers Anonymous to set up chapters in the student union of every college campus in the country.

offthemark.com

22

A Courtship with Anabolic Steroids

A few years ago I was asked by administrators of the National Institute of Drug Abuse (NIDA) to participate in a symposium on anabolic steroid abuse. The symposium, which was held in Washington at the National Press Club, was attended by other scientists as well as various news agencies. Eight other scientists and I delivered talks on our specialties and highlighted the most recent research from our respective laboratories.

My talk was entitled "Causes and Consequences of Anabolic Steroid Abuse: Animals Models" and it reviewed research from my laboratory. I spoke about the aggression-promoting quality of anabolic steroids and how our research in animals was generally supporting the many reports by athletes of "roid rage" — the extreme aggression and violence shown by those who chronically abused steroids. I also spent time talking about some exciting research we were doing in which we were finding that certain anabolic steroids were apparently producing euphoric states in animals. I noted that these findings were preliminary, but if we continued to confirm what we were finding and it was supported by other scientists, then the results would suggest that human beings may be taking anabolic steroids for some of the same reasons that addicts take cocaine and heroin. Namely, in addition to liking the added muscle and strength produced by taking anabolic steroids (psychologists refer to this as a secondary reinforcing effect), abusers also like the pleasurable subjective state produced by the drug (called the primary reinforcing effect). Thus, some of the reasons why people choose to continue to seek out and self-administer anabolic steroids may have to do with the "good feeling" engendered by continued use.

In the audience during my talk, but unknown to me at the time, was a former NFL football player for the Pittsburgh Steelers by the name of Steve Courson. Sitting quietly in the back of the room, Courson seemed to listen intently to each of us as we outlined what we knew about the potential dangers of using anabolic steroids. Following our talks, Courson posed the first comment from the audience. "My name is Steve Courson and I used to be an offensive lineman in the National Football League," he said. "The research that all of you are doing is very important. We have to get the message out to our youths that these things can do irreparable harm. I am living proof of the devastation that anabolic steroids can produce. For me, it is too late. I have cardiomyopathy, I am permanently disabled, and I need a new heart. Although it is difficult to prove, I am convinced that it was the steroids."

I was stunned by Courson's confession but then remembered a story about him in *Sports Illustrated* a few months earlier in which he had chronicled his anabolic steroid abuse. The picture of him in the article, one taken during his playing days, showed a beefed up 300 pound lineman who looked like a man of steel with the fierceness and physicality of a Viking warrior. His appearance to me that day was that of an average 200 pound man who was no more threatening than anyone else in the room.

Following the symposium, I approached Courson and asked to speak with him. He obliged and was only too happy to share with me some of his incredible story. Courson began his courtship with anabolic steroids when he was at the University of South Carolina where as a sophomore he started taking them to build up his size and strength. He played seven years with the Pittsburgh Steelers and Tampa Bay Buccaneers, won two Super Bowl rings, and was a Pro Bowler. Courson's strength was legendary in football circles. He could bench press 600 pounds and routinely won the NFL's Strongest Man competition in the early 1980s. It is a different story for him now, however, as his heart problems have limited his life. He has difficulty walking up a flight of stairs without getting winded and works out with 15 pound weights while waiting for a new heart.

Courson reminisced about his playing days. "You have to win, fight, and survive in the NFL," he said. "I was not out to be an average player; I was out to be the best. When other people in your arena are using an advantage from a tactical point of view, not an ethical point of view, it really narrows the choice. It is a lot easier to be ethical and spiritual when you're not in the trenches trying to survive whether it is on a battlefield of war or in the NFL. What has bothered me the most is when I worked at various sports camps with young kids putting on weight lifting exhibitions. I could see the gleam in the kids' eyes and their desire to be like me but I knew the reality behind it. Today, as I go around talking at high schools, I tell the kids that it is ethically wrong to use anabolic steroids. I tell them to be true to yourself and to remember that some things are not at all what they are made out to be."

Courson was very thoughtful and articulate in his remarks that day. I was impressed with his honesty and his ability to accept the consequences of what was admittedly a very poor choice—a choice that was now costing him his health. To his credit, he now spends much of this time coaching high school football and lecturing about the evils of performance enhancing drugs like anabolic steroids.

Courson's experiences are now being repeated among scores of younger athletes in a wide variety of sports at almost all levels of competition. Recently I received a telephone call from an area athletic director. He asked, "What can you tell me about Nandrolone?"

I responded, "It is one of many anabolic steroids that are being abused by athletes today. It is primarily used to bulk up and promote muscle growth. Are you having some problems with an athlete? Do you have some suspicions?"

The athletic director continued, "We found a marked vial of Nandrolone in the locker of a football player the other day. He has shown a dramatic increase in body weight, strength, and muscle mass since one year ago—and a transformation in his personality. He is very aggressive, picking fights all the time even with teammates, and is being penalized for unsportsmanlike conduct in games. Could it be the steroids?"

I responded, "Yes, probably, these are all classic signs of anabolic steroid abuse. This young man is headed for some very severe health consequences down the road if he continues on this path. I would suggest that you have a talk with him and his parents as soon as you can."

The true tragedy of Courson and his flirtation with anabolic steroids is that few lessons have been learned. Our present sports landscape, with its win-at-all costs culture, is even more intense today than it was when Courson competed in football during the 1970s and 1980s. Sadly, the pressure to use performance-enhancing drugs is escalating and remains unabated at almost all levels of sports and in almost every aspect of athletic competition.

©2003 MARK PARISI, DIST. BY UFS, INC.

23

The Up Side and the Down Side of Title IX

One of my most pleasant sports memories was the year I served as a basketball coach for a young sixth grade girl by the name of Nicole Conway. The year was 1990 and I was coaching a travel team from Bethlehem, New York in the Capital District Youth Basketball League (CDYBL). Nicole was getting her first taste of competitive basketball and she was part of an all-boys team that went on to win the league championship that year. A phenom from the start because of her shooting, dribbling, and rebounding skills, Nicole was one of the best players in an all boys league. She showed right away that she would be a tremendous success at the game; she loved it, practiced hard, played tenaciously, and had a sense for the team nature of the game that was unparalleled.

Nicole went on to have one of the most spectacular high school basketball careers of anyone in the history of the Albany Capital District Area. At Bethlehem Central High School, she played on the varsity girls team for four years and finished her career with 1,267 points, 563 rebounds, 295 assists, and 320 steals—to this day, all records for her high school. She earned all league honors four times and was named MVP of the league as a junior and a senior. She also was named to numerous area all-star teams and during her era was recognized as the best all-around player in the entire Upstate New York area. In her senior season she was a member of the all New York State third team. Nicole was a tremendous all-around athlete and also participated in soccer and track at her high school. In short, she could have done well at anything but she opted to specialize in her first love and that was basketball.

A talented athlete but also a superb student, Nicole graduated from high school with high honors, was named to the honor society, and

157

excelled in all subject areas but especially math and science. Her goal from an early age was to be a doctor and she seemed to be positioning herself well for this career aspiration. Named a prestigious scholar-athlete by the *Albany Times-Union* newspaper in her senior year, she could have elected to play basketball almost anywhere. And, because of Title IX legislation and the increased emphasis on delivering athletic scholarships to female athletes, Nicole was in an ideal position to call the shots in the recruiting wars that were inevitable for one so intelligent and physically gifted. She was the envy of most major collegiate basketball programs and eventually signed to play at Boston College early in her senior season.

Almost from the start, Nicole excelled at BC. A 5 foot 11 inch off guard and small forward, she was extremely versatile because she could deliver scoring from both the inside and outside. Her tenacious ways also made her a rebounding threat whenever she was on the court. Midway through her freshman season she started and ended up having a major impact upon an NCAA tournament team. BC reached the round of 32 before losing to eventual winner Tennessee. In that game, Nicole was high scorer with 16 points. She finished the season averaging 6.9 points and 3.4 rebounds in 28 games.

Like many freshmen, Nicole found adjustment to college and the task of balancing academics and athletics challenging. Intending to prepare for medical school, she took the normal pre-med curriculum of science and math courses in her freshman year. In the fall of her sophomore year at Boston College, Nicole was interviewed by *Albany Times-Union* staff writer Celina Ottaway about her experiences as a student-athlete. The interview is revealing about the demands placed upon collegiate athletes in general and those experienced by Nicole in particular. A portion of that interview is excerpted below.

Q. *You took honors classes in high school and played basketball. How did you first learn to balance academics and sports?*

A. I was very strict about my schedule. I would do my homework as soon as I got home. Or if my practice times switched, I would go right to practice and then come home and do my homework. I was very strict about it. I was never one of those kids who would put it off till later.

Q. *Do you think that's essential if you want to be a college athlete?*

A. It's hard. I didn't know right away. In high school you can wait until the night before or two nights before the test and start studying and you're fine, but in college it's not that way at all. You can't just sit down the night before and study a whole semester's worth of stuff. So freshman year, we, meaning freshmen athletes, we had a lot of problems. But this year's totally different. We haven't really started the season yet, so we'll see how that goes.

Q. *What's your schedule like now?*

A. At college, you have practice for two and a half hours. You have to get there an hour beforehand—if you need treatment. Like if your ankle's bothering you, you have to get there early to get treatment for it. You don't leave for a half an hour, 45 minutes afterward. We always have meetings, especially once the games start. After practice we'll meet for an additional hour or so to go over other teams' personnel or whatever they have to talk to us about.

Q. *What's your travel schedule like now?*

A. Last year, second semester I wound up withdrawing from a class—it was calculus—because we traveled so much. Calculus is the kind of class where you have to be there every time to stay on top of it. I took it in high school, but it is different in college. I wound up falling really behind. There was a period where we missed a couple weeks of class because we traveled so much.

Q. *How many days in a semester do you miss?*

A. I think we are going to miss five days this (fall) semester, but next semester we will miss a lot more. It's when our league games pick up. We haven't gotten the official schedule yet, but last year, my Tuesday-Thursday class I missed two weeks in a row. That killed me because I missed so much of it. I wound up doing OK, but I had to work a lot harder to keep up.

Q. *How do you manage to get your academic work done?*

A. If you have something due the day of a game you do it beforehand so you're not worrying about it. We have to do it ahead of time or if we do it on the road, some of the teachers are understanding about it—you might get an extension——if we're away or if we get in really late. But other teachers are really strict about it and they give you no leeway whatsoever. They feel you should be treated the same as any other student.

Q. *Is there any room for a social life in all of this?*

A. Preseason and postseason we don't have stuff on the weekends. But once the season starts we practice six times a week, and the one day off could be like a Wednesday, and we could find out the night before. So you can't really plan anything. It's very hard to do anything during the season. I never go home. I don't go into Boston. The most I'll do is go to a movie or something. We're always so tired that we don't have the energy to go to the clubs or anything. We just want to rest.

Q. *How long does the season run?*

A. October 16 until we lose, usually sometime in March. It's pretty long.

Q. *When you started college you had plans to go to medical school. Why did you change your mind?*

A. I've always wanted to be a doctor. I mean I still do. Science and math, they've always been my stronger points in school. I just enjoyed them more than history and English and stuff. I tried last year; I took the Intro to Bio class for pre-med majors. In college they are trying to weed through the pre-med students; they have one big lecture and three tests the whole year and that's it, so if you do bad on one you're not going to do well. It was really hard for me. Every night they would give me chapters and chapters to read. I just didn't have the time. It's hard enough being pre-med without being on an athletic team. I just have so much less time than everyone else. So I kind of gave up on that idea halfway through the semester.

Q. *You are talking about two life dreams there. How did you choose between them?*

A. I had no choice. I am not going to not play just to do pre-med. I am on scholarship and basketball is definitely my first love. I'm not really bitter about it. I kind of wish that I had the chance to do it. I mean I know that I could, but I'd have to kill myself. We don't have time to do the labs, so I'd have to stay all summer and do the labs. I could hypothetically do both, but I wouldn't want to. So I decided to look at what else was out there that I would want to do.

Q. *Was that hard?*

A. At first, I was kind of mad. I felt like just because I was on a sports team I had this huge disadvantage. All these other students were studying for hours. They can stay up late, I have to go to bed by like midnight or else I'm dead the next day. I have all these early classes and then I have practice. I was always so drained last year, physically and emotionally, I was just dead. It annoyed me that I couldn't do it just because I was on a sports team. As I said, academics have always been very important to me. I don't want to be just one-dimensional. I hate the stereotype of the dumb jock. It really bugs me. I really wanted to do the pre-med thing, but it was not realistic. But I'm over it now. I am actually really excited about the whole elementary ed. thing. I love working with kids. It's not like I'm going into a field that I don't want to go into. Otherwise I might be a little more bitter.

Q. *What's it like to love something as much as you love basketball?*

A. It's hard, especially in college, where this love gets tested a lot. There were times last year when I honestly thought that I didn't want to play anymore. And I know that that happens to probably every college freshman who plays basketball. It's so hard, not just physically. Physically it's hard, but I can definitely take that more than the emotional and psychological. It is so hard being a freshman. Coaches tend to yell at freshmen more. Freshmen are not as good, obviously, and they are trying to make them better, so they yell at them more. You really get tested—how much do you really love the game? I knew as soon as postseason hit and I was away from the monotony of the game that that was really stupid and I really do love it. I could never just walk away. During the season, there were times when I was like, I hate this, I just want to be a normal student here, but then I think about it now and I'm like, that's ridiculous.

Q. *It sounds like even though you worked hard in high school, your freshman year was a whole other level of stress both on and off the court?*

A. High school prepares you for it, but it can't prepare you all the way. But in high school if academics are important to you it will definitely help you. I've seen some of my friends who are on sporting teams, they didn't have to do anything in high school because they were some big shot at their school. They went to college, they didn't know how to deal with it. I mean most teachers don't care who you are. Granted, some will give some leeway because you are an athlete, but most will just treat you like you are any other student. So the fact that my mom was always on my case about my studying really helped. Now even though she's not with me, I'm programmed that way.

Nicole made the difficult decision to switch her major from pre-med to elementary education. She arrived at that choice after weighing her love of basketball with her career desire to become a doctor. By changing her major, she was able to have success in both areas——sports and academics. While at first she was troubled by her decision, she became more comfortable with it as time went on and eventually embraced the transition to a different career path. Her maturity in reaching one of the most important decisions of her life was admirable and consistent with the good judgment that was always a trademark of her personality.

On the basketball court, Nicole's remaining three years at Boston College were as impressive as her freshman season. With the exception of her sophomore year, BC made the NCAA tournament each year and Nicole's starting role and steady play were big reasons for that success. In her senior season, which was perhaps her best overall, she started in 29 of 31 games and averaged 9.0 points and 5.0 rebounds.

I was able to attend a number of Nicole's games during her collegiate career. One game that sticks out in particular was an early December contest in her senior year when BC played top-ranked Tennessee. Nicole did it all that evening with a solid performance at both ends of the court. She had 6 rebounds, 5 assists, and 14 points in a game that BC ultimately lost 75–66. At one point late in the fourth quarter, she scored 2 3-point goals in the span of just 11 seconds, thus catapulting her team to a 4 point deficit. There was no question in my mind that she was the best player on the court that evening.

Nicole Conway finished a spectacular basketball career at BC in 2002 and graduated cum laude that spring with a degree in elementary education. Among her academic and educational accomplishments were being named Big East Scholar Athlete of the year, Verizon Academic All-District, Big East Academic All-Star, All Big-East honorable mention, team MVP, Women's Basketball News Service All-Freshman third team, Big East/Nike All-Stars, and Sun and Fun Classic Tournament MVP. She is ranked in several career record categories at BC including tied for 1st in games played (121), 5th in steals (149), 7th in assists (260), 9th in 3-point field goals made (60), and 11th in rebounds (533). At Boston College's All-Sports Banquet, she was named senior female athlete of the year.

Presently, Nicole is continuing her basketball exploits by playing professionally with the Springfield Spirit of the National Women's Basketball League (NWBL). The-six team league, which started in 1997 but has struggled somewhat to stay financially viable, plays its games from the end of January to the beginning of April. Because of the timing of their season, the league does not compete with the other U.S. professional league, the Woman's National Basketball Association (WNBA). I recently attended one of her games where her team downed the Tennessee Fury 97–87. Nicole scored 8 points and at one stage of the second half executed a momentum shifting 3- point play. At one point, her teammates on the floor included some of the greatest names in the history of women's basketball, including Sue Bird, Rebecca Lobo, Swin Cash, and Kara Walters.

As I watched Nicole sign autographs for youngsters following her recent game, I thought about what a fantastic role model she is for young girls who are just getting their feet wet in sports. Simultaneous with her professional basketball activities, she is completing work on her master's degree in education. She continues to have the drive and acumen that will guarantee success at whatever she does. Somehow, it comes as no surprise that she is even considering going on for her doctorate degree in the field of education. This is a woman who can do it all; she has performed this way ever since she was a young child playing basketball and performing in the classroom.

Title IX, the federal law passed in 1972 that forbids sex discrimination at schools and universities receiving federal funds, has been both a blessing and a curse for young women like Nicole Conway. On the one hand, the receipt of an athletic scholarship allowed Nicole to continue playing a sport that she loved while simultaneously obtaining a free education at a top-notch college. On the other hand, like many men before her, it forced her into choices in which her academic options were narrowed considerably. Ultimately, she was placed in the position of changing an educational and career path in order to accommodate the rigorous demands of playing the sport she loved at the highest level of big-time collegiate basketball.

Life is about choices and everyone has a free will when it comes to career aspirations. Nicole Conway could have opted to play basketball at the Division III level or perhaps in the Ivy or Patriot League, where the demands of playing a sport would not have been so great and the opportunity to pursue a pre-med career path less difficult. Although nothing stands in her way in the future should she still want to become a medical doctor (i.e., the requisite undergraduate coursework needed for admissions tests could be completed in a few additional years), it is nonetheless bothersome that young college athletes like Nicole Conway should be confronted with such difficult options.

Should a young person, boy or girl, be placed into a forced-choice situation that pits a lifelong career path against athletics? Have we skewed the demands of collegiate sports so severely that academics by necessity become second-class citizens to athletics in our institutions of higher learning? In short, what is college for these days? Is it a training ground for professional sports or preparation for a career in science, business, education, government, medicine, the law, or innumerable other professional careers? Where is the balance when we insist that many college athletes spend most of their waking hours in training for their sport with education sometimes an afterthought?

Because of Title IX, the athletic opportunities available to women have certainly increased. At the same time, however, I am not so sure that those who shaped this legislation back in the late 1960s and early 1970s had as their intent that women should become more like men in the manner in which athletics control their existence. Already there are reports that admission standards are declining for blue-chip female athletes, educational options are narrowing to less demanding majors, and grade point averages of woman athletes at some institutions are actually declining. Though these data are nowhere near as pitiful as that seen for male athletes, the trend is cause for alarm. It is the same trend that was seen for men when college athletic scholarships began to mushroom back in the 1950s.

Male and female athletes, like their nonathlete counterparts, should be able to realize their ultimate career dreams whatever they may be. It is not acceptable that student-athletes should feel pressured to change a career goal because sports training occupies too much of their daily existence and exhausts them both emotionally and physically. This seems to happen on a regular basis in our present system of sports and much of it occurs because nobody is really looking after the interests of the athletes. Clearly, if we are to bring a level of sanity back to an out-of-control system of competitive athletics in this country, a major overhaul of our warped sports culture is needed.

Part Five

ROOT FOR YOUR TEAM

Every time I sit in an NCAA Tournament press conference and hear the moderator—under orders from the NCAA—ask if there are questions for the "student-athletes," I want to jump up and ask them exactly what they have done to be students while the multibillion extravaganza known as March Madness has been going on. Been to class lately, Mr. Student-Athlete? Did you bring any books on the trip with you? Tell me, what are your plans for the day you can't play basketball anymore? The answers in, I would say, about 90 percent of the cases would be: No, why would I do that? And, be a TV commentator, that's national TV, none of the local stuff.

John Feinstein, *The Last Amateurs*

Sport is becoming so disconnected from educational values and foundations that it is in grave danger of becoming educationally irrelevant.

John Gerdy, *Sports in School*

The most obscene dimension of the whole situation is hidden from public view. It's that so many African-American high school students, not just recruited athletes, have low SAT scores. The reason that happens is that so many inner-city kids have been brainwashed by the NCAA and the TV networks into thinking that the way out of their predicament is not to go to the public library and check out two or three books a week, but to throw something or kick something or slam dunk something in a way that will make men like Harrick (U Georgia basketball coach) and Chaney (Temple basketball coach) want to give them an athletic scholarship.

William Dowling, *Chronicle of Higher Education*

———————

It has been said that a chain is only as strong as its weakest link. With the glorification of sports, it turns out, the edification of students is diminished. And if education becomes our weakest link, and entertainment our strongest, then there is trouble festering.

Ira Berkow, *New York Times*

———————

24

About Second, Third, and Fourth Chances

He was, quite simply, the best scholastic basketball player I have ever seen in the Albany Capital District Area. Devonaire Deas, 6-foot-5, 195 pound point guard out of Albany High School could do it all on the basketball court. He could shoot threes with accuracy, get a step and slash to the hoop for a jam, and effortlessly set up his teammates for an easy assist. Although his defensive performances were often only average, he could turn up the intensity on this part of his game whenever he wanted.

From 1992 to 1994 I watched Deas play a number of times and always came away impressed with his athleticism and court sense. He started as a sophomore and junior and his Albany High Falcons were sectional Class A champions for both of those years. As a junior, he averaged 19 points a game and was named MVP in the Section II tournament. A game that especially sticks out in my mind was the Class A Sectional Final that year in which Albany beat Shaker High School 58–54. Deas only had 5 points in a lackluster performance during the first half of that game. His shooting was off, he wasn't setting up his teammates as a good point guard should, and he wasn't playing good defense. However, his play in the second half more than made up for it. With only a few minutes remaining in the game, Deas made a 3-point play to put Albany ahead, then forced Shaker into a turnover for an easy Albany basket. As *Albany Times-Union* writer Joe Layden described it: "It was Deas who came out of the pack on a breakaway and, while falling down, flipped a blind pass from halfcourt into the waiting hands of teammate Russell Johnson, who was fouled going into a layup. It was Deas who scored Albany's final six points to ice the victory." This was vintage Devonaire Deas. He took over the game as great players do and

170

put the team on his back. He finished with 19 points, five assists, and four rebounds and was named the MVP.

The story behind Deas was much more complicated than the successful basketball picture that was portrayed on the court. Frequent reports in the *Albany Times-Union* kept everyone abreast of the latest developments in his career. He and his mother Dionne escaped to Albany from an unstable life in Harlem when he was 12 years old. He was helped in Albany by Ron Peeks, who later became his guardian, as well as local Bishop Gibbons basketball coach, Herb Crossman. As time went on, problems in the classroom increasingly held him back. Deas was suspended for the first half of his junior season for failing three of his six classes. At the time, Crossman's words in a *Times-Union* interview proved to be prophetic. He stated: "The only one who can hold Devonaire back is Devonaire. Any Division I program would want a player like that. The way Devonaire sees the court, handles the ball, he's strong, cocky, aggressive. He's got all the tools. You see this in kids like Devonaire, kids who can play, but when it calls for real down-to-earth focus, will they do the work? They love to go on raw talent, but the higher you go, you can't rely on that."

Devonaire Deas left Albany before the start of his senior year to play at St. Thomas Moore Academy in Oakdale, Connecticut. Deas, who reportedly had stopped attending high school classes once the New York State High School Basketball Tournament had ended in March, was in need of academic rehabilitation. At the time, Albany High basketball coach Paul Lyons commented: "Devonaire will have no trouble playing basketball there. Academics are his problem. That's the main reason why he's going there, to pick up his academics. If it helps him, it's a good thing. I just hope he gets his grades in order and isn't a Prop 48 when he goes to college."

Deas averaged 17 points, 11 assists, 9 rebounds, and 5 steals a game, and was named MVP as St. Thomas Moore won the New England Prep Championship. He was recruited by most major college programs and could have gone just about anywhere. Wanting to play at the highest possible level, he eventually signed with Florida State of the ACC. Unfortunately, things did not work out well for him in his first year (1995–1996) at FSU. He was benched after starting his first five games and averaged only 10.6 minutes and 2 points per game for the season. The next fall he was suspended for academic reasons and finished the second half of his sophomore season (1996–1997) averaging 7.5 minutes and 2.5 points per game. A rift with head coach Steve Robinson resulted in less playing time as the season went along and eventually Deas left Florida State for greener pastures.

With two years of eligibility left, Deas landed on the doorstep of Iona basketball coach Jeff Ruland. While academic problems seemed to plague him at almost every stop along the way, Iona looked like a place he could find a home. Ruland, a coach with high expectations for his players both on and off the court, was willing to give the talented Deas another shot but it was clear that he was on a short leash. Recognizing his problems in the classroom, Jeff Ruland analyzed Deas's situation in the following way: "He has some issues. We want to get him to trust us here. Right now he is having a problem making classes and when you don't make classes, there is a problem. He has some demons with him and we are trying to help get rid of them. He is a stud; there is no question he would be a major player for us. But we can't worry about that right now. He has some unfinished business to take care of. He will have five or six good days and then he'll have a bad one. We can't have any bad ones. One of the reasons people come to this school is to get an education and he has to understand that. The ball is in his court." Commenting on his academic problems, Deas remarked: "I know I have a long road to go, I know there were times (at FSU) when I was real lazy and didn't go to class."

In late October 1998, Coach Ruland dismissed Deas from the team after he missed classes for two straight weeks. By Ruland's estimates, he missed 40 to 50 classes over a two month span of time. Ruland was disappointed but at the same time realistic: "We've had a lot of heart-to-heart talks with him. I wish him the best, but he would not go to class and that was part of the agreement when he came here. At Iona, you're a student first." However, at the same time, Ruland was so impressed with Deas's athletic abilities that he predicted he would have been a lock for MAAC player of the year for two straight years. It was clear that he was deeply disappointed in losing a player who could have gotten him the MAAC championship and a possible NCAA run in the Final Four tournament.

Deas returned to Albany where his girlfriend and their 7-month-old daughter lived. However, he quickly got into trouble of a more severe nature in December of that year. Following a botched robbery and shooting that took place near a Denny's restaurant in Albany, Deas was arrested and pleaded guilty to a reduced charge of attempted third-degree criminal possession of a weapon—a felony—and to possessing a firearm in which the serial number was removed. The plea was bargained down from a more serious charge of attempted murder and robbery. At the time, Assistant District Attorney Paul Clyne explained: "Other than Deas' presence (as the alleged driver of the getaway car), there was not a lot linking him to the robbery or the use of the gun." Deas was sentenced to 90 days in jail and five years of probation. His co-defendant pleaded guilty to second-degree criminal possession of a weapon—a violent felony—and was sentenced to 13 years in prison.

While many thought that Deas's basketball career was probably over at this point, he surprised many when it was reported in November 2000 that Winston-Salem State College, a Division II college in North Carolina, had offered him an athletic scholarship. However, things once again became complicated for Deas in the interim as he was arrested for violating his probation, skipping appointments with his probation officer. While he could have been sentenced to up to four years in prison, County Judge Larry Rosen instead reinstated his probation, citing his admission to college as the determining factor. Deas had survived again and his new college coach Rich Duckett proclaimed, "Everyone should have an opportunity to have a second chance."

Devonaire Deas did very well on the basketball court at Winston-Salem State College. Leading his team deep into the Division II playoffs, he averaged 16 points a game for each of his two seasons. From that point on, however, news about his life has remained sketchy. I have asked many about Deas to find out whether or not he ever graduated from Winston-Salem State College and what he might be doing now that his athletic eligibility has ended. Nobody seems to know. Curiously, the *Albany Times-Union* newspaper did not publish a single report on Deas to update his basketball career once he left the Capital District Area for Winston-Salem State College.

Rest assured, however, that there are always other potential Devonaire Deas waiting in the wings. In our area, Emmanuel "Tiki" Mayben, a phenom 6-foot-3, 165 pound point guard out of Troy seems to be duplicating many of Devonaire Deas' exploits both on and off the court. As just a freshman, he led his team to the sectional title and was named MVP for his performance. He was ranked as the ninth best high school sophomore player in the country by *Hoop Scoop Online*. He is considered by some in this area as the best freshman point guard ever in Section II of Upstate New York.

In *Albany Times Union* interviews, Mayben's coaches love his game but are only cautiously optimistic about his potential down the road. His high school coach Jeff Sitterly remarked: "If he stays on pace, I think he's on track to be at that (high) level. I know it's always been his dream to play for a major Division I team. He sees that it's all right there. The only way he could mess it up is by doing things that turn coaches off. My biggest fear with a kid like this is that if things don't go well, how will he react? He always can't look at wins and losses as the most important thing. His future is pretty bright for him, but he can't take any steps backward, and I'm hoping he understands that."

Mayben's AAU coach Jim Hart chimed in with a similar evaluation: "At that position (point guard) we've never seen anyone with his talent (in this area). He's just the best point guard we've ever had here. He needs to improve mentally by not taking the highs so high and lows so low. The great ones tend to keep an even temper, where he can wear his emotions on his sleeve." This area has produced some tremendous point guards in the recent past, including Willie Deane (Purdue) and Lionel Chalmers (Xavier) so the pressure clearly is on Mayben to live up to those very high expectations.

Things have not been easy for Tiki Mayben. In his sophomore year, he was suspended for one game early in the season for academic problems. Later in the season, he was terminated from the team by Coach Sitterly for "conduct not acceptable for a Troy High athlete." The termination from the team followed from some heated discussion between Mayben and spectators following a close loss to Ballston Spa in a tournament game. Mayben had to be restrained by teammates and helped off the court. Three weeks later Mayben's suspension was lifted by the Troy Superintendent of Schools Armand Reo and he was given yet another chance to come back to the team. He played the remainder of his sophomore season without incident.

Mayben announced in early December, 2003 of his junior year that his choice for collegiate basketball would be Syracuse University. While the announcement was a nonbinding oral commitment, it was considered by some to be premature since, as a junior, he could not technically be offered an athletic scholarship by any college. Nonetheless, the local media vigorously covered his press conference at Troy Boys Club as if the hoopster was the next coming of Alan Iverson. In mid January however, things again turned sour for the troubled Mayben and he quit the Troy High School basketball team under a cloud of undisclosed circumstances. He is now attending the Winchendon Prep School in Massachusetts.

Although he is very young and perhaps he will be able to learn from his mistakes, Tiki Mayben appears as though he could benefit from some anger management classes. However, the negative academic and behavioral incidents in his young life are disturbing and in some ways reminiscent of Devonaire Deas. As the pressure builds and more is expected of him, my hope is that I am dead wrong about what may be in store for Emmanuel Mayben down the road.

There are inumerable stories from every walk of life about individuals who have turned personal adversity and failure into eventual triumph and success. As humans, we should never lose sight of the fact that we are not perfect and that we can frequently make regrettable mistakes that cost us dearly. However, life in America is all about second chances and redemption and I, like many, strongly believe in that cherished principle. At the same time, I am not naïve. I know what high school and college sports are all about these days. I know that many coaches don't repeatedly rescue players from academic, legal, and behavioral problems unless they know that the athlete can help them win.

On the one hand, there is a growing sense of entitlement that young athletes have in their early years. Everything is done for them and they are used to hearing the answer "Yes, it is OK" for every twist and turn in their young lives. They don't grow up and their development into a complete human being is permanently arrested. On the other hand, our high schools and colleges do nothing to promote maturity by holding athletes responsible for important events in their lives. In particular, education becomes an afterthought and it is instead all about majoring in sports and getting better on the playing fields.

Just how many chances do we give athletes who have shown continually that they don't want to be in school and don't want to abide by the laws of our society? Should ability in sports necessarily guarantee an athlete second, third, and fourth chances? Whose interests are really served when we bail out star athletes time and again with the hope that things will change when in fact nothing ever does? Do we give a kid who can't dunk a basketball or catch a touchdown pass the same opportunities, or do we instead allow them to fall by the wayside and perhaps learn the hard way that if they want to make it in life they have to get their act together or become a casualty? When does enabling behavior stop for top athletes and why do we persist in compromising our educational system for those who really don't want to be there and probably don't belong in the classroom to begin with?

I don't pretend to have the answers to these ethical questions but perhaps we should begin to explore them soon. What hangs in the balance are future Devonaire Deas and Emmanuel Maybens—good kids who are failed by a system that can't get it right and won't reform itself because those in leadership positions think about everything else except the best long-term interests of the kids playing the games.

©2003 MARK PARISI, DIST. BY UFS, INC.

25

The Ephs Versus the Lord Jeffs

In the winter of 2001, I attended the Amherst—Williams college basketball game in Williamstown, Massachusetts. This rivalry, which is one of the oldest and most storied in the nation at the Division III level, pits the Ephs (Williams) and the Lord Jeffs (Amherst) against each other in a home and home series each year. Though I had never been to one of the contests, I was frequently told that the games were always a sellout and usually a good matchup between two very well coached teams. Forewarned that seating would be at a premium, I showed up before the girls varsity contest that was held before the men's game. Not a moment too early, I managed to get one of the last of the 1600 seats in jam-packed Chandler Gym.

My principal reason for going was to watch Chuck Abba, a boy that I had the pleasure to coach for several seasons in a high school summer basketball league in the Capital District of Albany, New York. Abba, a top student at Williams and a starter on their basketball team, was a superb high school basketball player at Bethlehem Central High School, where he was coached by his father, Chuck Abba Sr. There were many nights that I watched him play when he completely dominated the game with his outstanding offensive and defensive skills. He was an excellent perimeter shooter and could also slash to the hoop because of his quick first step and toughness. He also played great man-to-man defense and frequently guarded the opposing team's best player. In short, he was one of the best all around players that I had ever seen.

The game I saw that night was hard fought and well-played. The spectators were rabid on both sides and the gym was alive with partisan rooting for both teams. The coaching was every bit as good if not better than Division I coaches I had observed in the past and the athletes were intense and totally focused on playing the game. As Division III schools, Amherst and Williams typically get athletes who are first and foremost serious about their studies and secondarily interested in continuing their athletic careers. Blue-chippers don't usually end up at these schools but the players I saw that night were very good and played a superbly executed team game that was enjoyable to watch. Yes, they weren't as tall and skilled as Division I players and perhaps not as athletic either, but the quality of team play made up for any deficits in individual talent.

The game itself sea-sawed back and forth, with Amherst holding a 4-point advantage at the half. A 12-point run by the Lord Jeffs to start the second half proved to be an insurmountable difference, however, as Amherst ultimately was victorious over Williams 73–64. Chuck Abba played a solid game with his scoring, defense, and rebounding. I was glad to see him play and even happier to spend a few minutes with him after the game. We briefly talked about his team's defeat and I knew he was disappointed in the outcome. But he was not so disconsolate that he couldn't also tell me about his academic life and how things were going in the classroom. Political science, history, and English seemed to be his real interests, with perhaps a leaning toward law school in the future. With his superior grades and his focus I am sure that he will position himself for just about anything once he graduates.

On my ride back to the Albany area after the game that night I thought about some Division I basketball games I had seen a few years earlier in the opening rounds of the NCAA Final Four tournament at the Knickerbocker (now Pepsi) Arena in Albany, New York. In particular, I recalled being one of 15,000 spectators who paid dearly for the privilege to witness a UMass victory over Stanford to make it to the round of 16 in 1995. That was the year that Coach John Calipari rode the performance of his star and future NBA player Marcus Camby.

Allegations of academic corruption as well as recruiting violations dogged Calipari and the UMass program and eventually the school had to give back $151,000 to the NCAA for its appearance. On top of this, it was later reported that Marcus Camby had accepted $40,000 in cash and gifts from two different agents, thus further tarnishing the school and John Calipari. Soon after, Calipari escaped the NCAA investigators and left for a multimillion-dollar deal with the NBA Nets; Marcus Camby declared early for the draft and was selected in the first round by the Toronto Raptors. Both got what they wanted and both left a mess behind them on the UMass campus. The Minutemen basketball team has been in the doldrums ever since Calipari and Camby left the program in shambles.

In watching the Amherst—Williams contest that night, I knew that I had witnessed real students playing the game and not the exploited mercenaries that seldom crack a book or enter a classroom at many Division I colleges like UMass. I knew that I had watched students who would graduate from college having done meaningful classroom work in sound curriculum. Amherst and Williams are two of the best higher institutions of learning in the country and they don't cut academic corners with their athletes. Not only are these schools outstanding academically, but athletically they boast some of the best teams in the country. For example, Williams has won six of the last seven Sears Director's Cups, an award given annually for athletic supremacy in Division III.

So, unlike Duke versus North Carolina, Xavier versus Cincinnati, or UConn versus Syracuse, match-ups between professionals-in-training for the NBA who often don't know what the inside of a library looks like, who are trained by highly paid professional coaches, and who take phony "jock" curriculum, I knew that Amherst versus Williams represented an amateur athletic contest the way it was meant to be—a matchup between kids who are first and foremost interested in getting a good education and secondarily interested in playing a sport.

Though I don't like to use the term "student-athlete" (do we ever use the term "student-musician" or "student-thespian?"), the basketball players I watched at the Williams and Amherst game came as close as you can get to the original intent of the words. If more colleges possessed the same academic values as Williams and Amherst and they were as strongly enforced by college presidents and trustees as they are in the New England Small College Athletic Conference (NESCAC), then intercollegiate sports would not be in the fix that it presently finds itself in today.

Academic corruption and commercialism are rampant at big-time Division I colleges and universities. The link between education and commercialism is straightforward; the likelihood of serious academic training diminishes as the amount of money at stake increases. That is why a degree at Williams and Amherst (Division III) means something while one at UMass, Cincinnati, and Tennessee (Division I) or countless other big-time universities means little.

When "March Madness" arrives each year it has all the trappings of the highly commercialized event that it really represents. A made or a missed foul shot can result in a school gaining or losing several hundred thousand dollars. It can also result in millions of dollars changing hands through both legal and illegal sports gambling. During this media extravaganza, athletes miss lots of classes in "jock" curriculum designed to keep them barely eligible, millionaire celebrity coaches give us sound bites that their program is clean and ethically run, and the NCAA blitzes us with the myth of the "student-athlete." In reality, graduation rates are worse than ever for college basketball players and cheating and bending the rules by coaches is at an all time high. All this, so the NCAA can fulfill its end of the bargain for the $6 billion dollar, 11 year contract it signed with CBS in 2003 to televise March Madness.

Admittedly, many Americans love to be entertained by superb, professionally-trained athletes. So, we are willing to put up with academic hypocrisy and the lie that big-time collegiate sports factories are really trying to educate athletes. This is an illusion that many are willing to put up with in order to get their yearly dose of "madness" from the Final Four basketball tournament. But many like myself are beginning to question whether or not the mission of higher education has been irretrievably corrupted by commercial interests and whether or not we can bring back any semblance of balance between athletics and academics. In short, will reforms ever occur or we will continue to see the exploitation of college athletes, especially African Americans, for the ostensible purpose of providing the public with commercialized entertainment?

An increasingly vocal group of individuals who call themselves "sports reformers" want to see some changes in intercollegiate sports. Made up of professors, former athletes, coaches, and parents, this group has gathered momentum in recent years. Many reform proposals are being floated but none stronger and more sensible than those by the Drake Group, the National Alliance for College Athletic Reform. They want to take back the classroom that they have lost to the athletic department. Their agenda seems realistic. Get rid of the phony term "student-athlete" that was created by the NCAA to prevent workman compensation claims and any possibility that athletes might be considered employees of the university. Restore freshman ineligibility such that athletes have the necessary time to transition into the demands of a rigorous academic life. Insist that students attend classes and shorten sports seasons so students don't have to miss so much class time. Schedule games on weekends and over vacation periods so that they never conflict with classes. Place academic counseling centers for athletes back in the hands of educators instead of the athletic department. Force universities to disclose the courses and grade-point averages of athletic teams. And, get rid of one year, renewable athletic scholarships in favor of guaranteed four year, need-based financial aid. Adopting these changes would go a long way to returning the primary mission of our universities to education as opposed to sports training.

Athletes on our college campuses are not stupid though often they come unprepared for serious learning. Likewise, for those that are academically qualified when they enter as freshman, many end up underperforming in their classes. Quite simply the demands of a 30 hour a week commitment to sports exhausts them physically and mentally. They have little time to really sample what a complete college life is all about. As a result, they miss out on some of the most culturally valuable experiences one can have in an important growth period of their young lives. This situation, combined with an athletic scholarship that is renewable from year to year based upon athletic performance, forces athletes to prioritize the playing field over the classroom. This unbalanced system all but guarantees underachievement and academic failure.

Other more radical sports reformers are drawn to a fantasy that sparks their collective desire to see the whole charade end: Shortly before the tip for the championship game, the athletes from one or both teams strike and hold out for $100,000 per player before they take the court. The players' mantra of "pay up or we won't play" could finally bring the NCAA to its knees in what many consider to be the most lopsided employer-employee relationship in our country. Rumor has it that a strike almost happened a few years back but the team lost in the semifinals and never made it to the championship game. Too bad for those wanting to see the exploited athletes get what they deserve, but fortunate for the big boss NCAA which continues to serve as the master of the most effective cartel in the world.

How should prospective college athletes and their parents think about the continuing litany of commercialism and academic corruption on our college campuses? I am left to make a simple recommendation to those parents who think seriously about these important issues. If your son or daughter is an athlete considering the SEC, Big-Ten, or ACC versus a NESCAC, Patriot, or Ivy League school, the decision is an easy one from my perspective. Go to an institution where you can get a degree that means something instead of a commercialized sports factory where the likelihood of getting a meaningful education is uncertain at best.

As you tune in to March Madness each year, enjoy the pageantry, the excitement of blaring, high energy bands, the enthusiasm of kids with painted faces, the thrill of victory and the agony of defeat portrayed by shrill announcers, the excitement of tight games with buzzer beater endings, and the athleticism of the professionally trained players. At the same time, however, don't be duped into thinking that the players are actually students. It is time that we finally put that myth to rest and place it in the same category as Santa Claus and the Easter Bunny.

26

The Cheating Dome

As a member of the Drake Group, a recently formed national association of college faculty interested in reforming college athletics, I attended a meeting of our organization at the University of Tennessee (UT) in February 2001. Our purpose in convening was to further outline our national agenda for ending corruption in college athletics. On another level, however, our reason for meeting at Tennessee was symbolic. The University of Tennessee has been a high-profile collegiate athletic program for many years but, like many big-time sports universities, has been plagued by allegations of academic corruption in its athletic department. Dr. Linda Bensel-Meyers, a member of the Drake Group and associate professor of English and director of composition at Tennessee, had been waging a battle with UT regarding academic improprieties among athletes since the fall of 1999. The Drake Group's presence was meant to support Dr. Bensel-Meyers and other UT faculty as they battled academic fraud in upcoming faculty senate hearings.

Dr. Bensel-Meyers started her faculty position at UT in 1986 and became the director of composition in 1989. She taught a required freshman year writing course and quickly shaped it in the image of her own academic training. Dr. Bensel-Meyers received her undergraduate training at the University of Chicago, where the Great Books are emphasized; her doctoral work was conducted at the University of Oregon, where she further immersed herself in the area of Renaissance drama.

One of her principal tasks in her early years as director of composition was to train tutors whose primary responsibility was to help male basketball and football players. As time went on, she came to realize that many of the athletes were not receiving anything that even remotely resembled an education even though UT was making millions of dollars from their sports participation. Many of her tutors reported

183

that they were sexually harassed by athletes that they were helping; still others reported that they were also intimidated into writing term papers for them.

As time went on Dr. Bensel-Meyers also started to notice other patterns suggesting that athletes were being exploited instead of being given a real education. Because she had access to transcripts, which is common and indeed necessary for faculty involved with teaching and advising duties, she found extreme cases of grade changes, clustering of unusually high grades from faculty that were known to be "friends" of the athletic department, and abuses in the labeling of some athletes as having disabilities that would excuse them from having to read or write.

Dr. Bensel-Meyers informed her superiors but she was ignored by those who were most in a position at UT to investigate her allegations. She soon realized that she would have to go public with her findings if she was to have any impact upon the continued pattern of academic hypocrisy at UT. She contacted ESPN and made public her own investigation. Not surprisingly it revealed that there was an endemic problem at UT that ostensibly cheated both athletes and professors. In one particularly revealing pattern of results, she showed that football players with the lowest academic standing were 31 times more likely to receive an incomplete than those players not on academic review. This suggested to many that the academic support arm of the UT Athletic Department was primarily concerned with keeping athletes eligible for competition but was not interested in providing equal access to a university education.

The University of Tennessee has a brand-new academic advisement and tutoring center a short distance from the stadium. The Thornton Center, a domed structure that is palatial in its appearance, is staffed and principally overseen by the Athletic Department. It is meant exclusively for student-athletes and is referred to by regular students as the "cheating dome." Centers like these are seen at many large Division I schools and their presence often raises issues of what entity should be responsible for their operation: academics or athletics. Because they represent an academic arm of the institution, most faculty logically feel that it is their responsibility to staff and oversee their operation. Curiously, however, in many big-time college sports programs such as UT, it is the purview of the Athletic Department. It is this conflict that Dr. Bensel-Meyers believes is the root of abuses at UT.

The response by UT President Wade Gilley was to close down records access and take over the investigation. He put the controversy in the hands of the administration instead of the faculty. This is not unlike what happens when a dictatorship shuts off all access to personal freedoms and does so in the name of the people. Colleges and universities are supposed to be about seeking the truth, not about suppressing it. The actions by the UT administration, which suggested that there was something significant to hide, were as disturbing as the initial allegations of academic fraud brought by Dr. Bensel-Meyers.

Life was not easy for Dr. Bensel-Meyers in her fight to restore some level of academic integrity to UT. She was sued by a former athlete for releasing information about a disability but this suit was dropped. Another lawsuit was lodged against ESPN.com and Robin Wright, a tutor supervised by Dr. Bensel-Meyers. A former football player and tutor sued because he claimed that it was untrue that the tutor had written a paper for the athlete. Dr. Bensel-Meyers pledged to pay the legal cost for Ms. Wright. Because UT would not defend Bensel-Myers or the tutor, a legal fund was established to help in their defense.

In addition to dealing with the stress of lawsuits and an unsupportive university, she was taunted, her office was broken into, and she received hate mail. Her husband stopped talking to her because he thought she was hurting their family, and her children were exposed to unpleasant remarks in school. She was afraid to leave her office late at night and most of all she was afraid that she would be fired. Many of her colleagues ignored her and still others who supported her did not want to come out publicly on her behalf; they feared that they would lose their jobs or advancements in the university. Several faculty members gave money to her defense fund but only by cash and not by check. They of course feared that they could lose their jobs if it was known that they helped to defend her.

Dr. Bensel-Meyers took her fight to the floor of the UT faculty senate (February 5, 2001). Some of her remarks, which are courageous, eloquent, and brutally honest, are excerpted below:

> I understand that reforming collegiate sports is a national problem, that "unilateral disarmament" is a dangerous proposition. However, as faculty at UT, we are charged with defending the educational mission of the institution, not with protecting the business of college athletics, a business that depends foremost on recruiting the best athletes who would not be admitted as qualified for college work were they not athletes. To enable these athletes to remain academically eligible, athletics programs around the country rely on

what they call "academic support." But the term is not to be confused with "remedial education." As any faculty member knows, there is a substantial difference between 'academic support' that enables underprepared students to "catch up" in their academic preparation by requiring additional time and study from them and that "academic support" that waives underprepared students from the university's educational requirements to free them for other activities. The "academic support" that many of our male athletes receive is not intensive study that constitutes remediation of underprepared students, who must put in more rather than less time into their studies, but the kind of crutch that enables them to spend less time on their studies and more time in the weight room or on the field of play. For this reason, I think it essential that we not assume graduation rates mean that athletes received the kind of education faculty of this institution work to provide, and we should not assume that statistics on grade changes that lump together all athletes in all sports reveal anything about the discrepancy between the kind of academic support academically-prepared athletes receive and the kind of academic "handling" the highly recruited, semi-professional athletes need to remain eligible.

The "academic support" provided by the Athletic Department is intended to keep athletes eligible for competition not provide equal access to an education at this university. And the system is not only non-democratic but exploitive: highly-recruited athletes, who tend to be African Americans who have sought sports as their ticket to college and the pros, often come to us unable to read and write and certainly unable to "catch up" academically with the training, practice, and competition schedules the Athletic Department demands of them. These are the athletes whose labor on the field of play ensures the economic success of our athletics programs; they are also the athletes who receive little in return, other than the offchance they will win the jackpot with a chance in the pros or a "degree" that represents an education in the values that drive sports competition, the belief that "might makes right" and how to bend the rules without getting caught. I would hope the majority of you would agree those are not the values the university should endorse or perpetuate to ensure the future of a civilized society.

We as faculty are part of this institution, and what we choose to do within the Faculty Senate should play a major role in the administrative decisions made at this university. We must accept responsibility to look at the evidence ourselves, to demand access to academic records that reflect our own performance as educators, to require responsible and equal enforcement of academic policies, and to protest when the evidence reveals a lack of integrity in the institution's distribution of justice. In the case of athletes, there is evidence that we are allowing students to be used as investment capital purely to serve the profit-interest of the business of athletics, without regard to the athletes' future welfare as players in the real "game of life." In the case of faculty, there is evidence that, when doing our jobs as educators threatens the business of athletics, we often choose to play the "game of the institution" rather than that of educators. Disclosure of our grading practices in the cases of athletes should not threaten but protect us from having to accept the Faustian bargain. It is only sensible that the Faculty Senate, not the administration, should be where we interrogate academic practices on campus.

Hence, I petition this body to open up its own investigation of the evidence, to address the issues that have not been addressed, to look at the records I have provided, to demand a revocation of the President's new records policy, which was put in place to protect those who released student names to the press not to protect the students, which was established to prevent faculty from knowing what will be going on behind the closed doors of the Thornton Center without concern for how it compromises the 25,000 other students' right to quality advising from informed faculty.

The faculty response to Dr. Bensel-Meyer's recommendations was lukewarm at best. The faculty senate placed her suggestions into committees where they still remain. In all likelihood they will never see the light of day. Unwilling to stake a claim to what is rightfully their territory—the maintenance of teaching and academic standards—the faculty copped out and washed its hands of the problem.

A member of the Drake Group, Dr. Allen Sack, wrote to other members about his impressions of UT and Dr. Bensel-Meyer's mission to restore academic integrity. He said: "Sport helps to promote the university, but there would be no academic product worth selling without faculty to defend academic standards and deliver quality instruction. Without the faculty, the institution would be an empty shell, or at best a massive sports camp. The problem is that faculty, either out of fear or complacency, have been unwilling to step forward to defend their turf from intrusions by the NCAA, the SEC, and other outside forces. If faculty merely defended their own turf, they could have a significant impact. Something tells me that when faculty can no longer tolerate the humiliation, the system is going to blow its top."

I had the opportunity to walk around Knoxville and the UT campus while I was there for the Drake Group meetings. There are reminders everywhere that sports are religion in this area. From the 107,000-seat Neyland Stadium to the streets named after former athletes and coaches, there is little getting away from the fact that everything revolves around the success of athletic teams. At least one UT faculty member told me that "it's kind of a joke around here that all the academic buildings could burn down with just the facades remaining and nobody would even notice as long as the football stadium was still standing." The message that this sends is undeniable. In the State of Tennessee most people bleed Volunteer orange and the culture of big-time athletics is so ingrained that almost nothing stands in its way, especially a lowly professor seeking to achieve some balance between academics and athletics.

In spite of almost insurmountable odds, Dr. Bensel-Meyers continued her struggle at UT in a dignified and courageous manner. She believed in her heart and in her mind that she was right. She continues to believe that college students, both athletes and nonathletes, have the right to receive a good education.

In May 2003, Dr. Bensel-Meyers resigned from the University of Tennessee to take a position in the English Department at the University of Denver. In her letter of resignation, she leveled a scathing indictment against the University of Tennessee administration in which she accused it of a cover-up in the athletics department and academic fraud. Portions of her letter are excerpted here:

> It is clear that the faculty and the students at (UT) will continue to be used as mere investment capital for the profitable business of its intercollegiate athletic program. As an educator, I cannot conscionably serve a university that has chosen to exploit rather than educate its students.
>
> To this day, no apology nor even a response has been made to the many members of my staff who filed formal complaints about physical and verbal abuse they sustained when attempting to report plagiarism in the athletic department office of student life.

No apologies have been made to athletes who attempted to access an education per the letter of their scholarship, discovering they were forcibly labeled "learning disabled" and told they had to let the tutors do their work for them.

The new director of the Thornton Center has not reviewed reports of how the athletic department systematized violation of academic policies. The new records policy (promulgated by former UT president Wade Gilley) has ensured that the problems can persist without detection.

The University of Denver will support my work in the renaissance of ethical education and in the national reform movement to prevent further exploitation of inner-city athletes.

No faculty member should ever find her attempts to do her job met with institutional threats and public attacks on her character.

Academic corruption in our colleges and universities is pervasive. Allegations of impropriety take front and center stage every year yet little seems to change in the culture of big-time college sports. A slap on the wrist with a few minor sanctions, a new coach is hired, the slate is wiped clean, and it is business as usual. When will we finally realize that this benefits no one and that our young athletes are being exploited and cheated in the process?

More important, why do we have athletics in our institutions of higher learning to begin with? Do we have colleges and universities to grow sports teams or are they there to foster intellectual curiosity and educational achievement? When you experience places like the University of Tennessee, the conclusion is inescapable. Athletics have taken over the mission of the university and everything else is subordinate.

College presidents talk a good game about reforming sports and changing the culture of intercollegiate athletics and then they create bogus academic programs to funnel ill prepared athletes through college. The drive to fill stadiums with fans and obtain more money through endorsements, ticket sales, bowl game receipts and alumni donations supersede any responsibility to academic integrity and the lives of college athletes. In short, many college presidents have all but abdicated their responsibility as leaders of reform. Just look at the University of Tennessee for a textbook example.

When the history is written on sports reform in this country, Dr. Linda Bensel-Meyers will lead the way as one of its shining lights. She is a hero; she is one of the main reasons why I have written this book.

27

Pulling the Plug on Baseball

My son Mark attended Providence College in Rhode Island and I won't forget his telephone call to me in October 1998 when he said the following: "Dad, you won't believe it. Providence is pulling the plug on the baseball team because of Title IX." Sure enough, I quickly went to the Internet and read all about it. It was confirmed the next day in newspapers and television reports.

The Reverend Philip A. Smith, president of Providence College, had sent a memo to the entire college community before the formal announcement to the press the next day. It squarely laid out what has become an often repeated sequence of events in many colleges and universities in our country today. Portions of his memo are reproduced here:

> As you are aware, Providence College has been undergoing a Self-Study for NCAA certification of its athletic programs. One of the NCAA standards requires that the College develop a gender equity plan to comply with the demands of Title IX as interpreted for intercollegiate athletics by the Office of Civil Rights in its policy statement of December 12, 1979.
>
> Under those guidelines, an institution may comply with the gender equity norms of Title IX in one of three ways: 1) provide participation opportunities for women that are substantially proportionate to their ratio in the full-time undergraduate student body; 2) demonstrate a history and continuing practice of program expansion for women; 3) fully and effectively accommodate the interests and abilities of women. The college has chosen proportionality as the only viable avenue for developing our gender equity plan. To comply with Title IX, our plan must ensure equity for women in: 1) participation, 2) athletic scholarships, and 3) other program areas.
>
> Over the past two years, the College has been developing the specifics of our gender equity plan. It achieves proportionality by the end of the 2003–04 academic year and affirms the College's

190

commitment to equal participation, scholarships and other forms of support for all our varsity athletes, based on an undergraduate student body ratio of 57 percent female and 43 percent male. The process has been very painful for everyone involved. We explored every available option thoroughly in an effort to retain all our varsity sports programs. Unfortunately, that was not possible. We reached that conclusion with deep sadness and regret.

At the end of the current academic year on June 30, 1999, the College will discontinue the varsity sports of baseball, golf and men's tennis. Providence College simply does not have the financial resources necessary to maintain its existing fiscal priorities and to achieve proportionality without dropping these sports. We rely heavily on tuition revenue for our operating expenses. If we were to retain the status quo in our varsity sports and to achieve gender equity by raising tuition, we would have to more than double the tuition increase of the current year. The College will honor its four-year financial commitment to all student athletes on these teams who are currently recipients of athletic scholarships.

Over the next four years, the athletic scholarships and other resources currently allocated to baseball, golf and men's tennis will be reallocated to strengthen resources in several women's programs. In addition, Providence College will explore ways to improve the current status of club, intramural and recreational sports programs. The College remains committed both to supporting a highly competitive Division I athletic program and to providing our students with an opportunity to engage in and enjoy the benefits of competitive athletic programs at various levels suitable to their skills and interests.

The Administration's gender equity plan has been reviewed and supported by the Athletic Advisory Council. It was also examined twice by the Varsity Athletic Committee of the Board of Trustees. At its meeting on October 6, 1998, the entire Board of Trustees of Providence College reviewed the plan and formally endorsed it as the best option available to the College for complying with the requirements of Title IX. Immediately after the Board meeting, those directly affected by the decision were informed personally of the College's action and the reasons for it: the coaches, the student athletes, their parents and the athletic staff. I wanted to inform each member of the College community of the steps we have taken before an official public announcement is made.

Dan Conway, a catcher on the Providence team, was taken by surprise along with the rest of his teammates. I had coached Dan during his Little League Baseball days and he was rapidly becoming a force in collegiate baseball. Dan and my son Mark had been friends since their youth and they played basketball, baseball, and golf together on a number of scholastic and youth league teams. My son felt bad for his friend; he knew that Dan's life would now be turned upside down with decisions about what to do in the wake of the unexpected announcement.

Raised in Bethlehem, New York, Dan Conway was an all-star baseball player throughout his development. He was captain of the baseball team in his senior season and earned all-state honors as well. In his sophomore and junior years, he also was named honorable mention all-state. In 1996 he hit .420 and led Bethlehem to the league championship. He also participated in the prestigious Empire State Games. By his own admission, he was a baseball junkie: "I've always loved baseball. I started real young, made all the all-star teams in Little League and Babe Ruth league, and when you're a kid who does that well at something, you just want to keep doing it."

Dan made the decision to attend Providence College in his senior year of high school. As a freshman at the school, he played in 20 games, batted .265 and performed well behind the plate. When the news came that baseball would be discontinued after his sophomore season, he was disappointed. However, like most of his teammates, he made the decision to stay through the end of the academic year and then transfer to another college once the season was over. This decision was not an easy one. "We had to practice all winter and play all spring knowing there wouldn't be any next year, while all the time also searching for another school," he said.

In spite of all the distractions, Dan hit .312, clubbed 10 home runs, and 11 doubles, and scored 59 runs. He was an ironman behind the plate, starting 64 of 65 games and committed just 10 errors in 382 chances. His team won the Big East tournament and went deep into the NCAA playoffs before bowing out in regional play. The team finished 49–16, the best in the 77-year history of Providence College baseball. In spite of a great season, it was the last one in the annals of Friars baseball. Title IX had taken its toll on yet another men's athletic program.

Dan Conway transferred to Wake Forest at the end of his sophomore year. Based upon his performance at Providence, the school offered him an athletic scholarship and he accepted. Named a co-captain of the team, Dan performed spectacularly in his junior year. He hit

.333 and led the team with 14 home runs and 56 RBIs. At the end of the year, he was named MVP by his teammates.

Dan performed so well that many major league teams were interested in his services. The Colorado Rockies drafted him following his junior season at Wake Forest and signed him for a substantial bonus. He bypassed his senior year at Wake Forest and is now working his way through the Rockies minor league system. In his first season with the A level Salem Avalanche, Dan performed well until he broke his leg in a play at home plate. Though he missed almost half of the season, the long-term prospects for Dan in the Rockies organization would appear to be excellent.

While Dan's college baseball career was disrupted, he was able to overcome the adversity of the Title IX changes at Providence by moving on to another college. In a sense, he was one of the lucky ones because his opportunity to continue his baseball career was only temporarily derailed.

Providence College had a difficult choice to make in 1998. They could continue to offer fewer athletic opportunities to women and risk a major discrimination lawsuit such as the one lost by crosstown rival Brown University a short time earlier, or they could pare their men's offerings and create more opportunities for women. The latter solution clearly won out and the quota system called proportionality became reality on the Providence campus.

Proponents of Title IX applauded the decision of Providence to move in the direction of creating more opportunities for women but a vocal minority decried the fact that it was at the expense of three relatively cheap, non-revenue- producing men's sports. The reality is that these decisions come down to money and it becomes a zero sum game: if you create opportunities in one part of an athletic program, then it follows that you must take them away from another part.

But, there is another way of looking at all this and it has to do with viewing big-time collegiate sports for what they often represent and that is highly professionalized entertainment and revenue for the institution. Providence has a long and storied tradition of basketball excellence and has fielded very competitive teams year in and year out. The high-profile team draws well in a downtown civic center and travels in style throughout the country for games against elite collegiate competition. Their coach, Tim Welsh, signed a seven-year deal in 2001 for $500,000 a year, which escalates to $700,000 toward the end of the contract. Indeed, he is the highest paid person at Providence College by a huge margin and his salary alone would probably be more than enough to pay for the entire women's athletic program. A quarter of his salary could have been used to defray the cost of the low-profile golf, men's tennis, and baseball teams.

The rub in all this is that men's basketball is revenue-producing and Providence, like many big-time collegiate programs, justifies expenses for the program as a necessary cost in marketing the school. Moreover, to keep up with the Joneses next door (Boston College, St. John's, UConn, Syracuse), the school must continue to do right by its basketball program and make sure that its players, coaches, and staff are being well taken care of.

When I grapple with the many problems surrounding Title IX legislation and its impact on athletics, I invariably come back to two fundamental questions. First, when universities are forced to make gender equity decisions in athletics, why is the solution always to take opportunities away from minor men's sports? Second, why do we continue to engage in an arms race that prompts colleges and universities to spend lavishly on professionalized college sports teams like football and basketball?

There is a simple, commonsense solution to many of the Title IX questions that have pitted men against women and have stirred up silly acrimonious controversy in our institutions of higher learning. The way out is to acknowledge once and for all that Division I collegiate football and men's basketball are professionalized sports. Before we destroy amateur athletics and further reduce men's sports offerings, let's get football and basketball out of our big-time colleges and universities and place them under the control and supervision of the NBA and NFL. By doing this, we can return our college campuses to amateur athletes and focus our attention and resources on where they rightfully belong and that is the education of true students.

The longer we obsess over the problems of professional athletes in training, many of whom probably don't want to be in a college classroom to begin with, the more we are blinded by Title IX concerns in higher education. The troubles associated with creating equal athletic opportunity on our college campuses are a smokescreen for the bigger issue of restoring institutions of higher learning to academic priorities. Our colleges and universities have been hijacked by athletic sports machines that utilize resources as if there were no limits. How about returning our college campuses to students desiring to receive a college education and pulling the plug on professionalized college athletic entertainment? Now there is an idea that is long overdue in this day and age of forgotten priorities in higher education.

28

Naming the Sports Complex

I received my bachelor's degree from Susquehanna University in the spring of 1971. Located in the lush green hills of central Pennsylvania in the rural college town of Selinsgrove, Susquehanna is a small (1,600 students), Lutheran-affiliated college. I was fortunate to have close contact with my professors. The small classes at the university produced a seminar like atmosphere in most of my courses. It was exactly what I needed in order to become a better student. Though I initially bounced from major to major over a three-year period, I eventually found a home in something I really liked and that was my present field of biopsychology. I received a good undergraduate education and immersed myself in fraternity and campus life. In short, I enjoyed four idyllic years of serious academic training mixed in with the right amount of social life and fun.

Though my football days ended in high school with a serious knee injury that required surgery in my senior year, I became a big supporter of the Susquehanna University Crusader football team. Some of my best friends played on the team and my fraternity roommate for my last two years in college, Steve Freeh, was the placekicker. We developed a close bond and during the spring months I served as his holder whenever he practiced his kicking out on the football field.

Susquehanna has a long and storied tradition in football. Though it is only a small Division III school with a modest endowment, it consistently fields very competitive football teams. In fact, the Grand Old Man of Football, Amos Alonso Stagg Sr., co-coached Susquehanna at the mature age of 84 from 1947 to 1952 with his son Amos Alonso Stagg Jr. The legendary Stagg Sr. is considered one of the greatest coaches and innovators in the game of football. The Division III national championship football game is called the Amos Alonzo Stagg Bowl in his honor.

However, by the time I arrived at Susquehanna in the fall of 1967, the football climate had turned sour and it continued that way until the fall of my senior year. In the four-year stretch from 1966 to 1969, the team did not win many games and was regularly outclassed by its opponents. Indeed, in 1968 and 1969 combined, Susquehanna scored only 172 points to its opponents 556. The interest in the team steadily dwindled, there was grumbling among the players I knew, and football alumni I happened to visit with on their return to campus voiced their concern.

Many traced the downturn in the team's fortunes to an event in 1965 that attracted national media attention. On Parent's Day that year, head coach Jim Garrett became frustrated by the poor play of his team. Just prior to the end of the first half, he punched his helmeted quarterback in the head in front of all in attendance. President Gustave Weber, a principled man and a top football player in his day, promptly fired Garrett and personally took over the team for the remaining two games of the season. Though I was in high school at the time, I distinctly remember reading reports of the incident in the *Boston Globe* and *Boston Herald*. Though the story was spun to make a hero out of President Weber for doing the right thing with his head coach and taking over the reins of the team, the damage to recruiting efforts was apparently significant. Susquehanna did not have a winning season again until 1970 when the team finished a respectable 7–2.

From 1960 to 1965, Garrett compiled a 39–11–1 record while at Susquehanna. This included undefeated seasons in 1961 and 1962, an unbeaten string of 22 games which was the longest in the country at the time, and a near impossible victory over nationally ranked Division I Temple in the 1963 season. In 1960, his team gave up only 17 points all season, a record that still stands. Garrett won 70 percent of his games and to this day has the best winning percentage of any coach in the 100 plus years of football played at Susquehanna. A legend at the university, he moved on to become head football coach at Columbia and later head coach of the Houston Texans of the World Football League. He spent 38 years in the NFL as an assistant coach with the New York Giants, New Orleans Saints, Dallas Cowboys, and Cleveland Browns. He presently is still active in football as a scout with the Dallas Cowboys and his son Jason is a quarterback with the New York Giants.

Garrett's name did not surface again at Susquehanna until 1999 when two former players that had been under his tutelage in the 60s made major gifts to the University to rebuild the football stadium and the physical education complex. Nick Lopardo and Rich Caruso, both Hall of Famers and active in the alumni association and board of directors, wanted to honor their former coach by naming the athletic complex on his behalf. Their wishes were endorsed by the board and in October 2001, the James W. Garrett Sports Complex was dedicated at homecoming with the former coach present for the festivities.

In their remarks, Lopardo and Caruso called Garrett "one of the most important influences in our lives." From all accounts, Garrett was genuinely touched. In his speech, he commented: "What will they say 30 years from now when people ask 'who was Jim Garrett?'" At that point, he pointed to his name over the entrance to the sports complex and then said that he hoped the answer would give proper credit first and foremost to "the football players and coaches who played for and worked with me." He went on to say: "they were amazing football teams and they were amazing young men."

At the dedication, University President Jay Lemons was effusive in his praise of Lopardo and Caruso: "The greatest reward for any teacher is to hear from former students that you made a difference in their lives. In a magnificent and generous way, Rich Caruso and Nick Lopardo have expressed their gratitude and affection for Jim Garrett's role in their own learning and development. We hope that it is a special joy for Coach Garrett and his family to learn about this magnificent expression of their appreciation for the difference he made in their lives."

Another former player from Garrett's era, Rich Derrick, wrote a letter to the *Susquehanna Today* alumni magazine. In it, he praised Garrett as "a leader and a teacher and well-deserving of the honor. He was passionate and enthusiastic about teaching football and how to win—and from him we learned lessons of life. Coach Garrett is about winning— but not just on the field. He taught us how to be winners in life; how to win and succeed in our relationships with family and friends and in our careers. When you are honest with yourself, you tend to be honest with others, and that is how Coach Garrett operated. He treated everyone the same on the field. He didn't show favoritism. You had to earn his respect—along with that of your teammates—by the way you performed. He motivated you to work hard, and if you did, you would most often achieve your goals."

But at least one person gave another view of Coach Jim Garrett and a different perspective on the naming of the sports complex on his behalf. Former Susquehanna faculty member Joe Carter expressed his disappointment in a letter to the same publication (*Susquehanna Today*). Portions of that letter are excerpted here:

> Most of us tend to look back appreciatively upon our undergraduate years—often nostalgically. In my experience, recollections of athletes are especially prone to sentimental revisionism. And so, perhaps, it should not surprise me that Board Chair, Nick Lopardo has championed naming the new sports complex after Garrett and elected to sweep under the carpet evidence that raises tall doubts about the wisdom of that decision by suggesting that critics are remembering only the notorious Parent's Day incident in 1965 and overlooking the larger impact of coach Garret's career at the university.
>
> I remember Coach Garrett as a bright, articulate and dynamic individual who ardently urged students to give their best to their studies as well as the playing field. By his energy and intensity of purpose he was no doubt a positive influence. But I also remember how there was a lack of even temperament in his zeal that raised concerns long before October of 65. I recall Dean Reuning's dismay over the sign at the entrance to the practice field beneath which players daily passed, an equation for victory with three ingredients: Pride, Guts, Desire. Embarrassed that the sign was easily observed by anyone in the vicinity, he threatened to remove it himself. An overreaction? Perhaps, but rather than mindlessly visceral by-words, why not ones of deeper meaning and character: Dedication, Courage, Teamwork. No doubt Garrett preferred the passion of his words to ones of greater import. Emotional intensity was a key ingredient for winning. But like many another zealot, he had trouble stepping back from the thick of matters at hand and allowing himself a reasoned view. His assault on his quarterback's helmet that Parents' Day was not a unique occurrence. It was a fair representation of the man. To name the new facility for someone who did not demonstrate the kind of excellence that the university strives to instill in its graduates is a slap in the face of all those coaches who have dutifully and unspectacularly done so.
>
> It's a fine thing that Mr. Lopardo's love for the University and the value of its athletic programs has moved him to make a large gift of naming magnitude. But why spotlight one whose actions

and character were not representative of the best that the University stands for?

I don't begrudge Richard Caruso and Nick Lopardo for wanting to name the Sports Complex after their coach. After all, when you donate a sizable chunk of money to a college you should have a major say in the naming rights game. But money does not necessarily buy good will and respect, especially when a decision is made to permanently enshrine an individual who publicly embarrassed a young man, his family, and an entire university. Accomplished sports figures, whether they are coaches or players, often seem to be immune from the usual standards of conduct and accountability that most of us have to live by in our lives.

Jim Garrett's name will be on the façade of the Sports Complex for many years to come, a permanent testament to the victories he marshaled on the Susquehanna University gridiron in the early 1960s. For some, however, the façade will instead be a constant reminder of how much we value winning, how easily we forget the past, and how willing we are to absolve deplorable behaviors exhibited by coaches who go over-the-top in their professional behavior. Why? The easiest answer to that question is that success on our playing fields too often translates into elevated stature and immunity from the normal consequences that the average person must endure from illegal, unethical, or immoral behaviors. That's just the way we do things in our presently flawed sports culture.

29

Moving Up to Division I Athletics

As a professor of psychology at the State University of New York (SUNY) at Albany for over 25 years, I eagerly read the *Albany Times-Union* each day in the spring of 1997. The long awaited announcement trumpeting the school's upgrade to Division I athletics was made with all the fanfare of an Oscar nomination. "We have strong academic support for our student-athletes, outstanding coaches and excellent athletic administrators. I am confident that the transition from Division II to Division I will be successful," announced President Karen Hitchcock.

Also backing the decision with his own strong endorsement, Vice-President for Student Affairs Jim Doellefeld added, "Athletic competition at the Division I level will enrich campus life, advance our connection with the Capital-Saratoga Region, and provide another rallying point for the University's students, alumni, faculty and friends. We will move this upgrade process forward while maintaining the school's academic standards, and continuing both a commitment to gender equity and support for recreational and intramural activities." Not to be outdone, then athletic director, Milt Richards, chimed in with his own platitudes about the impending transition: "This town wants big-time and what they perceive to be big-time. Sports is the one thing that can unify a community. Everyone can relate to sports."

There was little surprise in the final announcement since the university had been moving in that direction since 1995 when it jumped from Division III to Division II status. A nonbinding referendum of students had voted 1,437 to 156 in favor of the move to Division I. Although this represented less than 10 percent of the student population, the vote was still viewed as an overwhelming positive statement by the university and the capital region community. The university senate, which is made up of faculty members, also voted 30–10 to endorse the jump. Thus, in spite of having many years of great success at the Division III level where athletics are secondary to academics, the university was deciding to take the plunge into the murky waters of big-time sports.

Outspoken critics were few but in some cases very vocal. Ivan Steen, a history professor and head of the United University Professions (UUP) stated his opposition emphatically. He remarked: "I think we are going in the wrong direction. I'd rather have the publicity for some great academic achievement." Jarka Burian, professor emeritus, also voiced his opposition after reviewing recent events at the university in which several low-profile, but highly successful, varsity athletic teams that boasted a number of all-Americans (wrestling, swimming, and tennis) were eliminated due to Title IX concerns. To make matters worse, the German department also was axed in a cost-cutting move even though many considered it to be essential for a university that considered itself a research center. He noted: "Coming from a university which prides itself on being a major research center and a traditionally rigorous scholarly institution, the proposal is ironic. The proposal to move the University at Albany into Division I sports competition perhaps may have one thing in its favor: it would clearly echo the bread-and-circus games climate of our culture, and thus bring the university closer to the mainstream—if that's where it wants to be."

With little significant opposition from faculty, students, or the Capital Region community at large, athletic directors, coaches, and administrators sold the move on three grounds. First, it was stated that the university would receive more regional and national media attention from coverage of sporting events. Second, it was proposed that the heightened profile could significantly increase the pool of students who might apply. Third, the pitch was made that sports programs could generate revenue from TV rights, ticket sales, promotions, and sponsorships. Finally, it was argued that higher-profile sports teams could be a more effective tool for generating contributions and job networking opportunities from alumni.

The above arguments are trotted out whenever the merits of Division I athletics are discussed. But, they largely represent pie-in-the-sky thinking as well as specious and downright erroneous claims. Notably absent during these discussions at SUNY-Albany was any serious talk regarding the appropriate place of big-time college sports in an academic environment, the difficulty of attracting good athletes when you are a bottom feeder in the recruiting food chain, the abuse that results when passing grades are given to star athletes in "mickey mouse" majors, the negative effects on student applications and image that losing college sports programs can have, and most important, the additional money that is always required down the road for expanded facilities, scholarships, and staff.

That being said, the university had to come up with significant additional money just to make the move up to Division I. To upgrade, the university was forced to bump up its sports budget from $2,275,000 to $2,900,000, an increase of $625,000. Most of the additional money has gone to more sports scholarships. They were funded by increasing the student athletic fees of the 16,000 students from $83 to $128 over a three-year period. What will happen in the future when more money is needed to prime the pump is unknown. For example, most recently there has been talk of moving football to the Division I-AA scholarship status, which would necessitate much more money for scholarships as well as upgrades in stadium and locker room facilities. These moves will undoubtedly require significant additional funding. However, with a university system that is still reeling from budget cuts over the past 10 years, it is unlikely that a bailout from the state will occur.

The jury is still out on whether or not the move to Division I will eventually be successful for UAlbany. The football team under long-time coach Bob Ford has been competitive in the nonscholarship Northeast Conference. However, as one might expect, the team regularly gets thumped when going up against scholarship programs in non-conference games.

The PR so far has been largely negative for the high-profile basketball teams that are now in the lowly rated American East conference. In its first year (2001–2002), the men's team was 8–20 (5–11 in conference play). In its second year (2002–2003), the team finished a dismal 7–21 (3–13 in the conference) with an embarrassing final RPI ranking of 295 out of 327. Attendance figures have been slim with only about 1,100 spectators per game. Students and the Albany community generally seem to be disinterested. Only about 10 to 15 percent of the 16,700 student body actually goes to sporting events. In spite of trying all kinds of gimmicks, such as free pizza, tee-shirt and visor giveaways, and lotteries for free tuition and preference for dormitory rooms, the students are apathetic. The team was also plagued by some well-publicized personnel changes in the 2001–2002 season that included the firing of the head coach, Scott Beaton, early in the season as well as a high turnover of players for both personal and academic reasons.

The women's basketball program did not fare any better. The team posted a woeful record of 4–23 (0–16 in conference play) in 2001–2002. The team slightly improved to a 9–18 mark (3–13 in the conference) in 2002–2003 but their RPI rating was a dismal 283 of 324. Long-time coach, Mari Warner, who had enormous success as a Division III coach at UAlbany, was axed at the end of the 2001–2002 season.

Because blue-chip athletes tend to go elsewhere, both the men's and the women's teams have difficulty attracting top players. Leaders at UAlbany may be realizing that the journey to respectability at the Division I level may take many years, a great deal of patience, and a lot more resources than the university can presently provide. Many in the academic community are left to wonder whether or not the resource investment required for Division I athletics is really worth it. Indeed, those same resources perhaps could have done wonders for graduate and undergraduate educational programs that are the real purpose of a university.

The push for a Division I athletic program coincided with another major effort by the university to attract big-time sports. The New York Giants football team was looking for a new summer practice facility. In 1996, SUNY-Albany and the entire Capital Region fell all over itself to get them here. Politicians, university administrators, and business leaders put together a package for President Wellington Mara that the New York team simply couldn't refuse. The State Dormitory Authority and the State University construction fund spent more than $2 million to improve UAlbany's facilities, including the resodding of football fields and the installation of air conditioning in dormitories and the Recreation and Athletic Center (RAC). The Albany Local Development Corporation as well as sponsors such as the *Albany Times-Union* coughed up additional funds to help the university defray the $162,000 price tag for housing the team.

During the Capital Region's courtship of the Giants, the Center for Economic Growth (CEG) projected that the camp would bring in nearly $18 million to the area's economy during the first year alone. This projection was based upon out-of-area fans flocking to the practice facility from all over the Northeast, staying overnight in hotels, eating in local restaurants, and spending money locally. This number was widely questioned at the time and indeed there is very little evidence to indicate that the economic spinoff has been even remotely close to this figure. The spectators visiting the camp tend to be local people who do not spend additional money for restaurants and hotels. Also, the number of spectators visiting the training camp has declined steadily since the reported 50,000 people in 1996.

Being a sports enthusiast all my life as well as a college professor, I felt as though I was sandwiched between a rock and a hard place throughout these developments. On the one hand, I was intrigued by the prospects of having a big-time Division I sports program and my beloved Giants football team training just 200 yards from my office. On the other hand, I knew the ugly realities of what was happening with scandals in big-time college sports programs on other campuses. Also, as a person who regularly taught in both our graduate and undergraduate psychology programs, I experienced firsthand the effects of limited resources in our academic programs.

The university is enrollment driven for its funding from the state and is accepting more students all the time, but the basic resources (faculty, staff, equipment and supplies) to support these numbers have lagged behind. The department to which I belong, psychology, has suffered from a faculty shortage for some years now. Good professors have left for more prestigious and lucrative positions elsewhere and their lines have not been replaced. Our psychology classes are bigger than they have ever been and our undergraduate students, though eager to learn, come in less prepared every year. More and more remedial help seems to be needed before many can respond to the demands of a rigorous academic life.

Our graduate program in psychology has turned out many fine Ph.D.s through the years but increasingly we are having a tougher and tougher time attracting the best students. Our state-supported assistantships are meager compared to other public and private institutions. The best graduate students go to other institutions where there has been more of a commitment to graduate education and higher assistantship stipends.

I have sat in my office many times and have mused about the shortcomings of our present educational environment at UAlbany. Clearly, things on my end of campus aren't anywhere near as good as they are for the up and coming athletic department these days. Wouldn't it be nice if the whole community got behind education the same way they got behind Division I sports and the Giants summer training camp? Wouldn't it be something to see some significant resources devoted directly to enhancing graduate and undergraduate education instead of the paltry sums of money budgeted for this purpose each year? Moreover, is it a defensible position to support an expensive top-level sports program when basic educational objectives are not being met because of inadequate funds?

I have come to the inevitable conclusion that my institution, like so many others in this country, may care more about sports entertainment than it does about the stated purpose of higher education. The most recent *US News and World Report* rankings of comprehensive doctoral universities show that SUNY-Albany is still mired in the third tier of their four-tier classification system. There are over 130 schools that are ranked ahead of my institution. The rankings do not use the quality or quantity of intercollegiate sports teams or whether or not we host a professional sports team for summer training camp. Instead, the measuring stick relies upon academic indices.

The last time I looked, the goal of a university was to properly educate our next generation of young people so they can effectively compete in an increasingly sophisticated world. I don't think that any objective observer could possibly say that we are doing our best to address this vital societal function. Will institutions of higher learning get back to their original charge before it is too late? Given the pace of our continuing romance with big-time athletics, often at the expense of education, I am skeptical that those in a position of authority will ever take a more realistic and enlightened perspective on the proper role of sports in an academic environment. As one of my colleagues recently said "our administrators are doing all the wrong things to build up the visibility of the university."

Part Six

TRAVELING THE ROAD
TO REFORM

Most of these kids (college football and basketball players) don't want to be in college but it's their only avenue into the pros. That's whom intercollegiate sports are being run for: the one-half of one percent. We should run the sports programs for the 99.5 percent. Sports used to be part of the educational process. Now it is the process.

Bill Cleary, *Sports Illustrated*

———————

In fact, short of a precipitating event—one comparable to the fall of the Soviet Union—it is difficult to imagine what could bring about reform of such a national obsession.

Allen Sack, *Chronicle of Higher Education*

———————

The competitive athletic programs that now drive many school schedules and budgets is a paradigmatic example of misplaced priorities—perhaps the most important example of how our schools try to do too much, to the detriment of learning. Athletics should be administered by organizations and institutions other than our public schools. The benefits for school budgets and school schedules could be enormous.

Etta Kralovec, *Schools that Do Too Much*

While the move to the European club sport system may sound radical, it is not. The fact is, our school systems and universities would survive without highly competitive sports and so would our elite athletes and coaches. Interestingly, America is the only country in the world where athletics is so intimately intertwined with the education system. Could it be that our concept of the role and purpose of school- and university-sponsored athletics is, after a century-long experiment, misguided?

John Gerdy, *Sports: The All-American Addiction*

30

Lessons from Singapore
and Australia

Needing a fresh perspective on my own sports-obsessed country, I arranged to spend some time in other parts of the world where sports have a different organizational structure and therefore a different pulse than that of the United States. Between 1999 and 2001, I spent time in Singapore and Australia and my experiences in both countries enabled me to assess the present American sports culture in some new ways.

My first stop was Singapore. Through the National University of Singapore, the National Institute of Education, and the National Sports Academy and Olympic Training Center, I had arranged to give a series of lectures regarding the perils of anabolic steroid abuse by athletes as well as the changing nature of sports in the United States

As part of my fact-finding mission, I asked to speak with as many people as I could regarding the sports atmosphere, culture, and the economy of Singapore. I also wanted to view some Singaporean athletic contests so I could get a firsthand look at what sports were like there.

Singapore, a small nation of only 648 kilometers, is inhabited by 3 million Chinese and Malaysians. It gained independence from Britain in 1965 and soon thereafter, through the leadership and policy making of Prime Minister Lee Kuan Yew, Singapore became the primary economic engine of Southeast Asia.

Because the country has virtually no natural resources and everything must be imported, Singapore built a world-class port facility that is the busiest in the world in terms of shipping tonnage. The small country has developed a strong high-tech manufacturing base especially in the area of computers and technical equipment. Its stability, self-reliance, and high standard of living are the envy of every Asian country. Its residents have average monthly earnings of about $1,500 in U.S. dollars and the unemployment rate is at a very low 1.8 percent.

The government, nicknamed "Singapore, Inc." for its businesslike manner, is among the most stable in the world. Even with the downturn in most Asian economies in the past few years and the political instability of surrounding countries, Singapore continues along with a remarkable level of efficiency and resilience. The World Economic Forum, a Geneva-based international center dedicated to improving business and government, regularly ranks countries based upon their economic competitiveness. The forum uses measures of finance, government policies, infrastructure, technology, management, labor, institutions, and barriers to trade in its rankings. In 1996 to 1999, Singapore ranked number 1 while the United States was far down the list until recently.

However, the country does exert a heavy level of control over its people. Regardless of their occupation, all citizens are expected to work 5 and a half days a week. Pornography is banned, speech is not free, and almost all residents (90 percent) live in government-built apartments. Public transportation is inexpensive, very efficient, and plentiful. The streets are clean, there are little or no slum dwellings such as those observed in many large American cities, and food hygiene is very strict. Crime is virtually nonexistent. Indeed, in my stay in Singapore I did not see one policeman on the streets during the day or night. Quite frankly, I felt safer in Singapore than I have in many American cities.

The pride of Singapore is what is referred to as Singapore One. This is a high-bandwidth computer network that brings the Internet to its residents five times faster than the more traditional dial-up modems seen in our own country. The government is providing many of its services over the Internet already and the goal is to provide computer access for almost all goods and services, education, and entertainment within the next few years.

The government is spending $1.2 billion over the next few years to ensure that one of every two students has a personal computer by the year 2004. Likewise, the government is spending $4 billion over the next five years to train high-tech workers and promote research and development in science and technology.

With electronic commerce world-wide expected to be in the neighborhood of $70 billion in 2004, Singapore is banking on the fact that they will be able to cash in on the growing global cyber economy. Already, 40 percent of Singaporean homes have PCs. Even Microsoft chairman Bill Gates has declared Singapore to be a world leader in developing a futuristic Web lifestyle. In fact, many computer companies are relocating to Singapore in order to test out and develop new technology since the business climate and the resources for success are already in place.

Singapore's public educational system appears to feed into the government's futuristic goals. For many years the curriculum in its schools was heavily dependent upon rote learning with little opportunity for creative thinking. This has all changed recently to the point where the government, through substantial financial grants, is now encouraging an entrepreneurial spirit in its educational system.

Through its 400 elementary schools, 135 high schools, and two colleges (National University of Singapore and Nanyang Technological Institute (NTI)), Singapore's educational system leads the way among Asian countries. The country's literacy rate stands at 83 percent, which positions it among the best in the world.

Students go through compulsory education from ages 6 to 16. This consists of 6 years of primary school and 4 years of lower secondary school. Higher secondary education in preuniversity institutes goes from 16 to 19 years of age. After this, students compete for university level studies (bachelor's, master's, doctorate), teacher's education, and higher vocational/technical studies.

Singaporean college students are among the best trained in the world especially in the area of semiconductor and technical knowledge. They are prized throughout the world not only for their expertise but for their dedication to their jobs. As our economies become more global and we become more dependent upon high-end technological training, there is little doubt that Singaporean workers will become even more valuable in the years to come. In contrast, in our own country, it is common to see jobs requiring technological skills going to foreigners such as Singaporeans. We have neither the infrastructure, nor the motivation apparently, to provide what will soon be the most valuable resource in the world: a technically trained labor force.

As you can imagine, there is enormous pressure among Singaporeans to compete for entry in university-level studies. Starting at an early age, students are administered national exams, which determine whether or not they will be allowed to enter university-level studies. Graduates of university-level studies attract the best paying positions. Though Singapore is rapidly expanding its university-level educational system by adding more facilities and faculty, its two universities don't provide room for everyone who wants to go to school. As a result, it is not uncommon to see parents spend much of their money on tutors in order to position their children for accomplishment on the national exams.

Based upon what I saw, read, and experienced there is little doubt that the Singaporean people have staked their country's success as well as their own personal happiness and well-being on their nation's business and educational system. How does all this interplay with athletic pursuits in this tiny country? What is the role of sports in the lives of young kids as they travel from elementary schools on up to college? Are there any parallels to our own country or lessons to be learned from life in Singapore?

As I gave my lectures and interacted with students, parents, and educators in Singapore, I was provided with some unique opportunities to answer many of the questions I had posed prior to my trip. One of the first informal lectures I gave was in a graduate class in sports psychology at the National Institute of Education. Dan Smith, on a two-year leave from his faculty duties at SUNY-Brockport, was teaching the class at the institute and invited me to come for the day.

The title of my talk was "Parents and Coaches from Hell: Sports in the USA" and much of it was based upon some of the material discussed in this book. The students were very attentive and laughed at my jokes. However, for the most part they looked at me as though I had two heads as I launched into stories about out-of-control-parents and win-at-all-costs coaches.

Upon the completion of my talk, I invited comments. The first student to respond asked a simple question: "Why are sports so important in your country? Why does it cause coaches and parents to act in such strange ways?"

I contemplated the answer only briefly and then replied:

"There are three reasons I believe. First, athletic participation in its purest form can be an important vehicle for human expression. To get good at something that you really love and have fun doing it at the same time is satisfying to one's ego and striving for self-fulfillment. Sports participation can have a way of rounding you out as an individual and complementing the development of your mind and body in new ways."

"Second, Americans have a way of wanting to be the best at every-thing they do. Athletics is no exception and the urge to win, in contrast to just participating, is ingrained in our athletes at a very early age. Unfortunately, this has spilled over to a win-at-all-costs attitude that is becoming more pervasive at all levels of sports."

"Third, beyond just participating, athletics for some can bring sig-nificant economic rewards. Over the past 30 to 40 years, this reason for sports participation seems to be gaining enormous momentum in our country. In terms of college scholarships and professional contracts, there are enormous monetary gains. But, these economic gains are often short-lived and tend to exist for only a very small proportion of the total number of athletes participating in our country. Moreover, the commit-ment that it takes to becoming a good athlete in the United States is getting greater and greater every year. Ask any top athlete in high school, college or the professional and amateur ranks and they will tell you that it often requires an enormous investment of time, money, and dedicated practice. Of the three things I have listed, the last two (win-at-all-costs attitude and the striving for economic gain) are the ones that have caused most of the evils in American sports today."

I thought that my response was adequate but it seemed to open up a whole new line of additional questions. Students in the back of the room then asked: "But, if you have all of these problems, doesn't it cease to be fun at some point? At what point do you say that the benefits derived from sports are no longer worth the costs that are involved? Also, there are many sports in which you cannot play your entire life and for many there are no economic rewards. Aren't you emphasizing the wrong things in your culture? After all, you can't play football or baseball for your whole life."

At that point I was stumped because the Singaporean students in Dan Smith's class were beginning to verbalize many of my own reser-vations about what happens when sports are sometimes emphasized over everything else.

Before I could begin to defend what was happening in the United States, another student piped in: "Sports just aren't that big of a deal in Singapore. If you are a very good athlete it is not going to help you get ahead. The problems you have in the United States just don't exist here."

At that point the class ended and it was time for the students to move on to another period. I continued discussions with some of the students who could stay. Their ideas and perceptions of my country were important for me to hear.

Later during my stay, I met with Dr. Steve Wright and Nick Aplin, both ex-patriots who were on the faculty at NIE. Aplin had lived in Singapore for many years and was very knowledgeable regarding the culture and sports atmosphere there. Steve Wright was an expert in the teaching of sports and was very involved with physical education majors at NIE. Both explained to me the role of athletics in the modern culture of Singapore.

Aplin remarked: "You have to understand that although sports are valued here as a component of educational development, they are not put on a pedestal like they are in the States and other countries. In the United States, there is a strong desire to be visible on a national and international level through sports. In Singapore, the motivation to be visible is obtained through other means. For example, our government structures economic rewards such that academic success is placed number 1. If children in Singapore do not do well in school, then they will not go on to college. If they do not go on to college, then they will not get a good paying job. Parents therefore place great pressure upon their children to succeed in school. It is not uncommon, for example, to see parents pull their kids from sports programs when they realize that their kids are getting good at something. They get afraid that their children will like it too much and then will devote all of their time to it. They (the parents) feel that the time they devote to sports is more properly directed toward academics. Getting ahead with respect to college and ultimately getting a good job is a goal more valued than becoming a good athlete."

Aplin and Wright went on to explain how Singapore's educational system emphasizes physical education classes and intramural sports in contrast to interscholastic competition. Wright remarked: "The emphasis is upon participation and fitness training above competition. Though schools do compete with one another, it is much more low-key than it is in the United States. Likewise, outside of school there are travel team and select team programs but the level of play is not anywhere near as good as it is in the United States and European countries. Because there are no college scholarships for athletics and only two colleges, competition is strictly at the club and intramural level. In this way, Singapore has followed the European system regarding a strict separation between competitive athletics and higher education."

At the regional and world class levels, Wright and Aplin informed me that Singaporeans have competed in the Asian games and the Olympics in such sports as swimming, wrestling, weight lifting, badminton, and table tennis. However, their participation has never been very note-worthy. Indeed, Singapore has won only one medal in the modern Olympics and that was for wrestling. In soccer, the most global of all sports, Singapore has never qualified for the World Cup and has never performed very well in the Asian games. Professional, minor league, and college sports are nonexistent.

I also had the opportunity to lecture in Singapore regarding anabolic steroid abuse and other performance-enhancing drugs used by athletes. My audience consisted of medical school students and faculty, coaches, parents, and athletes. Each time I gave my lecture on this topic, I was met with keen interest and attentiveness. Curiously, however, not one person felt that it was an important issue in Singaporean sports even at the world class level of competition. "Those things just don't happen here" was the comment I heard from most of those in the audience. Indeed, they were probably right as no one could recall any instances of Singaporean athletes at any level testing positive for a banned sub-stance. With such strict drug laws in effect, it is not surprising that this country experiences few problems in what has become an epidemic in the United States.

During my visit to Singapore, I was also able to view some intra-mural athletic events as well as some club team competitions in soccer and basketball. I saw both elementary school aged kids playing as well as kids that were comparable to our high school aged students. I was not impressed at all by the skill level of either group. However, what I did see was some pretty good teamwork and a lot of happy kids having a good time blowing off some energy on a Saturday morning. There were very few parents and the coaches were generally unobtrusive by-standers. Everything seemed to regulate itself quite well with few argu-ments or disagreements resulting in stoppage of play. In fact, there were no referees—they didn't really need any since everything was on an honor system.

Singaporeans love American sports and through satellite TV they are able to see professional and college basketball, baseball, and foot-ball. Michael Jordan, Mark McGuire, and Muhammed Ali are as much icons there as they are in other parts of the world. The merchandising of American sports was all around me. I saw lots of New York Yankee hats and Los Angeles Laker jerseys as well as the Swoosh on many Nike sneakers. Tee-shirts with well known and successful college sports pro-grams also were plentiful. In spite of this exposure to the western sports world, organized sports are still light years behind the United States and other countries.

As I reflected upon my visit to Singapore I soon realized that I had viewed a culture and lifestyle that in some respects was like our own about 100 years ago. Before sports exploded in this country in the 1960s, 1970s and 1980s, athletics were not unlike Singapore's of the 1990s. Sports were not as organized back then. There was more emphasis placed upon participation in contrast to individual improvement, competition, and winning. Academic success was more valued than winning teams and all-star participation. The "scholarship chase" usually referred to academics and not athletics. Parents and coaches were in control and were not living their lives through young kids. Performance-enhancing drugs were not an issue. Media attention was not excessive and people were more likely to read about important world events in contrast to which athletes were behaving badly and which ones were likely to be all stars and attract a college scholarship down the road. Burnout of athletes was rarely seen since young kids were not asked to devote their lives to a sport 12 months out of the year. Sports gambling certainly existed but it was not the mega-billion-dollar industry that it is today. Athletic injuries occurred but their frequency and severity were not as high as they are today. Importantly, college student athletes were actually there to get an education as opposed to training for professional sports careers. Sports just weren't that big of deal back then—they were low-key, almost an afterthought, just like in Singapore today.

I also thought about some interesting studies that were done in which television programming was examined for its influence on human behavior. When I want to highlight the importance of technological and cultural changes on human motivation, I always make it a point to talk about these experiments in my introductory psychology classes at SUNY-Albany.

In an older study conducted in the 1960s, the effects of television violence were examined in a small Canadian town (called Notel . . . meaning no television) several years before and several years after TV was brought to the community. Not surprisingly, the researchers found that acts of aggression and violence dramatically increased in school-aged children with the advent of television in the community. Likewise, small town values and social communication also seemed to suffer as more and more television was watched by community members.

In a more recent study conducted in the South Pacific Fiji Islands, television programs that depict slim and trim actresses such as "Melrose Place" and "Beverly Hills 90210" are apparently having a profound effect on Fijian teenage girls. This type of programming, which has only been made available by satellite recently, has produced an epidemic of serious eating disorders such as anorexia in a culture where few such problems previously existed.

In each of the aforementioned studies, something was certainly gained through the transmission of information, entertainment, and news programming provided by TV. However, something also obviously has been lost. Did the benefits resulting from the presence of televised American culture outweigh the negative consequences of this information? This of course is a question that will be debated for some time to come. The answers certainly are not clear.

And what would happen in Singapore if a technological and cultural change in the country suddenly vaulted sports to a vastly different role than it now occupies? What would happen if athletics suddenly received the exposure and exalted status that it now receives in the United States? For example, if there were significant economic rewards like athletic scholarships and professional contracts, what would happen to the people of Singapore? What would happen if the Singapore lifestyle ever became more like our own? Would the Singaporean sports culture then evolve and produce many of the same ugly by-products that now exist in our own country today?

Like the famous television studies, Singapore may someday provide the ideal natural laboratory for studying what happens to a culture when sports begin to take on an inflated presence in a society. While this obviously is far from happening in this relatively new country, there are some indications that such a change may not be too far off in the future. Nick Aplin, who serves on the Singapore Olympic Committee, pointed out that "there are rumors that the Singapore government plans to launch a major soccer initiative in the near future. This will be done by developing a more extensive youth program and by recruiting heavily from the rest of the world in order to become more competitive in future World Cups." Likewise, he also pointed out that the recruiting of top badminton players already exists in Singapore secondary schools. These events could be the very early signs of a more permanent changing role for sports in the life of the average Singaporean citizen.

I would love to do the 100-year study to answer my questions. I would lay odds on the possibility that Singapore may someday experience some of the same sports-related problems that are now prevalent in the United States. As a culture that is relatively new as an independent country, Singapore is continuing to experience growth and prosperity. When leisure time increases and the economic and individual rewards of sports success become greater and more valued, things are bound to change in this tiny country. Just give it some time.

Notwithstanding the few changes I have noted above, Singapore really represents the antithesis of sports in the United States. We can be sports crazed oftentimes to the detriment of cultural and educational objectives; Singaporeans are education and technical training obsessed at the loss sometimes of the enrichment that can be gained through athletic and leisure time pursuits. Singaporeans define their national and individual identity in terms of their economic and business success; Americans have a tendency to define their collective identity in their athletic successes and failures. Each extreme no doubt fits the prevailing culture. Each extreme has costs and benefits. One extreme is not necessarily better than the other. However, I am enough of a social scientist to know that extremes eventually wreak havoc with norms, roles, institutions, cultures, and most import, human relationships and self-identity. Achieving some balance and moving away from these extremes could be enriching and productive for the cultures of both countries.

Though my time was much more limited, I also recently visited Australia with a similar mission. I wanted to learn more about the country and its system of sports. I arranged to spend time at the Australian Sports Commission (ASC), which is in the capital of Canberra, and I also visited with faculty members in the sports science department at the University of Canberra.

Before spending time in this country, I boned up on some basic history, learned about the people, and tried to familiarize myself with Australia's economy and culture. The last landmass to be discovered by European explorers, Australia was officially discovered in 1870 by Captain James Cook. The land was found to be rich with vegetation and native wildlife and was considered to be highly suitable for colonization. Lord Sydney, the secretary of state of Britain's home affairs, believed that the land could be a strategic base for the Royal Navy and an ideal entry point for economic opportunities in the area. Also, because of overcrowded prisons in England as well as disruption in the country caused by the American Revolution, a British penal colony was established in New South Wales (Australia) in 1788. Australia Day, which is held on January 26 each year, commemorates the landing of the first boat of prisoners at what is now Sydney.

The British colonizers were not the first inhabitants of Australia. For more than 50,000 years, Australia's Aboriginal people thrived on the land. It is commonly believed that the Aboriginals are the world's oldest civilization. Forced to give up their land, the Aboriginals became paupers in their own country. They were required to live in subsistence living conditions and many of the population died out in the years of European colonization. While some groups of Aboriginals managed to retain their customs and survive, others died out and the population almost became extinct. In the 1950s and 1960s, the Australian government began to redress their wrongdoings and enfranchised the Aboriginals by land rights acts, grants, and self- determination assistance.

Australia is made up of six states and two territories with each having its own parliament. Australia became a federated nation after the union of the six colonies in 1901. Today, Australia is a thriving country with its economy specializing in tourism, the exportation of beef and precious stones, and the production of 70 percent of the world's supply of wool. It is also a country made up of people who are fiercely patriotic and important allies of the United States and England. Their soldiers, known for their bravery and proud tradition, have fought alongside Americans in World Wars and other armed conflicts.

If there is a country whose inhabitants love sports as much as American citizens, then that land is certainly Australia. Australians are health and fitness conscious and represent one of the most active populations of humans in the world. This follows from the temperate climate and low cost access to tennis courts, golf courses, beaches, waterways, and open spaces for hiking and other recreational pursuits. Australia has more than 120 national sporting organizations and thousands of state, regional, and club bodies. The most recent statistics show that an estimated 6.5 million people, about a third of the population, are registered sports participants and almost two-thirds of 5 to 14-year-old children play sports annually. Many other Australians are involved with activities such as fishing, bushwalking, recreational and competitive boating and sailing, horse riding, and lifelong fitness programs. Australians also love to watch sports and it is not uncommon to see crowds of over 100,000 at Australian football competitions. An average of about 6.25 million Australians age 15 years and over attend at least one sports event or competition as a spectator each year.

Australia has hosted two Olympic Games—in 1956 (Melbourne) and 2000 (Sydney). They have also hosted the Commonwealth Games three times and they are one of only three nations to have competed in every modern Olympic Games and all Commonwealth Games. Australians have won 78 Olympic and 396 Commonwealth gold medals and have produced world record holders and international champions in many different sports. Indeed, the Olympic records of female Australians is especially impressive since women have won more than 40 percent of the gold medals won by Australians. This is a remarkable achievement since only 23 percent of Olympic events between the years 1948 and 1992 were available to women.

Sports in Australia are overseen by the Australian Sports Commission (ASC), a statutory authority created in 1984 that is funded by the Australian government. The ASC oversees the government's efforts on behalf of both elite and local community sports participation. Among other responsibilities, the ASC supervises the Australian Institute of Sports (AIS) for elite athletes and teams as well as programs like Women in Sports, which encourages female participation; Active Australia, which promotes sports participation, health and fitness for all ages at the grassroots level; Indigenous Sports Program, which promotes sports among the Aboriginal population; and the Disability Sports Program, for those with physical handicaps who want to participate in sports. All told, the government outlay for sports has risen significantly since 1984 and is presently close to $3 billion a year.

My reason for choosing Australia for my admittedly nonscientific examination was quite simple: no country other than the United States has been more successful in producing world-class athletes than Australia. In the 2000 summer Olympic Games in Sydney, the United States led the medal count with 97 (40 gold) while Australia was next in line with 58 (16 gold). Australia is the sixth largest country in the world and about the same size as the mainland 48 states of the United States. Importantly, however, its population is only about 20 million people in contrast to 285 million in the United States. Therefore, Australia has performed at the Olympics with astounding success that is disproportionate to the size of its population. The secret to that success was what I was after. In particular, I wanted to know if athletics were a key element of the educational process and if Australian sports were riddled with the same kinds of problems as American sports.

My first meeting was with Professor Alan Roberts of the sports science department of the University of Canberra. He filled me in on how sports really works in his native country. He stated: "Australia has really followed the European model of sports. There are sports authorities and organizations at all levels of government, within the private sector, and in communities throughout regional and metropolitan Australia. The key element of the Australian sport system however is the club—this is a single sport local body which is run by and for its members. Importantly, its members range in age from very young kids to older adults—it's for everybody—it represents every age group for competitive sports. Clubs are affiliated with regional and state associations which in turn unite to form National Sporting Organizations (NSOs). Volunteers administer sport at all levels, in particular at the club level, but at state and national levels professional administrators begin to play a more important role."

At this point I was beginning to see some major differences emerging between sports in the United States and sports in Australia. However, it was not until Roberts went on to tell me about professional and school-based sports that I began to realize just how different the Australian sports system really is from ours in America. He continued: "Professional clubs exist outside this system in the major sports like rugby, cricket, soccer, basketball, and baseball. They belong to state or national leagues and are staffed mostly by full-time professional administrators and coaches. There are some sports and physical education classes in our elementary and secondary schools but these provide little more than a basic introduction to sports as well as health and fitness education. Some private schools have a bit more exposure to sports but nothing compared to what you have in the States. Sports at the university level consist of informal club activities at each university and then something called the University Games held for five days in late September and early October each year. All sports are contested but quite frankly it is more of a social event than anything else. The kids party a lot and the games are really just a way for students to blow off some steam. Overall, I would say that there is almost a total disconnect between sports and our educational system. I know that this is quite different from the way in which it is done in America."

I was surprised to learn that sports are not a significant part of the Australian educational system. There are 9,596 secondary schools in Australia with 72 percent public and 28 percent private. There are 43 publicly supported universities and colleges and 85 private colleges. In none of them is there anything that remotely approaches scholastic and collegiate sports as it is known in the United States. In spite of this, Australian athletes are as successful as ever and their participation rates are soaring among all ages of their population.

I also asked Roberts if Australia has experienced any of the problems that have been so destructive to the American sports culture. He commented: "We certainly don't have problems with academic corruption and commercialism and unethical recruiting because sports are out of the schools. Performance-enhancing drugs, like everywhere, are a problem but we have an aggressive testing policy and I think that we have a pretty good handle on it. Gambling on professional sports is pervasive but it really is not an issue below the pro ranks. Coaches, athletes, and fans misbehave of course and there are serious sportsmanship issues from time to time, but I do not think that it has reached the epidemic levels that it has in your country. We are always concerned with issues of sports injury and we are trying to do more preventative work in that area. We do have problems with overbearing parents from time to time and early specialization, but for the most part there is a premium placed upon getting an education and we are able to tailor academic programs for our athletes that are in serious training such that they do not lose out on getting a meaningful education. This obviously calls for a tremendous amount of cooperation and organization between athletes and their school teachers and professors (primary, secondary, and university) but there is a tacit agreement that education comes first. We certainly foster elite instruction of athletes and we select out kids at early ages for specialized coaching and training, but we devote even more resources to the teaching of lifelong physical activities and fitness education. Australians have a rich tradition of supporting and participating in health and fitness activities. They realize that these are skills that are far more important since they can enhance the quality of living of the average Aussie citizen."

After listening to Alan Roberts, I was beginning to think that we could learn a lot from the Aussie sports system. However, I needed to investigate a bit more and I wanted to hear from administrators that were high up in the system. To accomplish this purpose, my next stop was the Australian Sports Commission (ASC) in the national capital of Canberra. Because the Australian Institute of Sports is located on the same campus, I first viewed some elite athletes in training. I saw very skilled swimmers, wrestlers, and gymnasts training in facilities that were state of the art and every bit the equivalent of those in the United States. Following my tour of the facility, I was fortunate to have the opportunity to meet with Mark Peters, the CEO of the Australian Sports Commission. I asked him to give me a brief synopsis of what Australian sports were all about. He stated: "First and foremost, we stress participation and involvement at all age levels. We want kids to start learning early that they can have fun with sports throughout their entire life. This is reflected in the grassroots club programs that are so effective in starting and keeping athletes involved throughout the lifespan."

I also wanted to know what Peters viewed as his chief challenges, his proudest moments at the helm of the ASC, and his biggest fears for the future of Aussie sports. He responded: "Our biggest challenge right now is further incorporating our underprivileged Aboriginal population in sports. We have a huge initiative going on right now at the grassroots level in which we are fostering the development of sports in this population. It is long overdue and we are finally seeing the fruits of our concentration in this area. As you know, the Aborigine runner Cathy Freeman won an Olympic gold medal recently in Sydney. This was a defining moment for Australian sports. However, we need to do much more in this area before we can say that we have truly succeeded. I have had many proud moments while serving as the CEO of ASC. Clearly, the recent Sydney Olympic Games and the success of our athletes stand out, but there are also other moments. We are constantly asked by other countries in Asia and Africa for assistance in developing their sports systems. This is flattering to us and it is something that we are only too willing to do. My fears are ones that have to do with where our sports system may be headed in the long term. Quite frankly, there are times when many of us feel that we may become as corrupt as the Americans. There are forces within Australia that are now talking about athletic scholarships in schools and all the trappings of the intercollegiate sports programs that you have promoted so heavily over the past 30 to 40 years. There is also talk of modeling the scholastic athletic programs seen in the United States. I don't think that it will happen because of our government investment in the organization of sports in our country and the emphasis upon the club system, but it is nonetheless worrisome."

I then asked Peters what he thought of American sports. He halted for a few moments and then spoke these words that I will never forget: "Well, please don't take offense, but for those of us involved with sport in Australia, we are always astounded at how the Americans do things. We admire your country and your athletes. However, with all of the resources you have available, we cannot understand why you are not the best at every sport and why you continue to have such problems. If the Americans ever get their act together, they will have the best sports system on earth and they will be unbeatable in every individual and team sport."

Peters did not directly answer my question and later on he could not be coaxed into expanding upon what he had said. However, by limiting his comments to some well chosen words, his answer spoke volumes about the disastrous state of my own sports culture.

The U.S. system of sports is unique in that we are the only country in the world where competitive athletics are an integral part of secondary and university education. Moreover, the United States is a nation that prides itself on its athletic accomplishments. We routinely do well in international competitions such as the Olympics and our athletes lead the way in setting new records all of the time. With a huge financial investment in improving athletic competition and sports opportunities for our kids, the American ego demands that our athletes win and be the very best.

In spite of this, however, we have failed our youths in many ways because we tend to emphasize athletic accomplishment over academic achievement in our communities and in our schools and we overemphasize elite and select team play in contrast to participation in lifelong fitness-based and recreational activities. Moreover, our present sports system exploits our athletes and frequently does not educate them. What good is a superb sports system if many of our athletes cannot read and write and cannot get a good job once their playing days are over? What good is a sports system in which nonathletes are left behind at an early age, with few continuing or returning to significant exercise and fitness once they reach their adolescent years? The answer is that ours is a sports system out of whack with the more important goals of our society.

U. S. school children are largely outperformed by children in industrialized Asian and European nations, scoring only at average levels on international tests (International Association for the Evaluation of Education Achievement, 1999). The United States ranks 12th in the world for science and math scores of 8th graders and 18th in the world in math and physics scores of high school students. Equally alarming is the fact that only 3,826 bachelor's degrees were awarded in physics in 1997 (the lowest figure in 49 years) and half of the Ph.D.s awarded in physics go to foreigners, many of whom return to their own country. While we are winning the race for producing the best athletes, we are losing the contest for educating the minds of our young people. Which competition is more important? Which competition is more likely to produce a stable, wealthy, and productive nation in the long run?

Students in many foreign countries, including Australia and Singapore, outperform Americans in the key areas of math, science, and technical skills. These attributes are precisely the ones that are in high demand by the increasingly sophisticated global economy of today. While many Americans can probably dribble a basketball, hit a baseball, or catch a football far better than their foreign counterparts, these are not skills that will help them to compete for the best jobs in today's world. In spite of this realization, which is probably recognized by most Americans at some level, the out-of-control sports bandwagon keeps rolling along in this country at a breakneck speed.

My short visits to Singapore and Australia will not be forgotten. I met many wonderful people involved with sports in both countries and I was afforded the opportunity to observe two sports cultures that were radically different from each other. Singapore is a country that is still in its infancy regarding the development of sports. In many respects, the sports culture I found there was primitive at best and not unlike our own early development in the 1920s and 1930s. In contrast, Australia appeared to be on the cutting edge of a sports culture that is highly evolved and focused on providing sports opportunities in ways that benefit everyone without detracting from the total development of the individual. Indeed, there are features of the Australian sports system that probably should be adopted in the United States. Clearly, if we continue to fail our young athletes in important ways such as education and if we continue to fall behind in promoting lifelong habits of fitness and health in our young adults, then it is time to scrap our current sports system and look elsewhere for more effective models.

My experiences in each country permitted me to open a window into sports cultures that were radically different from my own. It also provided a basis of comparison for evaluating what may be right and what may be wrong about sports in the United States. Lastly, and perhaps most important, it was not until I visited these countries that I became more focused and committed to articulating my recommendations for changing youth, amateur, scholastic, and college sports in my own country.

31

Problem Areas

The problems surrounding preprofessional sports are pervasive in our society. Every level of sports contains a dark side that threatens to weaken the core values of athletics and render it meaningless. My experiences are probably a representative reflection of what goes on across our country. My journey through our runaway sports landscape leads me to conclude that we have significant problems on our hands that will require major work if we are to save athletics as a valuable institution. Summarized below are the major problem areas as reflected by the essays that you have just read. For additional documented evidence for the claims below, the reader is directed to the detailed companion volume to this book entitled: *Crisis on Our Playing Fields: What Everyone Should Know About Our Out of Control Sports Culture and What We Can Do to Change It*. Additionally, other important books are cited in each subsection as well as in the references to this book.

Specialization and Professionalization at an Early Age

One of the biggest problems that we have in our current sports culture is that athletics have become too much of a serious pursuit for our youths. The end result is that we rob them of the carefree years of their early development. This is a time that should be devoted to unstructured play and the exploration of a variety of different athletic and nonathletic pursuits. Instead, more and more, the early years of development are devoted to a single-minded obsession with getting better at one particular sport. In a recent *New York Times* article, Dr. Alvin Rosen-feld lamented: "We're taking children and making them professionals. We're stealing their childhood. Childhood was supposed to be a preparation, not a full performance."

Fueled by pressures from parents, young kids are pushed into specializing in one sport at an early age. Frequently the pressure is provided by a parent who is living out his or her own misspent sports career through the accomplishments of a son or daughter. With an athletic scholarship or professional contract at stake, many parents push their kids into one sport year round and spend lavishly on traveling, specialized training, coaching, and equipment. The by-products of this competitive culture are often reflected in the destructive forces of youth sports. Misguided in their goals, adults single out talented athletes at younger and younger ages and favor their development and training through elite travel and select teams. The collateral damage in this selection process is countless kids who aren't physically mature at a young age, aren't the best at their sport at that time, and who eventually become discouraged and quit. Dr. Chuck Yesalis pinpoints the problem in his book *The Steroids Game*. He says: "The available data indicate that misguided parents and coaches help perpetuate the idea of the "Rocky" story when the reality is that they have almost as good a chance to win the lottery as to guide a child into professional sports. Moreover, this attitude sends an unspoken message that participating in sports is not worth anything unless the participant can parlay that into a paying job."

The economics of a carefully calculated decision to foster the athletic training of a young child is unpalatable but certainly understandable in many regards. The tuition costs of many colleges and universities these days are astronomical and parents rightfully view an athletic scholarship as an opportunity to lessen those burdens. Thus, with the money that it now takes to develop a young athlete, a son or daughter is not just a player, but instead becomes an investment. Those individuals that should be the first to protect their children from exploitation and abuse are actually those that first promote it. Material gain and status is the name of the game for many parents who intentionally channel their kids into one sport and the unrelenting pursuit to get better.

In spite of unrealistically long odds, the stimulus for much of the insanity in our sports culture is the possible reward of an athletic scholarship or a professional contract. The probability of a high school athlete getting a college scholarship is roughly 1 in 1000; the likelihood of obtaining a paycheck in the NFL or NBA is about 1 in 10,000; the chance of cashing in on an Olympic medal is roughly 1 in 1,000,000. Capitalizing on a short-lived career in professional sports is very risky business, especially compared to other lifelong professions where one's chances of becoming an engineer, a doctor, an educator, or a lawyer are statistically much greater.

Critics of our current sports landscape refer to this phenomenon as "early specialization" or "professionalization" and it is becoming more of a problem with each passing year. Burnout at an early age, injury due to overtraining, and substance abuse can be the result of unrealistic expectations and the intense pressure to succeed in athletics. The misguided notion that youths should concentrate on one sport at an early age is pervasive and severely damaging to our developing youths.

Several well-written volumes have detailed the problems in this area. They include the following: *Just Let the Kids Play: How to Stop Other Adults from Ruining Your Child's Fun and Success in Youth Sports* by Bob Bigelow; *Why Johnny Hates Sports: Why Organized Youth Sports are Failing Our Children and What We Can Do About It* by Fred Engh; *The Cheers and the Tears: A Healthy Alternative to the Dark Side of Youth Sports Today* by Shane Murphy; and *We Own This Game: The Little Kids, Big Dreams, and High Stakes of Pop Warner Football* by Robert Andrew Powell.

Exploitation and Academic Corruption

In many respects it is correct to say that the conditions under which athletes compete today are much better than they have ever been. We certainly know more about the science of sports than we ever have and it is reflected in greatly improved equipment, nutrition, and training methods. However, in other respects the conditions are far worse since our sports culture is exploiting athletes like never before. Our young athletes are often exploited by parents who are living through their children's athletic accomplishments. They can become abusive monsters when they engage in a relentless pursuit for athletic scholarships and professional contracts. Likewise, exploitation of athletes can occur when coaches only have winning and the satisfaction of their own ego as their principal objective. This can take the form of physical, emotional or even sexual abuse.

However, the most widespread exploitation that takes place today is that practiced by many of our academic institutions with big-time sports programs. Scholarship athletes at these universities and colleges are often heavily exploited; they are entertainers in every sense of the word since colleges, the NCAA, and many college coaches are making millions of dollars off their dedication and hard work. While the athletes receive a scholarship in return and a paved road to a college diploma, it is often the case that no education is actually delivered. Athletic scholarships often become avenues for increased athletic opportunity but not educational gain.

Many college athletes do not attend classes or they take phony courses in watered down and often meaningless curriculum. This "hidden" curriculum is designed for the sole purpose of keeping athletes barely eligible. Still others that are academically capable simply do not have the time to spend studying because of the demands of their sport. It is not unusual to see wholesale cheating in these situations where academic tutors become involved in completing work for athletes in order to keep them eligible.

Many athletes do not graduate and only a very small percentage make it to the professional leagues. This exploitive system is especially damaging to many African American athletes whose graduation rates are especially low. There are frequent stories of athletes being kept eligible by a complicit faculty, only to end up with no diploma and no prospects for a good job down the road. One of the biggest myths in our current sports culture is that these individuals are student-athletes. It is sad to say but nothing could be further from the truth. In fact, the term "student-athlete" should be retired from our vocabulary altogether since it is a condition that rarely exists at big-time colleges.

Dr. Jon Ericson, founder and former director of the Drake group, a national organization of faculty working to end academic corruption in our colleges and universities, summarizes the hypocrisy in the following way: "At the heart of the academic corruption problem in college sports is the lie that a university can enroll an athlete who is woefully under-prepared for higher education, allow him to miss numerous classes, come tired to many others, work him 30 hours a week in a demanding and distracting business, spend millions of dollars to hire graduate assistants to sit in classes and take notes for him, surround him with tutors who select his courses, help with research and writing papers, place these helpers in athletic departments because they (the athletes) won't go to the tutors if they have to walk up to campus, engage in special pleading for him with his professors, and say that we provide this athlete with a college education."

While it is a perfectly worthwhile goal for a boy or girl to want to play a sport while in college, parents should not be deceived into thinking that academics are the top priority at many institutions. At the highest level of college athletics such as Division I, where athletes receive scholarships to play their sport, it is more like a job than anything else. The pressures to win are enormous and, as noted above, academic expectations are low or absent. Even in cases where athletes enter an institution with solid academic credentials and high expectations, they soon learn that their sport must come first if they are to retain their scholarship. As a result, this means that there is far less time to spend on academics. Unless their young athlete is a certifiable "blue-chipper" with professional potential, many parents should probably consider a program for their son or daughter where the pressures are not as great and the environment for academic success is more serious. Many Division III schools, especially the colleges of the New England Small College Athletic Conference (NESCAC), fit this profile as well as some Division I programs such as those institutions in the Patriot and Ivy Leagues.

A disturbing recent trend, as evidenced by the landmark research of Dr. James Shulman and Dr. William Bowen in their book *The Game of Life*, is that even academically select schools are caving into the demands of fielding superior athletic teams at the expense of academic preparation and training. They found that at academically prestigious liberal arts colleges, sports stars were more likely to be admitted than minority students and children of alumni. They also found that recruited athletes not only entered selective colleges with weaker academic records than their classmates as a whole but that once in college they consistently segregated themselves from the mainstream college culture and underperformed academically. Moreover, compared to athletes of earlier decades, the Shulman and Bowen data showed that present athletes are less likely to take on community leadership roles in their lives once they graduated.

Shulman and Bowen concluded that, "Intercollegiate programs in these academically selective institutions are moving steadily in the direction of increased tension with core educational values, and more substantial calls on the tangible and intangible resources of their host institutions." The longer-term effects that this has on the next generation of applicants is profound. Shulman and Bowen state, "High school students, their parents, and their schools watch attentively for the signals that colleges send. The more that leading institutions signal through their actions how much they value athletic prowess, the greater the emphasis that potential applicants will place on those activities. The issuing of rewards based on sports accomplishments, supports— and, in fact, makes real—the message that sports is the road to opportunity."

The problem of academic corruption and exploitation is not just a college issue. Our public schools and prep schools are like colleges and universities overemphasizing athletics and perpetuating academic corruption. Today's public high schools are more like sports camps and players are identified by sophisticated recruiting services as early as their elementary and middle school years. Lured by high school coaches that see winning as the most important goal of athletics, such players regularly transfer in order to build dominant teams in some communities. Their educational experiences are fractured by frequent moving and few schools have rigorous minimum standards for athletic participation. Chronic failure in the classroom combined with gross educational deficiencies results in the need for academic "deals" to be struck for a high school diploma. Indeed, few public and private high schools have rigorous standards for athletic participation and gross educational deficiencies frequently result. It comes as no surprise that many high schools athletes are ill-prepared for college work. Some attend prep schools and phony academies where they major in SAT preparation and staying eligible. They train and travel even more intensively in order to position themselves for a college scholarship in their sport. These young athletes are just like their college counterparts; they spend an inordinate amount of time on their sport and are seeking a professional career even though it is absurdly unrealistic.

Ira Berkow, writing in the *New York Times*, has written: "It has been said that a chain is only as strong as its weakest link. With the glorification of sports, it turns out, the edification of students is diminished. And if education becomes our weakest link, and entertainment our strongest, then there is trouble festering." Former Harvard hockey coach and athletic director Bill Cleary, writing in *Sports Illustrated*, has also weighed in on the issue. He says, "Most of these kids don't want to be in college but its their only avenue into the pros. That's whom intercollegiate sports are being run for: the one-half of one percent. We should run the sports programs for the 99.5 percent. Sports used to be part of the educational process. Now it is the process."

A number of excellent volumes detailing the problems associated with exploitation and academic corruption in our schools have recently appeared. They include *Unsportsmanlike Conduct: Exploiting College Athletes* by Walter Byers; *College Athletes for Hire: The Evolution and Legacy of the NCAA's Amateur Myth* by Allen Sach and Ellen Staurowsky; *Intercollegiate Athletics and the American University: A University President's Perspective* by James Duderstadt; *The Game of Life: College Sports and Educational Values* by James Shulman and William Bowen; *Reclaiming the Game: College Sports and Educational Values* by William Bowen and Sarah Levin; *Beer and Circus: How Big-Time Sports is Crippling Undergraduate Education* by Murray Sperber and *A New Season: Using Title IX to Reform College Sports* by Brian Porto.

The Drive for Commercialization

In *The Last Amateurs*, John Feinstein accurately depicts the present state of intercollegiate athletics and the cancer of commercialism. He says that college sports today, "are about chasing millions—no billions—of dollars; it's about a win-at-all costs mentality that more often than not starts in the President's Office and works down; alumni and fans who could care less what a school's graduation rate is as long as they're winning championships; illegal payoffs that go way beyond what is reported because they are so hard to prove; academic fraud that only occasionally comes to light; and pampered players who expect everyone to kiss their butt twenty-four hours a day because that's the way their lives have been since the day their talent was discovered."

Athletics and academics exist in two parallel universes in many of our institutions of higher learning today. On the athletic end of things, just about everything that big-time colleges and universities do in intercollegiate athletics smacks of professional entertainment. From the marketing of the product to the millionaire salaries that are paid to coaches to the outlandish TV contracts that are signed by colleges and the NCAA, it has been clear for quite some time that we are no longer talking about amateur athletics. Moreover, colleges and universities are very clever at cooking the books and making the public think that revenues from sports have a positive spin-off for the rest of their institution.

Athletic revenues help athletics, pure and simple; they do not assist the main function of a university and that is academics.

There is a great deal of misinformation as well as some myths regarding the effects of athletics on educational programs and college finances. First, contrary to what the public thinks, only a very few institutions actually make money on their athletic programs. The vast majority of colleges and universities in this country lose money or break even on their sports programs. Second, revenues from sports programs go right back into athletics and rarely if ever go into academic programs. While it is true that athletic revenues are also used to support nonrevenue sports, ask any collegiate soccer player, golfer, or volleyball player if they enjoy the same scholarship commitments and comforts as their classmates on the football field or basketball court. The fact is that they are not treated the same and they are largely second-class citizens in the college athlete hierarchy. Third, because of the lavish salaries paid to college basketball and football coaches and the arms race to see who can build the best sports facilities and therefore get a leg up on the recruiting wars, there is a never ending sea of red ink at most institutions. Fourth, donations from boosters and large corporations don't come without any strings attached. Colleges and universities are beholden to these large contributors to athletic programs and increasingly they call the shots when important decisions need to be made within the institution. Fifth, successful college athletic programs do generate enhanced giving from alumni but usually that money is targeted for athletics and not academics. Sixth, successful college athletic programs also generate more applicants in the short-term but often they are qualitatively inferior candidates. Likewise, lack of success on the college playing fields can have the reverse effect of lowering the total number of applications.

The most alarming trend in this area is that commercialization is reaching down into the scholastic and youth ranks of sports. To support their athletic programs, many high schools as well as amateur sports teams now accept funds from large sports apparel companies. It is a slippery slope when we begin to view scholastic and youth sports as part of the athletic entertainment business in this country.

Colleges and universities were never meant to be in the entertainment business. This is antithetical to the major mission of institutions of higher learning. Clearly, they have sold their souls to the highest bidders and are now at the point of no return. As a result, many of our institutions of higher learning now focus more of their time and energy on athletic entertainment than they do on academics. Our public schools and universities need to refocus their efforts on their principal mission and that is education.

We have promoted a system of sports in this country which has commercial entertainment as its major underpinning. Because of misplaced priorities by our educational system, we are much more interested in satisfying the needs of coaches, fans, corporate America, the media, and sports governing bodies in contrast to the athletes themselves. In his book *A New Season*, Brian Porto has effectively argued that we must shed the commercial model of sports in our schools for a participation model. By doing so, we could discard many of the ugly trappings of the business side of collegiate and scholastic sports and return to an emphasis upon the athletes' enjoyment of the games. Athletes therefore would be the primary beneficiaries of the games instead of those seeking to make money from their sweat and dedication on the playing fields.

Recent volumes addressing the problems associated with commercialism in our educational system include *College Sports, Inc: The Athletic Department vs the University* by Murray Sperber; *Keeping Score: The Economics of Big-Time Sports* by Richard Sheehan; *Sole Influence: Basketball, Corporate Greed, and the Corruption of America's Youth* by Dan Wetzel and Don Yeager; and *Unpaid Professionals: Commercialism and Conflict in Big-Time College Sports* by Andrew Zimbalist.

Sports Gambling

Robert Lipsyte, columnist for the *New York Times*, describes the pressures and temptations that presently exist on college campuses, "The scenario is so simple it's banal. But it keeps athletic directors up sweating at night, especially on college campuses so wired that a student can click into a gambling site before he has gotten the top off his beer can. By midnight, he can be maxed out on his credit cards. Trying to get even, he bets with a local bookie, and loses. Salvation is the disaffected varsity player down the hall who can't understand why the coach makes a million a year while he can't afford an Escalade or, in the more populist version, fly home for his grandmother's funeral. No one expects the player to actually tank a game or even miss a crucial 3-pointer. By slacking off on defense, he can reduce the spread, the number of points that bookmakers have predicted his team will win by. This can be accomplished in the blink of an eye by pretending to be faked to the left so a sprightly guard can cut right to the hoop. There are Cassandras who say it happens all the time and will bring down college basketball."

The cancer of legalized gambling poses a major threat to the integrity of college athletics and increasingly high school contests. Millions of dollars are legally and illegally bet every year on college football and basketball games, and there are numerous examples of how organized crime has persuaded some college athletes to throw games and shave points. Sports gambling has also become a major problem on college campuses, where it ranks right beside alcohol and drug problems as disruptive factors in the lives of both athletes and nonathletes. Gambling and the seedy environment that surrounds it is the antithesis of what we are trying to teach in our colleges and universities. The integrity of sport is constantly being challenged if we continue to allow legalized gambling on college sporting events. It is further exacerbated when point spreads for both college and high school games are routinely published in newspapers.

An excellent account of the disruptive effects of sports gambling on one college athletic program is found in *Fixed: How Goodfellas Bought Boston College Basketball* by David Porter. Also, important information on the cancerous effects of sports gambling is found in *The Money Sucker Machine: The Truth About Gambling and How It Destroys Students Lives* by Arnie Wexler and Mark Isenberg.

Supplements and Performance-Enhancing Drugs

Our sports culture is now filled with stories about high school, collegiate, Olympic, and professional athletes abusing anabolic steroids and other performance-enhancing drugs. Indeed, some would argue that it is the number one problem facing athletics today both in our nation and world-wide.

Dr. Chuck Yesalis, an expert on performance enhancing drugs, has captured the essence of the problem in his groundbreaking book *The Steroids Game*, "The fact is that the appetite for steroids and other performance-enhancing drugs has been created predominantly by a societal fixation on winning and physical appearance. This behavior is learned. Children play games for fun, at least as long as they can before adults intervene to tell them that winning is what's important. One of the strongest reasons we should not give up the struggle to make sports contests fair and to encourage young athletes to be good sportsman is because their ethical conduct on the playing field lays a foundation for later ethical conduct in life. Life is a team sport. Competitiveness and fierce desire to win are qualities that have made this nation great. But before we allow our children to compete, we must first establish in them a moral and ethical foundation so they have boundaries they will not cross in pursuit of victory."

While anabolic steroids initially were used by super-athletes as a means for adding an edge to a performance already close to perfection, the word gradually spread that they could be effective in any sport that required strength. Though actual figures on the incidence and prevalence of anabolic steroid use among elite, amateur, and recreational athletes is just beginning to emerge, it is generally agreed that anabolic steroids are widely used by professional, college and high school football and baseball players, shot putters, discuss throwers, wrestlers, weightlifters, swimmers, sprinters, tennis players, bicyclists, and soccer and hockey players.

Anabolic steroids have been banned by a number of sports governing bodies in order to protect athletes. Regrettably, however, there is tremendous inconsistency in which ones are banned and how frequently athletes are tested. Some sports rigorously test their athletes by using random, unannounced tests while others get by with only minimal testing in which it is easy to cheat. Moreover, in college and scholastic sports, there often is little or no testing at all due to constrained budgets. While sophisticated detection procedures have been developed in order to enforce the bans, athletes continue to abuse anabolic steroids.

A growing area of concern is the nutritional supplement field in which products contain anabolic steroids such as androstenedione (called Andro) and dehydroepiandrosterone (DHEA). Through a loophole in FDA regulations, both steroids can be bought over the counter, the internet, or by mail order and are being used to aid in the building of muscle. Substances other than steroids like EPO and human growth hormone, creatine, and ephedra are also a major concern for those involved in maintaining the integrity of sports competition.

There is no justifiable reason why illicit substances should be tolerated at any level of athletics today. From an ethical point of view, it robs sports competition of any semblance of fairness. From a scientific and medical perspective, performance-enhancing drugs can have serious and long-lasting physical and behavioral effects. Our sports culture, with its win-at-all-costs attitude, has fostered the use of performance-enhancing drugs at almost all levels of competition in almost every sport.

Two recent books review the problems associated with performance enhancing drugs in our sports culture. They are *The Steroids Game: An Expert's Inside Look at Anabolic Steroid Use in Sports* by Charles Yesalis and Virginia Cowart; and *Faust's Gold: Inside the East German Doping Machine* by Steven Ungerleider.

Declining Sportsmanship and Escalating Misbehavior and Violence

The phenomenon of out of control parents, athletes, coaches, and fans is pervasive in our present sports culture. It is reflected in hideous displays of poor sportsmanship as well as distasteful and often violent behavior. Declining sportsmanship and escalating misbehavior of all those involved with sports is the backdrop for athletics in our present times. It results in a negative undercurrent that strikes at the core values of what athletics are supposed to be about. Clearly our athletes and the games they play may be fully enveloped by issues of declining sportsmanship and misbehavior if they are not rectified soon.

Caught in the middle of misbehaving athletes, fans, coaches, and parents are the men and women that officiate games. Most of them do it for the love of the game because the pay, especially at the youth and scholastic level, is not great. Increasingly they are putting their lives on the line to officiate games and more and more of them are leaving the ranks out of frustration.

The present emphasis on sports in our country has also produced a jock culture that fuels inappropriate and often illegal and violent behavior on the part of athletes. Sportswriter John Feinstein remarked, "Rules don't exist for great athletes. Often, LAWS don't exist for great athletes. Rarely are they prosecuted and when they are, regardless of how guilty they are, they usually walk away with probation or that famous catchall, 'community service' as in 'go and serve your community by winning some games.'" Brought on by the glorification of sports in our society, the jock culture is reflected in a sense of privilege and entitlement that is bestowed upon athletes from an early age.

The jock culture is also reflected in numerous cases of "hazing" and serious crimes that include homicide, rape, kidnapping, robbery, assault, domestic violence, and drug-related offenses. Sadly, athletes on college campuses commit a disproportionate number of serious crimes in comparison to the rest of the student body. The repeated cases of athlete misbehavior toward women and the disproportionately high incidence of athletes fathering out of wedlock children is a particularly troublesome finding in this area. Lastly, athletes are not the only ones in our sports culture that have been involved with drug and sex related crimes. Increasingly, there are reports that drug dealers and child molesters, posing as coaches, have infiltrated youth and amateur sports.

The question of course is, why has sportsmanship declined so dramatically and why do we see an increasing number of ugly incidents of misbehavior and violence among athletes, coaches, parents, and fans? There are multiple answers to that question. Clearly, the intensity and pressure of sports participation and winning and losing has been ratcheted up many times over what it was back in the 1950s and 1960s. Athletic scholarships and professional contracts hang in the balance and parents often live through their kids in the quest for the rewards of sports. At the collegiate level, the pressure for wins and scholarships in high profile, revenue producing sports can make a difference in the marketing strategies of an educational institution. There is too much money at stake on our playing fields these days and we take sports way too seriously.

The unrealistic expectations of winning by everyone involved, even at a very early age, propels fans, parents, players, and coaches to act in unethical and sometimes illegal ways. The media hype that accompanies almost all aspects of sports at every level also contributes to the problems. Bad behavior is recognized more than good behavior and it becomes the expected norm. Sadly, the misbehavior that often occurs is either ignored or dealt with only superficially. Often, athletes and coaches are allowed to continue in their roles even though they have engaged in illegal and violent behavior. Our young people see and hear what happens at the higher levels of sports and come to believe that it is OK for athletes to abuse the values of the game and engage in unethical and illegal behavior. Some athletes develop a sense of entitlement because they have been pampered by a society that treats them differently than normal citizens. This is a cocktail for disaster and it is surprising that our outlaw sports culture is not worse than it is. Clearly, something must be done to return our athletes, coaches, parents, and fans to a more sane sports landscape; one in which ethics, sportsmanship, and fair play become the focus instead of an afterthought.

The problems associated with declining sportsmanship and athlete misbehavior are dealt with in a number of interesting books on the topic including: *Our Guys: The Glen Ridge Rape and the Secret Life of the Perfect Suburb* by Bernard Lefkowitz; *Public Heroes, Private Felons: Athletes and Crimes Against Women* by Jeff Benedict; *Pros and Cons: The Criminals Who Play in the NFL* by Jeff Benedict; *Out of Bounds: Inside the NBA's Culture of Rape, Assault, and Drug Use* by Jeff Benedict, and *The Hazing Reader* by Hank Nuwer.

Excessive and Unbalanced Media Coverage

The media coverage of athletes in our present sports culture is both excessive and unbalanced. In particular, local media coverage over the past 10 years has done the same thing that parents and organizers of scholastic and youth sports have done: they have attempted to professionalize young athletes by reporting on them in the same way that they report on Michael Jordan, Bobby Bonds, and Brett Favre. There is no code of ethics when it comes to reporting on youth, scholastic, and college sports. The coverage is excessively detailed and distorted and tends to "hype" and make myths out of young players, many of whom have not even reached puberty. While a certain amount of media coverage is acceptable, good taste and setting limits have been erased in the name of selling papers and sensationalizing the lives of young athletes. An unfortunate by-product of excessive media coverage is that many young athletes develop huge egos and are ill-equipped to handle their newfound fame.

Jay Weiner, columnist for the *Minneapolis Star Tribune*, thinks that something needs to be done. He recently wrote: "To paraphrase sportswriter and author Robert Lipsyte, we sportswriters are the piano players in this tawdry preps brothel. As we move along this path of increased commercialism of school sports, it's clearly time for the nation's sports media to examine ourselves and reevaluate the time, space and energy we devote to games, athletes, recruiting news, and state tournaments. Cut the personality features. Shorten the game stories. Stop touting prospects. We feed the flames of premature fame."

The media coverage of young athletes is also unbalanced. We do not cover nonsports-related activities such as educational attainment or accomplishments in the performing and fine arts anywhere near as much as we cover sports achievements. As a result, we end up reinforcing and giving attention to athletes and their endeavors far more than we cover the exploits and accomplishments of nonathletes. Parents and young people rightfully conclude that athletic accomplishments are more important than educational accomplishments when they see such unbalanced media coverage.

The media also is at fault for the excessive amount of coverage devoted to the physical and violent aspects of sports. We are routinely bombarded with bone-crushing hits from football, grotesque blood-filled fights in hockey, unruly fans attacking players and officials with snowballs and bottles, and bench-clearing brawls in many sports. Nothing seems to be sacred, not even the reporting of just about every aspect of the private lives of athletes. The media to date has taken very little responsibility in policing itself in these important areas.

Excessive and unbalanced sports reporting is discussed in books such as *Just Let the Kids Play: How to Stop Other Adults from Ruining Your Child's Fun and Success in Youth Sports* by Bob Bigelow; and *Why Johnny Hates Sports: Why Organized Youth Sports are Failing Our Children and What We Can Do About it* by Fred Engh.

Unequal Opportunities

Title IX has definitely improved opportunities for women in athletics and has been a positive development in our sports culture. However, we should not be deluded into thinking that 100 percent equality for women has arrived. This clearly is not the case in many areas of our country in which women still lag behind men in terms of the resources devoted to athletics at the youth, scholastic and collegiate levels. Moreover, some believe that Title IX has also been used as an instrument for social engineering. In spite of the fact that real differences exist between men and women in their interests, quotas and preferences have been established to create new opportunities for women in sports where interest is marginal or absent.

One by-product of trying to create interest in sports for women is that opportunities in some male sports have dramatically diminished. A complicating factor however is that spending on some sports, especially football and men's basketball, is disproportionately higher than that on other low-profile, non-revenue-generating sports.

According to Jere Longman, columnist for the *New York Times*, there is an unfortunate and inaccurate perception about who is to blame for problems associated with Title IX enforcement. He states: "Women are not forcing the curtailment of some men's teams. Rather, it is a failure of imagination and commitment by many universities and an unwillingness to confront the money pit of football. Football should receive favorable treatment because it brings in millions of dollars, its supporters argue. Yet, according to various surveys taken by women's groups, half to two-thirds of football teams operate in the red, meaning they don't even pay for themselves, much less other teams on campus."

Apart from Title IX concerns, there are other glaring inequities in sports opportunities that are related to socioeconomic status. Poorer inner cities as well as rural areas often cannot provide the same athletic opportunities as middle-class and upper-income suburban areas. Also, the trend toward supporting select, elite, and other highly competitive teams means that community-based and intramural recreational opportunities are actually diminishing. Even traditional physical education classes in our public schools are becoming a thing of the past owing to budgetary considerations. Consequently, our sports landscape still has many inequities that are not even close to being resolved.

Several recent books have dealt with the controversy surrounding Title IX and athletic opportunities for men and women. Two excellent books are *Tilting the Playing Fields: Schools, Sports, Sex and Title IX* authored by Jessica Gavora; and *The Feminist Dilemma: When Success is Not Enough* by Diana Furchtgott-Roth and Christine Stolba.

Escalating Sports Injuries

Increased risk of certain health problems and escalating sports injuries have reached a crisis stage for many athletes. Dr. David Janda, Director of the Institute for Preventative Sports Medicine commented in his influential book *The Awakening of a Surgeon*, "Injury is a national and internationally unrecognized public health problem that transcends age, race, gender, and state and national borders. With increasing worldwide participation in sports, injuries have become an epidemic of global proportions. Those of us on the front lines of health care delivery feel frustrated and perplexed by the apparent inability of government, business, and medical research facilities to focus on the issue of injury and injury prevention."

One problem is that many believe that injury is simply a part of sports that will always be present. Dr. Janda disagrees with this interpretation. He noted: "The number one fallacy is that injuries are inherent: that they are going to happen no matter what you do. The vast majority of injuries are completely preventable."

With the rise in the popularity and competitiveness of women's sports, there has been a dramatic increase in serious knee injuries experienced by those involved in basketball and lacrosse. Likewise, the increase in head injuries for those involved in soccer has prompted concern. Clearly, more time, effort, and resources need to be devoted to the important area of prevention if this trend is to be reversed. Our athletes are becoming more skilled and are training harder than ever before, but we do not devote adequate resources and attention to health and safety issues. Many studies now show that equipment and training changes could effectively prevent many sports injuries. However, sports governing bodies do little to incorporate these changes because of cost, tradition, pressure from equipment and insurance companies, and the benign neglect of our federal government. Moreover, in addition to physical injury, we often subject our young athletes to emotional and overuse injuries. By failing to make an investment in prevention of sports injuries, we compromise the health and safety of our athletes and jeopardize their long-term development.

An excellent account of the field of sports injury and prevention is found in *The Awakening of a Surgeon: One Doctor's Journey to Fight the System and Empower Your Community* by David Janda.

Declining Health and Fitness

Dr. Andrew Miracle and Dr. Roger Rees sounded an alarm in their book *Lessons of the Locker Room*. They said: "It is an anomaly that our society is in the middle of what can be described as a fitness boom and yet our youth have never been less fit. In fact, there is a crisis in fitness among America's children." Those words, spoken in 1994 are as true today as they were nearly ten years ago.

There is little question that our athletes are becoming better trained and more skilled. Watch any Olympic, professional, collegiate, or high school sports contest and you will certainly notice a higher skill level than what was observed five or ten years ago. However, while our select and elite team athletes are getting better, overall fitness of the average young person is actually in a state of decline. This is due in part to the fact that we no longer place an emphasis upon lifelong fitness, physical education, intramural sports, and overall recreational and health-related activities. Instead, both locally and nationally, resources are being directed toward athletes-in-training versus those who are not. Because most school and college athletic budgets go to support competitive teams, the vast majority of individuals hardly benefit from the facilities and equipment that are available for sports activities.

If physical education and fitness-based curriculum in our public schools can be described as significantly lagging behind what it should be, then the situation in our colleges and universities could be characterized as virtually non-existent. The arms race on many college campuses is to build better facilities for competitive sports teams and athletes in training. Those facilities, which oftentimes are sold to the student body with the promise of more access to the average student, are frequently funded in part from student fees but usually end up as restricted areas and largely off limits to students seeking to improve their own fitness. As average students give up because access is so limited, the pattern of a sedentary lifestyle becomes even more entrenched. Sports and physical activity on our college campuses therefore becomes a spectator and not a participatory activity. As George Cowan wrote in the *New York Times* recently, "While billions of dollars are spent on new stadiums to nestle the rear ends of sports fans, our grammar school, high school and college kids are being deprived of the benefits and joy of sports at an ever-increasing rate."

As physical education declines, and competitive interscholastic and intercollegiate team sports mushroom and expand taking more resources along with it, the vast majority of our youths are left inactive. Our elite athletes get the benefit of physical activity through their respective sports but average kids are left behind in their health and fitness development. Indeed, if the benefits of fitness and participation in athletics are so important, then why do we continue to shortchange the many for the advancement of a few?

The author's more detailed volume in the area of sports reform, *Crisis on Our Playing Fields: What Everyone Should Know About Our Out of Control Sports Culture and What We Can Do to Change It* examines this area of declining health and fitness in our country.

The Need for Action by All Those Involved With Sports

Out of control and in serious danger of losing its relevance, preprofessional sports in America are at a critical crossroads. The major stakeholders in our athletic community need to come forward and share the burden of reforming sports before it is too late. This includes sports governing bodies, parents, coaches, athletes, administrators, media professionals, college and school athletic directors, and teachers and professors. Anyone who wants to become involved with sports reform must first recognize that there are multiple problems and they exist at every age level of sports, in every region of the country, and in every sport that is played. The health, safety, and welfare of kids should drive all decision making for preprofessional sports. Ironically, however, one of the most significant problems in sports reform these days is that there are not enough individuals involved in our sports culture that think this way. Too often, the policies that end up directly affecting young athletes are made by individuals who have competing agendas such as the winning of games or commercial interests. As a result, many reform groups are now actively seeking to change this unbalanced emphasis.

The National Institute for Sports Reform is poised to take a leading role in reforming sports in this country. You can find out more about this organization in Appendix I. Also, a list of the many other reform groups that are actively seeking change in our sports culture is found in Appendix II.

IT'S CALLED "SPORTS REFORM"... I HOPE IT'S EVENTUALLY MOVED INTO THE NEXT GALLERY...
ABSTRACT
REALISM
©MARK PARISI offthemark.com

32

Needed Reforms

Sport was never intended to occupy the position of importance that it presently has in our society. We revere athletes more than we do doctors, lawyers, educators, and engineers. We place them upon a pedestal, deify their persona, and talk of their athletic feats as though they were super-humans. In the process, we have compromised the integrity of our educational system in order to provide entertainment for the public and we have exploited and abused our athletes to accomplish this purpose. There is no longer a balance between sports and other more important aspects of our lives.

If our sports culture is so out of touch with traditional values and more important aspects of our lives, then how can we possibly return it to an acceptable level of functioning? How do we reform something that has grown so powerful, so addicting, and so all-consuming to our society that we apparently can't do without it?

Many helpful books have been written to guide parents, coaches, athletes, and sports administrators through sports. A sampling of some of the more important works on sports parenting and coaching include *The Encyclopedia of Sports Parenting* by Dan Doyle and Rick Wolfe; *Raising Winners: A Parent's Guide to Helping Kids Succeed On and Off the Playing Field* by Shari Kuchenbecker; *The Total Sports Experience for Kids: A Parent's Guide to Success in Youth Sports* by Aubrey Fine and Michael Sachs; *Catch Them Being Good: Everything You Need to Know to Successfully Coach Girls* by Tony Dicicco, Colleen Hacker, and Charles Salzberg; *Raising a Team Player* by Harry Sheehy; *Positive Coaching: Building Character and*

Self-Esteem Though Sports by Jim Thompson; *Just Let the Kids Play: How to Stop Other Adults from Ruining Your Child's Fun and Success in Youth Sports* by Bob Bigelow; *Why Johnny Hates Sports: Why Organized Youth Sports are Failing Our Children and What We Can Do About It* by Fred Engh; and *The Student Athlete Survival Guide* by Mark Isenberg.

Yet other excellent books have been written to specifically address the various ills of sports in our schools and institutions of higher learning. These works include *Sports in School: The Future of an Institution* by John Gerdy; *Lessons of the Locker Room: The Myth of School Sports* by Andrew Miracle and Roger Rees; *Schools that Do Too Much: Wasting Time and Money in Schools and What We Can All Do About It* by Etta Kralovec; *Beer and Circus: How Big-Time College Sports is Crippling Undergraduate Education* by Murray Sperber; *The Game of Life: College Sports and Educational Values* by James Shulman and William Bowen; *A New Season: Using Title IX to Reform College Sports* by Brian Porto; *Reclaiming the Game: College Sports and Educational Values* by William Bowen and Sarah Levin; *Intercollegiate Athletics and the American University: A University President's Perspective* by James Duderstadt; and *Unsportsmanlike Conduct: Exploiting College Athletes* by Walter Byers; and *College Athletes for Hire: The Evolution and Legacy of the NCAA's Amateur Myth* by Allen Sack and Ellen Staurowsky.

These books are excellent but many of them fall short of a comprehensive analysis of the systemic organizational problems that presently plague our sports landscape. A detailed examination of these issues, the important events that may lead to change, and the ultimate destination for our sports culture is provided in the detailed companion volume to this work entitled *Crisis on Our Playing Fields: What Everyone Should Know About Our Out of Control Sports Culture and What We Can Do to Change It*. In particular, I encourage the reader to examine this volume for critical study of the important legal and social events that may soon take place to reorder the organization of sports in our country.

It is one thing to criticize things as they are in our present sports system; it is quite another to provide some reform measures that will truly change our current culture. Knowing full well that no suggestions for reform are perfect and that a radical reordering of our priorities may be inevitable, I advocate a number of specific remedies for improving our out of control sports system. While some of these remedies have been advocated by others in the past, renewed emphasis upon them is necessary to bring about reform of our sports culture. Clearly, major reforms are necessary. We must propose real reforms rather than the pretend reforms that seem to proliferate in our educational institutions and sports governing bodies that have failed. In the words of columnist Robert Lipsyte, we can't continue to "put lipstick on a pig." We have to be bold in what we propose even if it means dismantling what we have and starting over again.

Establish a Federally Funded National Sports Commission

Youth, amateur, scholastic, collegiate, professional, and Olympic sports governing bodies in our country exist in virtual isolation from one another. This is unfortunate since answers to mutual problems that ultimately affect the health and well-being of our young athletes are often ignored. Likewise, if we move to the Australian and European club system of sports and move athletics out of our schools and institutions of higher learning (see below), our government should take a more active role in coordinating and promoting sports and fitness from the local community level to the elite stage. The creation of a National Sports Commission, with all sports governing bodies as members, would provide an important coordinating mechanism for athletics in this country. It would be charged with overseeing the entire spectrum of sports from the promotion of health and fitness for all to the training of Olympic athletes. The commission would also be charged with promoting sports, health, and fitness through the creation of partnerships with private corporations and professional sports organizations. The overriding goal of these associations would be to elevate the funding of sports and encourage the formation of a club system of athletics for the entire life span of our population. The establishment of a National Sports Commission is a must if we are to make any headway in our desire to reform sports to benefit all of our athletes and all of our citizens.

Establish an Independent Organization That Would Serve As a Think Tank, Research Center, Information Clearing House, Consultant, and Advocate for Sports Reform

With the many problems that our sports culture presently faces, there is a critical need for an independent organization to serve as a focal point for the sports reform movement. An institute made up of faculty fellows and scholars who are specialists in the study of sports reform issues would be called upon in the same way that the Brookings Institute is asked by our federal government to consult and do research on economics, foreign policy, and government. Such a "think tank" would serve many functions including serving as a consultant to sports governing bodies and the government, the issuing of position papers, the conduct of commissioned research, the support of conferences, symposia, and published work, and the clearinghouse and information resource center for the public and the media on all issues related to sports reform. Because considerable research and creative thinking is needed to provide long-lasting solutions to the difficult issues that plague our sports landscape today, the creation of such an entity is overdue and a high priority. The newly created National Institute for Sports Reform (NISR) is poised to serve all of these important functions (See Appendix I).

Get Youth Sports Programs to Eliminate the Fielding of Select and Elite Teams below the Age of 11

The single most negative development in our sports culture over the past 20 years has been the creation of elite and select teams for very young children in a wide variety of sports. This development has promoted an entire subculture and cottage industry of coaches, trainers, psychologists, educators, and nutritionists, as well as specialized sports academies for young athletes in professionalized year round training. All of the available information suggests that this type of focused and intense training is of little benefit for the vast majority of participants and arguably has many negative outcomes for young kids who are still developing their interests in athletic and nonathletic activities. By eliminating this practice, we signal that we are interested in taking the pressure off young children and normalizing their development in an age-appropriate manner.

Get Youth Sports Organizations to Eliminate State, Regional, and National Championship Games

Pop Warner Football, Little League baseball, AAU basketball, Youth Basketball of America, and Babe Ruth baseball regularly promote state, regional and national championship games. In some cases, national championships are held for kids as young as 8 and 9 years of age. Their purpose is dubious for a number of reasons. First, tournament and championship play necessarily emphasizes the winning of games and a coach's ego, with player skill development an afterthought. Second, because the resources devoted to championship game formats are restricted to only a few select players, the benefits of skill development for a wider group of athletes are prohibited. To enable broadly based skill development for more athletes at early ages, youth sports organizations should seriously consider eliminating state, regional, and national championships for kids younger than 13 years of age. By eliminating this practice, we will encourage a more rational perspective on age appropriate development of athletic skills. Likewise, it will allow for a deemphasis on winning as the only worthwhile product of sports participation.

Get Youth Sports Programs to Implement More Non-Results-Oriented Activities in Their Leagues

The focus on winning in our sports culture is excessive and has trickled down to the youngest levels of organized athletics. Winning and losing is a by-product of the games we play but there is no rational reason why it needs to be emphasized at ages younger than 12. Decisions to keep win-loss records in tournaments and games serves the needs of coaches and adults that are in charge but does not serve the needs of young kids. When winning is placed above everything else, it causes coaches and adults to make different decisions about who plays and who doesn't, it pressurizes the playing conditions for young athletes, it takes the focus off skill development and places it on game strategy, and it promotes an environment in which adults often lose their cool. We have pressurized and overorganized the lives of our young kids enough. In athletics, there is no reason why we can't back off and lessen the pressure on our playing fields. Player development and enjoying sports for the wonderful physical outlets they represent should be the focus of all athletic activities at least until the first year of high school.

Get Organized Competitive Sports Out of Our Public Schools and Colleges and Promote the European and Australian Club Sports System

Previous reform movements have tried endless measures to bring school and college sports back to some semblance of sanity. Many of these measures are well intentioned but doomed to fail. Previous history repeatedly has shown that traditional reforms from within the system simply will not work. Even if they are enacted, which is highly doubtful given the vested commercial interests that are involved, there is too much money at stake and cheating and other unethical behaviors are likely to occur. Likewise, at the public school level, our interscholastic sports programs are eating up school budgets like never before and little is being done to maintain academic integrity, amateurism, and the constant threat of exploitive commercial interests. It is time that we face the facts once and for all that the long experiment with sports in our high schools and colleges has failed; it simply is not worth adding new layers of reform measures that can never be enforced. The sooner we get over it and move on to a better system, the better off our athletes will be in the long run.

There is a better model and that is the European and Australian club sports system. Gradually moving toward this system should be a long-term goal for our organized sports programs. In many countries throughout the world, this system works well because it is outside the educational system; it works for everyone from recreational participants to elite athletes, from the very young to the very old. Nothing will change for our athletes under this system since the opportunities for athletic participation and development will be the same if not greater. The only difference is that our high schools and colleges will no longer have to devote considerable resources to a small number of elite athletes; they can divest themselves of the hopeless responsibility of meshing competitive athletics with education. As a result, professional leagues would then be more responsible for nurturing the development of their future players, thus lifting this burden from our educational system. Importantly, schools can then return to their job of educating our young people as well as providing enhanced fitness and physical education for all (see below). Importantly, we will no longer have to deal with issues of commercialism and academic hypocrisy in an educational setting.

Foster the Development of Minor League Sports Franchises for Football and Basketball

Our professional sports, especially football and basketball, have received a free ride in the development of their players for many years. Our public and private high schools and our colleges and universities have been doing their work at a considerable expense to our educational system, both in terms of resources as well as weakened educational objectives. Importantly, both the National Hockey League (NHL) and Major League Baseball (MLB) have created strong minor professional leagues for their respective sports. The NBA and the NFL need to follow their lead, step up to the plate, and create a true minor league system for their respective sports in which those athletes who want to specialize and train for the pros can do so without being burdened by educational requirements. Such a system could incorporate a small number of big-time college and university facilities that would be leased by professional franchises. Players for these franchises would have no educational strings attached and could be in training all year long for their sport. The National Developmental Basketball League, sponsored by the NBA, is a good departure point. However, the league needs to be greatly expanded to accommodate more players and the 20 year age minimum needs to be lowered so that athletes graduating from high school could be eligible. The development of minor professional leagues should not be restricted to men's sports nor should other sports be excluded. As women's sports expand and as "minor" sports such as volleyball, soccer, and lacrosse gain in popularity, there will be an evolving need for minor professional leagues to develop.

Get Our Institutions of Higher Learning to Turn Down the Volume on Intercollegiate Sports

There will undoubtedly be a transitional period as we move toward minor professional league development and the European and Australian sports club system. In this interim period, there are a few things that can be done at the college level to rein in sports. Some of the current proposed remedies include higher academic standards, penalties for low graduation rates, rewards for superior graduation rates, and equalization of monetary incentives for tournament/bowl participation.

While these measures may diminish academic hypocrisy, commercialism, and exploitation to some extent and they should be enacted, there are other remedies that I strongly advocate.

First, though it is only a symbolic move, the term "student-athlete" needs to be stricken from our vocabulary. Athletes are an important part of the student body but no more important than musicians, artists, or those involved in drama and theater productions. Created by the NCAA to avert workman compensation and lawsuits that could emerge if athletes were viewed as paid employees, the term needs to be replaced in all documents and popular news media accounts with "student" or "college athlete."

Second, we need to eliminate athletic scholarships and replace them with need-based financial aid. Athletic scholarships are nothing more than work-for-hire, one-year contracts. They have many negative features, not the least of which is that athletes soon realize that their performance on the playing fields is much more important for scholarship renewal than their performance in the classroom. As we move to a club system and a professionalized minor league sports model outside of our high schools and colleges, we need to eliminate athletic scholarships and replace them with the Division III model of guaranteed need-based financial aid. This will free students who play sports from the shackles of the present performance-based model, return them to some form of true amateurism, and, most important, permit them to more properly focus their time and energy on educational achievement.

Third, to boost graduation rates, a number of measures should be taken to provide greater accountability. To allow adjustment to college academic life, freshmen should be ineligible for athletic competition. Athletes should also be required to maintain a 2.0 grade point average throughout their academic careers. Also, while keeping the identity of individual athletes anonymous, colleges and universities should regularly make available information on the courses taken by athletes, their majors, and the average grade given in courses taken by athletes.

Fourth, the practice of establishing separate academic counseling centers for athletes needs to be eliminated. The location and control of academic counseling for athletes should be the same as that for any student on campus. This is an important measure to achieve the full integration of athletes into the student body.

Fifth, to allow athletes to get a quality college education, class attendance policies for coursework needs to be strictly enforced. Universities need to ensure that athletic contests are not scheduled in such a way as to conflict with class attendance; faculty need to enforce attendance policies to ensure that academic instruction takes precedence over athletic participation.

Sixth, to reduce conflicts with academic objectives, the length of seasons and the amount of time that athletes currently spend in practice and training (preseason and postseason) need to be dramatically curtailed. The present practice limits of twenty hours per week during the season and eigtht hours per week out of season needs to be cut in half. Also, the practice of voluntary unofficial workouts is one of the worst abuses in our present system of intercollegiate sports and should be eliminated altogether.

Seventh, employment practices for coaches and athletic directors in Division I programs need to be rethought. Coaching and athletic director salaries need to be reduced to the level of other faculty and restrictions need to be placed on outside income from sporting goods companies. Also, coaches should be allowed to stand for tenure and promotion in a manner identical to that of academic faculty. Finally, we need to restore the model of coach as educator. The academic credentials of coaches in higher education need to be evaluated in the same way that academic faculty are judged. Degree attainment validates educational credibility for faculty and there is no reason why this should not also be true for coaches. College coaches are hired as part of a larger academic community and their credibility as educational role models for athletes is associated with how well they have made a significant commitment to education. The attainment of advanced degrees is proof that a coach is committed to education as a mechanism for career fulfillment. By promoting more vigorously the attainment of advanced degrees among college coaches, we set the tone for reintegrating athletics with the academic community.

Eighth, the televising of school athletic contests should be determined solely by colleges and universities and not by TV networks. Consequently, intercollegiate games should be scheduled for weekends and vacation periods and not during weekdays while classes are in session.

Ninth, the amount of spending on football and basketball programs is too lavish and needs to be scaled back dramatically. For starters, roster size (scholarship players) in football should be dropped from 85 to 53 (the size of NFL rosters) and the practice of paying for extravagant hotel accommodations (for both home and away contests) needs to be eliminated. Also, the number of coaches allowed needs to be reduced.

Tenth, commercial contracts with schools should be eliminated and players should not be allowed to wear anything that constitutes advertising.

Eleventh, transfer rules need to be dramatically changed and the Division III model should be adopted. If students desire to transfer, they should become immediately eligible to participate at their new institution without having to sit out for a period of time.

Twelfth, sanctions on institutions that break major rules by increasing postseason bans and reducing scholarships need to be stiffened. For repeat offenders, of which there are many, administer the "death penalty" and do not allow them to compete in intercollegiate athletics for an extensive period of time. Finally, insist that sanctions follow coaches, athletic directors, and university presidents when they relocate to another institution.

Thirteenth, the IRS needs to tax the NCAA, collegiate conferences, and individual colleges and universities in the same way that regular profit-making businesses are taxed. There is no longer any doubt that these entities are cartels who make millions of dollars off the sweat and labor of college athletes. They have executive pay scales that equal that of major corporations, they engage in commercial takeovers (mergers and acquisitions) of conferences, and they have their own marketing and licensing offices. They can no longer claim that collegiate athletics is educational and nonprofit. In short, these activities are unrelated to the central mission of colleges and universities. Thus, any profits from engaging in these activities should be subject to a tax.

Fourteenth, for reasons of economy as well as renewed emphasis upon education, athletic conferences need to scale back on the number of members and their geographic reach. Far-flung travel is very expensive and the time taken from classes as a consequence of cross-coastal competition seriously compromises academic progress by athletes. Thus, conference alignments should be done regionally with no more than eight to 10 members.

Fifteenth, Congress should grant the NCAA an antitrust exemption so that it can jointly market TV rights. Importantly, however, Congress should insist that all Division I schools share equally in the revenue that is generated. Therefore, small schools would receive just as much as large schools in TV revenue.

Get Our Public Schools to Turn Down the Volume on Interscholastic Sports

Although we are slowly moving in the direction of the European and Australian sports club system (e.g. the extensive U.S. club system of soccer), it is unrealistic to think that it will happen overnight. We will have a significant transitional period and, during that time, we need to rethink the way we presently conduct scholastic sports. The specific changes I advocate consist of the following measures.

First, there should be strengthened standards regarding academic performance and the privilege to participate in athletics. Because academic hypocrisy has reached heightened levels in our high schools, new standards for educational progress need to be employed. Athletes should be automatically ineligible if they are not passing any of their courses; return to playing status can occur but only after passing grades are obtained. Athletes who are not passing two or more subjects should be suspended for the entire season with a return in the succeeding year contingent upon obtaining passing grades in all courses.

Second, to limit transferring of students for strictly athletic purposes, transfer students in their first year should be required to sit out the first half of the season and should be ruled ineligible for postseason play. As a correlate to this, any coach or other individual who is found to have engaged in recruiting or any undue influence should be permanently suspended from coaching.

Third, because they unnecessarily prolong sports seasons, state tournaments should end at the level of local regional play (usually called sectional play in most states) and state tournaments should be eliminated.

Fourth, because travel has become excessive and expensive, sports teams should not be allowed to travel any farther than 100 miles from their school for an athletic contest.

Fifth, because commercial interests are corrupting the integrity of scholastic sports, school athletic programs should not be allowed to accept any funds from corporate interests (e.g., shoe companies), nor should they be allowed to engage in contracts to have their games televised.

Sixth, because they serve no practical educational purpose and are principally showcases for college recruiters, all-star games should be eliminated.

Seventh, because athletic contests frequently interfere with proper academic progress, they should be restricted to vacation periods and weekends (e.g., beginning on Friday afternoons after the school day has been completed and extending through Sunday afternoons).

Eighth, because admission charges to athletic contests are highly variable from one school to another and because they are frequently used as sources of revenue to support athletics, they should be eliminated at the interscholastic level. If sports are an integral part of education then they need to be treated as such and not as commercialized entertainment.

The same holds true for other school activities like music and theater. Thus, schools should fully fund their athletic programs and should not count on gate receipts as a method to offset those costs.

Ninth, if athletics are considered an integral part of education, then school boards need to fully fund their sports programs and eliminate the practice of user fees. The cutting of sports budgets sends the message that the community considers interscholastic athletic programs to be a low priority and perhaps educationally irrelevant. It follows that a community should not be allowed to self fund interscholastic teams where an elected school board has determined that it is not an important part of the educational process.

Promote the Growth of Intramural Programs and Recreational and Fitness-Based Curriculum in Our Schools

Sports are an integral part of our everyday lives. This includes competitive organized sports as well as fitness-based recreational and intramural activities. They should be for everyone and not just a select few. Once organized competitive sports are eliminated from our school systems, both colleges and public schools, we can begin to devote our resources in physical education to all students instead of just a select few. By refocusing our attention on intramural programs and fitness-based curriculum for all, we signal that we are more interested in sports as a lifelong enhancement to the everyday lives of all individuals in contrast to an activity for a select few for a short span of time.

Enact Tough Legislation Against Sports Gambling and the Publication of Point Spread Information

Sports gambling is an immediate threat to scholastic and intercollegiate athletic events as well as to the athletes themselves. Legislation to limit sports gambling has languished in Congress for a number of years. A ban on legalized sports gambling on collegiate and high school events must be passed immediately. The legislation should also include a ban on offshore Internet gambling as well as a strict prohibition on the publication of betting lines for collegiate and high school sporting events.

Expand Testing for Performance-Enhancing Drugs and Toughen the Penalties for Their Use

The use of performance-enhancing drugs and supplements at all levels of sports keeps escalating in spite of the good intentions of our sports governing bodies. Additionally, the penalties for their use are ridiculously weak and the resources devoted to prevention, research, education, and enforcement are appallingly low. A new government-based initiative in all of these areas needs the cooperation and full monetary support of all sports governing bodies. As the only legitmate process for testing, there should be a renewed emphasis upon random, unannounced tests both within and outside of sports seasons. Most important, the penalties for the use of banned substances need to be dramatically stiffened. As a starting point, any athlete at any level of sports who tests positive for a banned substance should be suspended for two years with reinstatement contingent upon a sustained record of clean tests over the penalty period; a second positive test would result in a life-time ban from the sport. Perhaps we would lose out on watching a few exceptional athletes here and there but the long-term effect would be to make athletes think more critically about getting a performance edge with banned substances.

Establish an Age Minimum for Media Coverage of Athletes, Eliminate National High School Sports Rankings, and Prohibit Televised Coverage of Scholastic and Youth Sports

The coverage of young athletes today is excessively hyped by television, radio, and newspapers. It has reached new heights of over-the-top, unbalanced reporting. If the media will not step in and police themselves by limiting their coverage of "star" athletes, then get sports governing bodies (e.g., Federation of State Athletic Associations, Pop Warner Football, Little League Baseball, Amateur Athletic Association) to enact tough guidelines that prohibit media coverage. The guidelines should prevent individual athletes at the high school age and younger from receiving excessive media attention other than game reports. Newspapers and television should be allowed to make brief game reports but there should be no in-depth individualized attention until after the high school years are over. Television coverage of prep, high school, and youth athletics should be strictly barred by sports governing bodies. This especially holds true for state, regional, and national championship games that have become commercialized extravaganzas promoted by organizations such as Pop Warner Football and Little League Baseball. Finally, newspaper publication of national rankings for scholastic and youth sports programs should be eliminated.

Vigorously Pursue Sports Injury Prevention Research and Education

Many sports injuries could be prevented by more extensive education of parents and athletes as well as by using safer equipment and modified rules. If a sports organization does not incorporate the latest safety information in its equipment and rules because of tradition and/or cost, then that organization does not have the health and welfare of the athlete as its number 1 objective. To that end, we need to increase dramatically the amount of funding available for independent testing of new sports equipment so as to enable the safest possible conditions for our athletes at all levels of play.

Toughen the Penalties for Off-the-Field Misbehavior of Athletes and Stiffen the Penalties for Sportsmanship Infractions by Athletes, Coaches, and Fans

Sportsmanship violations during games and the general misbehavior of athletes, coaches, and fans has reached epidemic proportions. Often the penalties for these infringements upon the values of the game are weak or nonexistent. The punishment for the misbehavior of athletes off the field is often subverted by an educational system that is beholden to the sports machines on our high school and college campuses. Athletes should be treated by our legal system in the same way as average citizens. Playing a sport is a privilege and not a right. That privilege is one that is earned and subject to good citizenship and behavior on and off the field. Loss of those privileges should be swift and long-lasting for athletes. The same holds true for coaches, parents and fans. Thus, in combination with renewed efforts in the prevention area as well as added incentives for good sportsmanship, we must make the loss of the privilege to participate, coach, or view games a more severe and immediate threat.

Promote More Vigorously the Concept of Equal Opportunity for All in Sports

Our sports landscape is still filled with inequality. There are inequities related to gender, age, and socioeconomic status that persist in just about every region of our country. Title IX did a great deal to resolve some of these inequalities but women still lag behind in the resources devoted to sports. At the same time, we need to celebrate the differences that do exist between the genders in sports interests and not reduce opportunity for either males or females. Also, age and socioeconomic status are major stumbling blocks in access to sports. Opportunities in athletics decline for kids as they get older unless they are involved with competitive or elite teams. Likewise, youths in our urban and rural areas have far fewer sports opportunities than their suburban counterparts. Everyone who wants to participate in sports should have the opportunity to do so. To accomplish this purpose, there must be new initiatives spearheaded at the local and the national levels to more adequately fund sports opportunities. Thus, like the European and Australian model of sports, we need to develop partnerships between corporate America, local, state, and federal government, as well as private sports clubs.

Educate Parents and Athletes from an Early Age about Both the Benefits and the Costs (Risks) of Organized Sports Participation

The benefits of participating in athletic competition are considerable. Fitness, health, sportsmanship, fair play, teamwork, and ethics are wonderful outcomes of an experience in sports. However, the downside of athletic participation, the costs and the potential pitfalls elucidated in this volume, are rarely fully discussed at any stage of athletic participation. This information needs to get into the hands of our athletes and parents in an unfiltered manner. If this occurs, parents and athletes will be able to make better decisions regarding their future involvement in sports and nonsports related activities.

Encourage Individuals at the Local Level to Promote the Positive Rewards of Education and Act Against the Negative Elements of Our Sports Culture

Reforming our sports culture begins with those around us in our immediate sports environment. In our own homes and communities, individuals need to act forcefully and swiftly when they observe examples of exploitation and commercialism, academic hypocrisy, early professionalization and specialization, poor sportsmanship, sports gambling and point spread reporting, unsafe playing conditions, performance-enhancing drug usage, and unequal sports opportunities. They also need to promote the positive culture of educational achievement as the one tried and true method for career success and satisfaction. This can take on many different forms but what it really means is getting our priorities in order. We must ensure that the imbalance that presently exists between recognition for athletic achievement on the one hand and educational attainment on the other is reversed. This can be done by doing a better job of vigorously recognizing and rewarding educational accomplishments in our public schools and colleges.

Fatalists say that it is not possible to reform our current out-of-control sports culture. They say that the genie is out of the bottle and it is useless to even try to put it back in again. If we resign ourselves to this conclusion, then we must be prepared for more exploitation and abuse of our young athletes, more pressure for athletic achievement and winning, more incidents of academic corruption and hypocrisy in our institutions of higher learning, more usage of performance-enhancing drugs, more cases of self-absorbed athletes and abusive parents and coaches, more incidents of burnout, overtraining, and sports injuries, more unethical and unbalanced sports reporting, and more unequal sports opportunities.

My purpose in authoring *Reforming Sports Before the Clock Runs Out* and its more extensive companion work *Crisis on Our Playing Fields* was to convince the public, especially parents of upcoming athletes, that there is a major problem in our sports culture. We can't hide our heads in the sand about it any longer and say that it does not exist. We can't continue to ignore it because soon it may be too late to recover from the negative onslaught of the dark side of sports.

The clock is running and the problems faced by our young athletes at all levels of preprofessional sports have reached crisis proportions, threatening the integrity of sports and the young athletes who want to have positive experiences as participants. The crisis on our athletic playing fields will continue until the time comes when we have the wisdom and inner fortitude to recognize failed policy, reform sports, and return our athletes to a more rational athletic landscape. The reform measures advanced in this book, as well as those advanced by others before me, must be taken seriously if we are to reverse the dangerous and often negative culture of sports that envelopes us today. The rewards for making changes to an out-of-control sports bandwagon are considerable. What hangs in the balance are countless young people who should be learning that sports represent only a small dimension of their development and certainly not one that will determine their longterm health, happiness, and productivity. Those of us in the field of sports reform are determined to see that day finally arrive.

EPILOGUE

For the better part of five years, I have worked on *Reforming Sports Before the Clock Runs Out* and its companion volume, *Crisis on Our Playing Fields*. My daily routine was simple. I spent considerable time each day reading every book that I could get my hands on that dealt with sports reform. I also spent time each day reading the sports sections of a wide number of national newspapers on sportspages.com. I separated articles into 10 piles on a table in my home office, with each pile corresponding to one of the major problem areas of pre-professional sports. The small piles quickly turned into mountains. The volume of information I collected and read in this area was staggering by any standards of measurement. This simple fact alone—that so much is written on how bad things have become—is, in and of itself, an indictment of how terribly distorted our sports culture has become.

The negative culture of sports seems to be in our faces almost seven days a week and 24 hours a day. As I make final revisions on these two volumes, our sports culture is hemorrhaging once again. Let me mention a few of the many sports news items that have recently competed for national attention. As you will see, many are strikingly similar to the sports experiences I have reported on in this volume.

- In the past few months, academic fraud scandals have rocked intercollegiate sports. At Ohio State, Heisman trophy candidate Maurice Clarett was accused of receiving preferential treatment in the classroom because he was allowed to take a final exam by oral rather than a written test. Although Clarett was cleared of academic fraud, others in the class were not given the same option which is a fundamental violation of teaching ethics at any institution of higher learning. At Fresno State, a team statistician allegedly wrote papers for basketball players and was paid off by a sports agent who funneled money to the team's academic advisor. At the University of Georgia, an assistant coach who taught a course in the physical education department allegedly gave

267

credit to players even though they never attended. At URI, team managers allegedly wrote papers for players that were then typed by an athletic department assistant. And, in one of the worst cases of academic fraud in a long time, the St. Bonaventure president allegedly approved the transfer of a junior college basketball player from a community college even though he knew the student only possessed a certificate in welding. Coaches and college presidents have been fired in these scandals and seasons have been forfeited and/or terminated prematurely. These schools have either imposed sanctions on themselves and/or are awaiting news about their status following NCAA investigations.

- Graduation rates at big-time colleges and universities are still abysmal. A recent report shows that the four top seeded teams in the NCAA Final Four tournament had zero percent graduation rates for their male basketball players. The NCAA has proposed a package of incentives and disincentives that will tie graduation rates to NCAA revenue, postseason play, and scholarships. Skeptics of the plan suggest that it will never receive the necessary votes for passage since most big-time colleges and universities will not want to risk revenues for higher academic standards. However, the hypocrisy evident in college athletics is finally starting to have an impact on the general public. In a recent survey of public opinion conducted by the *Chronicle of Higher Education*, three-quarters of the respondents said that athletes "are not held to the same academic performance standards as other students," and two-thirds said that "four-year colleges and universities place too much emphasis on athletics."

- The elevated importance of athletics even at academically elite colleges and universities increasingly is being called into question. In their recent book *Reclaiming the Game: College Sports and Educational Values*, William Bowen and Sarah Levin report that two-thirds of small-college football, basketball, and hockey players finished in the bottom third of the class and more than a quarter finished in the bottom 10th.

- Issues of commercialism still plague preprofessional sports. Some college coaches and administrators are beginning to speak out about the length and timing of the basketball season. Increasingly, schedules are built around television contracts. Year end tournaments, which are huge cash cows for conferences, are increasingly taking students away from the classroom and examination periods for longer and longer periods of time. The NCAA has insisted that college athletes are amateurs when in fact they are professional entertainers in a multibillion-dollar industry. By putting a cap on room, board, tuition, and fees, the NCAA acts as a cartel by controlling salaries. The magazine *Business Week* recently voted the NCAA as the "best monopoly in America." It beat out OPEC, the U.S. Postal Service, and Microsoft. Because of the way that college athletes are exploited, two states, Oklahoma and Nebraska, recently have proposed legislation to have college football players paid for their services. Finally, in a blatant money-making move, the Atlantic Coast Conference raided the Big East Conference by issuing invitations to Miami, Virginia Tech, and Boston College to join their athletic conference. Not to be outdone, the Big East did the same thing by inviting DePaul, Marquette, Louisville, Cincinnati and Southern Florida to join their conference. These moves are all about greed and the ability to attract more TV dollars from the Northeast market. It has nothing to do with helping athletes to become better students. In fact, it will impede academic progress since it will result in more time out of the classroom due to additional costly and far flung travel.

- Controversy continues to surround the area of performance-enhancing drugs and supplements. A major league baseball pitcher dropped dead during spring training and the weight loss and performance-enhancing drug ephedra has been implicated. Also, major college athletes at the University of Maine and the University of Texas are being investigated for illegal possession of anabolic steroids, syringes, and prescription-drug bottles. Also, a recent study shows that chromium picolainate, a popular supplement taken by athletes to trim fat and build muscle, could cause sterility in a user's children and grandchildren. Finally, in perhaps the biggest drug scandal of any we have ever witnessed in sports, the designer anabolic steroid, tetrahydrogestrinone (THG), was produced in a San Francisco area laboratory and was routinely used by elite athletes. Upon reassessment of urine samples, many top athletes are testing positive for this previously unknown steroid. This development threatens to further undermine the integrity and credibility of many of our top athletes in a variety of different sports.

- The threat of sports gambling continues to be a focus in collegiate sports. A quarterback at Florida State is being investigated for his problem gambling behavior. Though all the facts have not yet emerged, some are suggesting that he may have bet on his own games and may have thrown a game he played in. Also, according to the results of a University of Michigan survey on collegiate sports gambling, more than 45 percent of male collegiate football and basketball athletes admit to betting on sports events, despite NCAA regulations prohibiting it. More than 5 percent of male student-athletes admitted to providing inside information for gambling purposes, bet on a game in which they participated, or accepted money for performing poorly in a contest. In another survey conducted by the University of Michigan, researchers found that 40 percent of division I-A football and basketball officials said that they had bet on sports and 22.9 percent had wagered on the NCAA basketball tournament. The authors concluded that "It is increasingly likely that some intercollegiate contests are not being legitimately contested." Lastly, some recent studies by the Paul Robeson Research Center for Academic and Athletic Prowess show that collegiate athletes do not know NCAA rules and do not believe that the organization represents their interests. Many feel exploited by their academic institution, overworked, undercompensated, and channeled into particular areas of study. This finding, in combination with the proliferation of sports gambling in general, suggest an ideal environment for new point shaving scandals to emerge in the future.

- The media continues to overhype and exploit young athletes. High school basketball player Lebron James, who was dubbed "The Chosen One" by *Sports Illustrated* and appeared on its cover as a high school junior, became a media traveling show in his senior year. His games were nationally televised by ESPN2 and his team traveled all over the country for games. His home games were moved to a larger arena that would seat more people, and ticket prices were hiked. Some of his games were broadcast on pay-per-view and his team received appearance fees for playing in some games. Because of the high ratings for Jame's games, ESPN is now considering the possibility of nationally televising a full slate of prep school contests in the future. Also, ESPN has recently ushered in a new era of over the top media reporting through its coverage of blue chip high school athletes announcing their college choices on live national television.

- Issues of sportsmanship, athlete and coach misbehavior, and violence continue to mar our sports culture. In a women's high school basketball game on Long Island, a player was punched in the face and knocked to the ground. Also, reports of blowout losses, some by more than 100 points, continue to plague high school basketball contests in some areas of the country, most notably in Michigan, Indiana, and Washington, D.C. Also, three high school football players from Mepham High School on Long Island, New York are alleged to have hazed three would-be freshman teammates at a preseason football camp. They used pine cones, golf balls, and a broomstick in the assault. Additionally, following several high profile federal law suits lodged by women who were allegedly raped by University of Colorado football players, the governor of Colorado and the Colorado Board of Regents is calling for an independent examination of allegations that the CU football program regularly enticed recruits with sex parties. Likewise, St. Johns University terminated one player and suspended several others for arranging to have sex with a prostitute in Pittsburgh following a Big East basketball game. Lastly, boorish baasketball coach Bob Knight of Texas Tech is in the news again for having bullied and verbally chastised the chancellor of the school in public in a grocery store.
- Certain types of sports injuries continue to escalate and compromise young athletes. Recent reports indicate that over 20,000 female high school athletes and 10,000 female college athletes will have anterior cruciate ligament (ACL) surgery each year. The epidemic of knee injuries among female athletes keeps escalating in spite of programs emphasizing specialized prevention training.
- The impact of Title IX on athletics continues to be a hot button issue. The findings of the recent Title IX commission have been severely criticized for being biased by big-time athletic interests and unrepresentative of those involved with lower levels of sports such as Division III and high school interscholastic sports. Both proponents and opponents of Title IX are pessimistic about the final outcome of revisions to the legislation. Also, more schools are opting to drop sports in order to satisfy Title IX legislation. Recently Fairfield College eliminated football and men's hockey while Canisius, Siena, and St. John's dropped football.

- The health and fitness of our young people continues to be at risk while we focus more of our resources and attention on elite athletes. A recent report from the Centers for Disease Control and Prevention shows that nearly 13 percent of children ages 6 to 17 are officially overweight, and increasing numbers are suffering from Type II diabetes and other obesity-related illnesses. A recent surgeon general's report found that overweight children have a 70 percent chance of becoming overweight adults and susceptible to life threatening diseases such as heart disease and high blood pressure. In spite of these reports, physical education and fitness programs are continuing to be cut from school budgets while interscholastic school budgets remain the same or grow larger.

The familiar nature of the recent sports news above is disappointing if not altogether depressing. The message is clear: the beat goes on and it is business as usual in our runaway sports culture. The conclusion is still inescapable: there must be major sports reforms before it is too late. Our failure to act could result in further abuse and exploitation of our next generation of young athletes.

Although my love for sports and the athletes who play the games is being challenged, my hope for a better sports culture is not diminished. In spite of all that I have written, I do not envision a time when I will give up on organized sports, throw in the towel, and walk away from an institution that has so much promise. As an important adjunct in our lives, sports involvement can result in wonderful life-changing experiences for our young athletes. Learning about teamwork, sportsmanship, ethics, the benefits of hard work, and physical fitness are some of the desirable outcomes of athletic participation. Sports remind us of our strengths and weaknesses; they are indeed a metaphor for life.

I am reminded of the true meaning of sports when I think about my college roommate, Steve Freeh. A place kicker on the football team at Susquehanna University, Steve had the misfortune of losing his left arm to cancer while he was in high school. He accepted his disability and made up his mind to continue playing the sport he loved. With his options somewhat limited, he turned his passion for the game into being a place kicker for the team. Not once did I hear him complain; not once did he utter "why me?" Instead, with hard work and determination, he made himself into the best field goal kicker that he could possibly be. As a result, his leg won many a Susquehanna football game back in the late 1960s. Steve had a few professional tryouts but decided to continue his education instead. He received his doctorate in biology and now teaches at the State University of New York at Binghamton. He has continued his athletic interests by becoming a top-notch racquet ball player and a respectable golfer. Remarkably, he has done it all with just one arm.

I am further reminded of the benefit of sports when I think of a local athlete by the name of Matt Quatraro. I came to know Matt some years ago when he was a high school student in Bethlehem. A superb baseball player and all-around athlete, Matt went on to Old Dominion College, where he starred as a baseball player and student. In his senior year of 1996, he was both an academic and athletic all-American. Matt's love for the game of baseball has taken him to many different places. He played in the prestigious summer Cape Cod baseball league and has also played professionally in Australia. Winding his way through the minor league system with the Tampa Bay Devil Rays, he has gone from rookie league baseball in Butte, Montana, to single A ball in St. Petersburg, Florida, to double A in Orlando, Florida, to triple A in Durham, North Carolina. Presently playing triple A baseball for the New York Yankees in Columbus, Ohio, Matt is ready for another season in which he hopes to realize his dreams. His journey has been derailed numerous times by injury. He fractured his wrist a number of times and missed parts of three seasons. He also endured a season-ending injury to his elbow, which required sophisticated surgery to repair his medial collateral ligament in his throwing arm. In spite of these setbacks, Matt, now 29, has persisted. He has kept his eye on the prize—a chance at the major leagues.

So, when I think of all the negative things that happen in athletics these days, I remind myself of what sports sometimes can do for us when we have the real meaning of the games as our number 1 goal. Steve Freeh taught us that sports are about overcoming hardship and focusing your attention on what you can do and not on what you can't do in your life. He reminds us all that anything and everything is possible in sports; you just have to have the heart of a champion. And Matt Quatraro has taught us that you must follow your dreams in spite of the odds that are stacked against you. You can't give up the fight for what you love because it is the love of the game that will ultimately carry you to the top.

My personal decision to get involved in sports reform has not been an easy one. Having sat on the outside looking in for many years, I believe that some of my actions (and mostly inactions) could have contributed in a small way to our continuing problems. My commitments now are fully front and center; I wish to be an activist and do something constructive about a crisis that seems to escalate with each passing day.

My work in the area of sports reform is only beginning. The NISR is in its infancy but already I am devoting much of my time and energy to its development. The journey I continue to take is not remotely near its completion but at least I can begin to see the shape of things to come and what the future might look like.

Through the NISR, it is my personal goal to carry my message to as many groups of people as I can. I want every parent and every prepro-fessional sports entity in our country to understand what is happening to our athletes and what the consequences are for failure to reform a sys-tem that has evolved into a monster. This will take time, energy, and resources but it is a task that must be completed before it is too late.

It is my dream that much of what was written in *Reforming Sports Before the Clock Runs Out* and *Crisis on Our Playing Fields* will someday be obsolete and there will be a better sports culture in place for our young athletes. The idealized sports environment that I envision will be one in which athletics assumes its proper place in a culture that values intel-lectual accomplishment as much as physical prowess. It will also be a culture in which athletes are not abused, exploited, and pressured to cheat. It will instead be one where ethics, personal responsibility, fair play, safe and healthy competition, sportsmanship, teamwork, and racial and gender equality and tolerance will be promoted. If this is ever achieved, and we return to the values on which sports were founded, then there will be no need for organizations like the NISR.

The question I ask myself daily is: Can anyone make a difference in our present runaway sports culture? My answer to that question is a resounding "yes!" Our nation is filled with well-intentioned, commit-ted, sports-loving people who want to make things better for our young athletes. By promoting reforms in countless community, state, regional, and national sports organizations, average citizens can be the instru-ments for change. All causes require this kind of grassroots effort and sports reform is no different. The alternative—inaction and continued apathy—will only hasten the growth of a negative sports system that is devouring everything in its path. Consequently, it is my sincere hope that many of you will seriously examine your own immediate sports environment, engage in "truth-telling" about what you experience, and answer the call for reform by joining me in a concerted effort to promote a better sports landscape for our young people.

November 2003

ESSENTIAL READING
IN SPORTS REFORM

Anderson, C. 2000. *Will You Still Love Me If I Don't Win*. Dallas: Taylor Publishing.

Benedict, J. 1997. *Public Heroes, Private Felons: Athletes and Crimes Against Women*, Boston, MA: Northeastern University Press.

———. 1999. *Pros and Cons: The Criminals Who Play in the NFL*. New York: Warner Books.

———. 2004. *Out of Bounds: Inside the NBA's Culture of Rape, Assault, and Drug Use*. NY: Harper-Collins.

Bigelow, B., T. Moroney, and L. Hall. 2001. *Just Let the Kids Play: How to Stop Other Adults from Ruining Your Child's Fun and Success in Youth Sports*. Deerfield Beach, FL: Health Communications, Inc.

Bissinger, H.G. 1990. *Friday Night Lights: A Town, a Team, a Dream*. Cambridge, MA: Da Capo Press.

Bowen, W.G., and S.A. Levin. 2003. *Reclaiming the Game: College Sports and Educational Values*. Princeton: Princeton University Press.

Bradley, B. 1998. *Values of the Game*. New York: Workman Publishing.

Byers, W. 1995. *Unsportsmanlike Conduct: Exploiting College Athletes*. Ann Arbor: University of Michigan Press.

Doyle, D., and R. Wolfe. (in press) *The Encyclopedia of Sports Parenting*. New York: Time Warner.

Duderstadt, J. 2000. *Intercollegiate Athletics and the American University: A University President's Perspective*. Ann Arbor: University of Michigan Press.

Engh, F. 1999. *Why Johnny Hates Sports: Why Organized Youth Sports are Failing Our Children and What We Can Do About It*. Garden City, NY: Avery Publishing.

Feinstein, J. 2000. *The Last Amateurs: Playing for Glory and Honor in Division I Basketball*. Boston: Little Brown and Company.

Ferguson, G. 2004. *Sports in America: Fascination and Blemishes*. Santa Fe, NM: Sunstone Press.

Fine, A., and M.L. Sachs. 1997. *The Total Sports Experinece for Kids: A Parents Guide to Success in Youth Sports*. South Bend: Diamond Communications, Inc.

Frey, D. 1996. *The Last Shot: City Streets, Basketball Dreams*. New York: Touchstone.

Furchtgott-Roth, D., and C. Stolba. 2001. *The Feminist Dilemma: When Success is Not Enough*. Washington: AEI Press.

Gavora, Jessica. 2002. *Tilting the Playing Field: Schools, Sports, Sex and Title IX*. San Francisco: Encounter Books.

Gerdy, J.R. 1997. *The Successful College Athletic Program: The New Standard*. Phoenix: Oryx Press.

———. 2000. *Sports in School: The Future of an Institution*. New York: Teachers College Press.

———. 2002. *Sports: The All-American Addiction*. Mississippi: University of Mississippi Press.

Goldman, B.P., J. Bush, and R. Klatz. 1987. *Death in the Locker Room: Steroids, Cocaine, and Sports*. Scottsdale: H.P. Books.

Hawkins, B. 2000. *The New Plantation: The Internal Colonization of Black Student Athletes*. Winterville: Sadiki Publishing.

Heywood, L. 1998. *Pretty Good for a Girl: A Memoir*. New York: The Free Press.

Isenberg, M. and R. Rhoads. 1999. *The Real Athletes Guide: How to Succeed in Sports, School, and Life*. Los Angeles: Athlete Network Press.

———. 2001. *The Student Athlete Survival Guide*. Camden: Ragged Mountain Press.

Janda, D.H. 2001. *The Awakening of a Surgeon: One Doctor's Journey to Fight the System and Empower Your Community*. Chelsea: Sleeping Bear Press.

Joravsky, B. 1996. *Hoop Dreams: A True Story of Hardship and Triumph*. New York: HarperTrade.

The Knight Commission. 2001. *A Call to Action: Reconnecting College Sports and Higher Education*. Miami, FL: Knight Foundation.

Kralovec, E. 2003. *Schools That Do Too Much: Wasting Time and Money in Schools and What We Can Do About it*. Boston: Beacon.

Kuchenbecker, S. 2000. *Raising Winners: A Parents Guide to Helping Kids Succeed On and Off the Playing Field*. New York: Random House.

Lancaster, S. 2002. *Fair Play: Making Organized Sports a Great Experience for Your Kids*. New York: Prentice Hall.

Lefkowitz, B. 1997. *Our Guys: The Glen Ridge Rape and the Secret Life of the Perfect Suburb*. New York: Vintage Books.

Llewellyn, Jack. 2001. *Let' em Play: What Parents, Coaches and Kids Need to Know about Youth Baseball*. Marietta: Longstreet Press.

Michener, J. 1976. *Sports in America*. New York: Random House.

Miracle, W.W., and C.R. Rees. 1994. *Lessons of the Locker Room: The Myth of School Sports*. Amherst: Prometheus.

Murphy, S. 1999. *The Cheers and the Tears: A Healthy Alternative to the Dark Side of Youth Sports Today*. San Francisco: Jossy-Bass.

Nuwer, H. 2003. *The Hazing Reader*. Bloomington, Indiana: Indiana University Press.

Porter, D. 2000. *Fixed: How Goodfellas Bought Boston College Basketball*. Dallas: Taylor Trade Publishing.

Porto, B. 2003. *A New Season: Using Title IX to Reform College Sports*. Westport, CT: Praeger Publishers.

Powell, R.A. 2003. *We Own This Game: A New Season in the Adult World of Youth Football*. New York: Atlantic Monthly Press.

Ryan, J. 1996. *Little Girls in Pretty Boxes: The Making and Breaking of Elite Gymnasts and Figure Skaters*. New York: Warner Books.

Sack, A.L., and E.J. Staurowsky. 1998. *College Athletes for Hire: The Evolution and Legacy of the NCAA's Amateur Myth*. Westport, CT: Praeger Publishing.

Sheehy, H. 2002. *Raising a Team Player*. North Adams: Storey Books.

Sheehan, R. 1997. *Keeping Score: The Economics of Big-Time Sports*. South Bend: Diamond.

Shulman, J.L., and W.G. Bowen. 2001. *The Game of Life: College Sports and Educational Values*. Princeton: Princeton University Press.

Sperber, M. 1990. *College Sports, Inc.: The Athletic Department vs The University*. New York: Holt.

———. 2000. *Beer and Circus: How Big-Time Sports is Crippling Undergraduate Education*. New York: Holt.

Svare, B. in press. *Crisis on Our Playing Fields: What Everyone Should Know About Our Out of Control Sports Culture and What We Can Do to Change it*. Delmar: Sports Reform Press.

Telander, R. 1989. *The One Hundred Yard Lie: The Corruption of College Football and What We Can Do to Stop it*. New York: Simon and Schuster.

Thelin, J.R. 1996. *Games Colleges Play: Scandal and Reform in Intercollegiate Athletics*. Baltimore: Johns Hopkins University Press.

Thompson, J. 1995. *Positive Coaching: Building Character and Self-Esteem Through Sports*. Portola Valley: Warde Publishers.

———. 2003. *The Double-Goal Coach: Positive Coaching Tools for Parents and Coaches to Honor the Game and Develop Winners in Sports and Life*. New York: Harpers Resource.

Tofler, I., and T.F DiGeronimo. 2000. *Keeping Your Kids Out Front Without Kicking Them from Behind: How to Nurture High Achieving Athletes, Scholars, and Performing Artists*. San Francisco: Jossey-Bass.

Toma, D. J. 2003. *Football U: Spectator Sports in the Life of the American University*. Ann Arbor: University of Michigan Press.

Ungerleider, S. 2001. *Faust's Gold: Inside the East German Doping Machine*. New York: St. Martin.

Wetzel, D., and D. Yaeger. 1999. *Sole Influence: Basketball, Corporate Greed, and the Corruption of America's Youth*. New York: Warner.

Wexler, A., and M. Isenberg. 2002. *The Money Sucker Machine: The Truth About Gambling and How It Destroys Lives*. Los Angeles: A-Game.

Yesalis, C.E., and V.S. Cowart. 1998. *The Steroids Game: An Expert's Inside Look at Anabolic Steroid Use in Sports*. Champaign: Human Kinetics.

Zimbalist, A. 1999. *Unpaid Professionals: Commercialism and Conflict in Big-Time College Sports*. Princeton: Princeton University Press.

ABOUT THE AUTHOR

Dr. Bruce Svare grew up in Milford, New Hampshire, and Gardner, Massachusetts, where his love for sports was nurtured by his father and friends. Like many New England youngsters at the time, he played basketball, football, and baseball and learned to love the Red Sox, Bruins, Celtics, and New York Giants. He received his bachelor of arts degree in psychology from Susquehanna University, his master's degree in psychology from Bucknell University and his doctorate in biopsychology from Rutgers University. After receiving his Ph.D., he completed a National Institute of Health postdoctoral fellowship at the Worcester Foundation for Experimental Biology in Shrewsbury, Massachusetts. He currently is a professor of psychology at the State University of New York (SUNY) at Albany, where he teaches and conducts research in the graduate and undergraduate behavioral neuroscience program.

He has specialized in the study of hormonal effects on behavior and most recently has been developing models for assessing the addiction potential of performance-enhancing drugs such as anabolic steroids. His research has been supported by the National Institute of Drug Abuse (NIDA), the National Institute of Mental Health (NIMH), the National Science Foundation (NSF), the National Institute of Aging (NIA), and the Harry Frank Guggenheim Foundation. A fellow of the American Psychological Association (APA) and the American Psychological Society (APS), he also holds membership in the Society for Neuroscience (SFN), the Society for Behavioral Neuroendocrinology (SBN), the Association for the Advancement of Sport Psychology (AASP), the North American Society for the Sociology of Sport (NASSS), the International Society of Sport Psychology (ISSP), and the Drake Group, The National Alliance for College Athletic Reform. He has authored 70 scientific papers in such scholarly journals as *Nature, Psychoneuroendocrinology, Behavioral Neuroscience, Hormones and Behavior, Developmental Psychobiology, Biology of Reproduction, Physiology and Behavior, Behavioral and Neural Biology*, and *Neuroscience and Biobehavioral Reviews*. He has also authored a number of book chapters and edited books including the frequently cited volume, *Hormones and Aggressive Behavior*.

The author has been actively involved in many different sports organizations over the past 25 years and is the founder and current director of the National Institute for Sports Reform (NISR). He was the founder and past president of the Bethlehem Basketball Club, the founder and current president of the Capital District Youth Basketball League, the founder and past president of the Albany City Rocks AAU basketball club, and the past basketball chair of the Adirondack region of the AAU. He has coached basketball from the youth to the elite amateur level and has also coached Little League and Babe Ruth Baseball, Pop Warner Football, and youth soccer. In recognition of his service to youth sports, he was named citizen of the year in 1991 in his community of Bethlehem, New York, where he resides with his wife Maryalice and his two sons, John and Mark. *Crisis on Our Playing Fields: What Everyone Should Know About Our Out-of-Control Sports Culture and What We Can Do to Change It* and *Reforming Sports Before the Clock Runs Out: One Man's Journey Through Our Runaway Sports Culture* are the first books he has authored for a general audience.

Appendix I

The National Institute for Sports Reform

Achieving reform of our runaway sports culture will not be easy. Indeed, four important events must occur before we can achieve true reforms that will benefit our young athletes. First, there must be a coalition of all the various reform groups from the youth level up to the collegiate level such that there is a centralized, strong voice advocating change. Second, in combination with a unified coalition, there must be a grassroots movement in which parents and athletes demand changes and become more actively involved in the development and implementation of reform measures. Third, there must be an active and continuing dialogue between representatives of national sports organizations and representatives of sports reforms groups. Fourth, there must be an independent organization that can serve as a think tank, research center, information clearing house, consultant, and advocate for sports reform.

To accomplish the above objectives, the National Institute for Sports Reform (NISR) was established in 2003. The NISR is a coalition of concerned Americans seeking to improve the athletic and educational experiences of our young people. The NISR is a nonprofit (501)(3)c organization whose mission is fivefold: to end the exploitation and abuse of youth, scholastic, amateur, and collegiate athletes; to promote safe and healthy sports activities for all individuals regardless of age, race, gender, religious background, socioeconomic status, or level of physical proficiency; to develop resources to aid individual researchers and institutions who are studying sports reform; to serve as a think tank, clearing house, and research center on sports reform issues; to educate the public regarding important reforms that are needed to improve the academic and athletic experiences of those who compete in sports; to bring under one umbrella organization the many different groups that are actively seeking to improve and reform sports in the

United States; and to promote discussion between national sports organizations and sports reform groups.

The specific goals of the institute are to end the academic corruption that routinely occurs in college and scholastic sports; curtail the growing commercialization of interscholastic and intercollegiate sports; end the inappropriate and overemphasized media coverage of young athletes; stop sports gambling and the reporting of point spread information for interscholastic and intercollegiate athletic contests; end the utilization of performance-enhancing drugs at all levels of athletic competition; end the win-at-all-costs attitude that pervades sports at the preprofessional level; reduce the growing trend of early professionalization and specialization of very young athletes; curtail the proliferation of poor sportsmanship, violence, unethical conduct, and misbehavior of players, coaches, and fans; and end the escalating incidence of burnout, overtraining, and sports injuries among athletes.

The NISR has established a faculty fellow and scholars program that will promote some of the main functions of the institute. Faculty fellows and scholars consist of distinguished individuals who rank among America's foremost experts in the field of sports reform. The NISR faculty fellows and scholars testify before congressional committees and private foundations, provide expert consultation to government and nongovernment agencies including sports governing bodies, conduct research on sports reform issues, and author position papers and white papers on critical areas of sports reform.

The institute also supports a biannual conference in which participants from around the country gather to discuss sports reform issues of national importance. Another purpose of the biannual conference is to honor at least one individual whose contributions to the sports reform movement have been particularly noteworthy.

As part of its research and education mission, the institute also supports a twice yearly, peer-reviewed scholarly publication entitled the *Journal of Sports Reform*. We welcome manuscripts for consideration that address issues surrounding the reform of sports in the United States. Submission should contribute to the public debate regarding the reform of youth, scholastic, amateur, and collegiate sports in the United States. Please contact NISR or our web site (www.nisr.org) for publication guidelines.

Another purpose of the institute is to sponsor an essay contest each year in which we ask the public to write to us regarding their ideas for sports reform. The contest is held in conjunction with National Sports

Reform Month in which the NISR strives to put the focus on needed sports reforms and the core values of sports such as participation, fitness, health, fairness, ethics, sportsmanship, and fair play. Contact the National Institute for Sports Reform (NISR) through our web site (www.nisr.org) for more information about both of these programs.

Finally, through an internet based survey, the institute provides an annual report card on the general health of the American sports culture. This is done by assessing the public's perception of the major problem areas in our sports landscape. The report card is made available to the public during National Sports Reform Month.

The institute operates entirely through tax-deductible contributions from individuals, foundations and corporations, and by grants from public and private agencies. Yearly membership in the institute entitles the individual to receive the *Journal of Sports Reform*. A biweekly online publication entitled *Sports Reformers' News* is free by registering on our web site at www.nisr.org.

NISR is the only organization in the United States that is specifically devoted to studying and promoting needed sports reform at the preprofessional level. Because of this unique role, the institute encourages a diversity of opinions and ideas from individuals in all walks of life. From educators and other professionals, to athletes, coaches, parents, fans, media representatives, and the average layperson, NISR needs the input and action of all people to study and promote change in our sports culture.

A portion of the proceeds from the sale of *Crisis on Our Playing Fields* and *Reforming Sports Before the Clock Runs Out* will be donated to NISR.

For additional information, contact the Director, The National Institute for Sports Reform, PO Box 128, Selkirk, New York 12158 or log on to our web address at www.nisr.org.

Appendix II

Sports Reform Resources

The Drake Group-National Alliance for College Athletic Reform (NAFCAR)
215 Foster Drive
Des Moines, Iowa
50312–2539
www.blommington.in.us/~nafcar/index.html

The Drake Group is a faculty reform organization working to restore and defend academic integrity in college sports. The members of this national organization believe that it is their ethical obligation to confront the sports corruption that occurs on their respective campuses and clean up college sports by taking back their classrooms.

College Sports Council (CSC)
PO Box 53356
Washington, D.C. 20009–9356
www.savingsports.org

A national coalition of sports associations that are devoted to the promotion of the student athlete experience, the CSC is serving as the voice of underrepresented college sports programs. The council works with coaches, associations, and alumni groups to preserve, promote, and expand opportunities for both male and female college athletes.

National Alliance for Youth Sports (NAYS)
2050 Vista Parkway
West Palm Beach, Florida 33411
www.nays.org

The alliance believes that youth sports can help to develop character traits and values but only if the adults that are in charge (parents, coaches, administrators) have proper training and information. NAYS has become the nation's leading youth sports educator and advocate with nine national programs that educate volunteer coaches, parents, youth sport program administrators, and officials about their roles and responsibilities in the context of youth sports.

Institute for International Sport (IIS)
PO Box 1710
Kingston, Rhode Island 02881–1710
www.internationalsport.com

The goals of IIS are to promote and improve relationships among nations, particularly those experiencing internal conflict, encourage individual growth and the development of human potential in young scholars throughout the world, develop global awareness in future world leaders, promote ethical behavior and good sportsmanship on an international basis, and facilitate among institute alumni a humanitarian approach in their actions as they develop as world leaders. The primary vehicle for the IIS to accomplish its mission is through the World Scholar-Athlete games and National Sportsmanship Day.

Sports Ethics Institute (SEI)
PO Box 1217
Laurel, Maryland 20725
www.sportsethicsinstitute.org

The mission of the SEI is to foster good conduct in sports and to elevate sports so as to endure a legacy of goodness for future generations. The objectives of SEI are to raise and explore ethical issues in sport, to provide opportunities for people to discover and examine the ethical dimensions of sport, to develop programs and activities that educate others on ethics in sports, and to create forums for the open expression and discussion of diverse sports ethics.

Institute for Preventative Sports Medicine (IPSM)
PO Box 7302
Ann Arbor, Michigan 48107
www.ipsm.org

The institute is a research organization dedicated to finding effective and practical ways to reduce sports injuries and speed rehabilitation of injured athletes. The institute has sought to achieve this goal by way of research and development of protective equipment, rules modifications in sports, changes in conditioning practices and injury treatment techniques, and instructional methodology.

Collegiate Athletes Coalition (CAC)
4740 Kester Ave. #24
Sherman Oaks, California 91403
www.cacnow.org

The goals of CAC are to achieve greater commitment to the education of college athletes so as to improve graduation rates, obtain year-round health coverage for sports-related injuries, obtain increased life insurance policies for
student-athletes, obtain increased monthly stipends for student-athletes, and
obtain an elimination of off-season salary caps.

National Student-Athletes Rights Movement
2006 Kasold
Lawrence, Kansas 66047
www.studentathletesrights.org

This organization is seeking to improve the welfare of collegiate student-
athletes by advocating a bill of rights. The most important goal of this organization is to restore the welfare of student athletes to their rightful place as the
first priority of the NCAA.

National Coalition Against Violent Athletes (NCAVA)
P.O. Box 620453
Littleton, Colorado 80162
www.ncava.org

The mission of the NCAVA is to promote positive character development in
athletes, to educate coaches, management, and the public on violence prevention and assessment, to be a voice for victims when they are reluctant to talk to
the media, to pressure the governing bodies of sports to take action against violent athletes, to track and release athlete charges and convictions, to educate
victims on prevention and the process of forcing accountability, to give support
to victims, and to endure the rights of victims.

Rutgers 1000
Box 410
Palmer Square Station
Princeton, NJ 08542
http://members.aol.com/rutg1000/colonial.htm

This organization is focused on seeking changes in the intercollegiate sports
environment at Rutgers University. Because members of the organization

believe that athletics has eroded the intellectual standards at the university, they believe that Rutgers would be a better fit both academically and athletically in the Patriot League as opposed to the Big East.

Knight Commission on Intercollegiate Athletics
John S. and James L. Knight Foundation
One Biscayne Tower
Suite 3800
2 South Biscayne Boulevard
Miami, Florida 33131–1803
www.knightfdn.org

The Knight Foundation has funded two separate commissions, one in 1991 and the most recent in 2001, to examine the athletic abuses that threaten the integrity of higher education. The recommendations in both reports are noteworthy since they advocate better institutional and presidential control, reduced commercialism, and greater academic integrity.

The New England Small College Athletic Conference (NESCAC)
86–88 Vernon St.
Trinity College
Hartford, Connecticut 06106
www.nescac.com

A model for the way in which collegiate athletics and academics can be blended to form a positive partnership, NESCAC schools play in the NCAA Division III and are some of the most prestigious academic colleges in the country. There are no athletic scholarships and financial aid is need-based. Athletics are kept in proper perspective and are subordinate to academic achievement.

The Patriot League
3773 Corporate Parkway
Suite 190
Center Valley, PA 18034
http://patriotleague.ocsn.com/

This northeast collegiate athletic league consists of prestigious Division I colleges and universities that place academics before athletics. Schools in this conference regularly compete successfully at the highest levels of competition even though many do not give athletic scholarships. The Patriot League is a good example of how rigorous academic training can successively coexist with intercollegiate athletics.

The Ivy League
Council of Ivy Group Presidents
330 Alexander St.
Princeton, NJ 08544
www.ivyleaguesports.com

The most prestigious academic institutions in the United States belong to the Ivy League and their athletic teams regularly compete at a very high level in the NCAA Division I. The League is another excellent model for how sports can succeed without compromising academic quality.

The Center for Study of Sport in Society
360 Huntington Ave.
Suite 161 CP
Boston, Massachusetts 02115–5000
www.sportinsociety.org

Housed at Northeastern University, the center aims to increase awareness of sports and its relation to society and to develop programs that identify problems, offer solutions, and promote the benefits of sport.

The Institute for Diversity and Ethics in Sport
University of Central Florida
P.O. Box 161400
Orlando, Florida 32816–1400
www.bus.ucf.edu/sport

Established at the University of Central Florida, the institute focuses on publishing the racial and gender report card, which is an annual assessment of racial and gender hiring practices of major professional sports, Olympic, and collegiate sports. The institute also monitors some of the critical ethical issues in collegiate and professional sports.

The Institute for Study of Youth Sports (YSI)
Department of Kinesiology
2131M Sports Circle Building
Michigan State University
East Lansing, Michigan 48824–1049
www.ed-web3.educ.msu.edu/ysi/

Formed at Michigan State University, the mission of the institute is to research the benefits and detriments of participation in youth athletics. The institute produces educational materials and educational programs for parents, coaches, officials and administrators.

The Paul Robeson Research Center for Academic and Athletic Prowess
University of Michigan
Ann Arbor, Michigan 48109–2214
www.umich.edu/~paulball/

Established at the University of Michigan, the goals of the center are to provide research and analysis of issues that affect African American student-athletes. The center also strives to promote the ideal that an athlete's lifetime career success can best be achieved by way of educational attainment.

The Woman's Sports Foundation
Eisenhower Park
East Meadow, New York 11554
www.womensportsfoundation.org

The principal goals of the foundation are to be recognized as the foremost worldwide resource and advocate for girls and woman in sports, to educate the public about female participation and gender equality in sports, and to increase leadership and sports and fitness participation among women.

The Citizenship Though Sports Alliance (CTSA)
23500 West 105th St.
P.O. Box 1325
Olathe, KS 66051–1325
www.sportsmanship.org

The alliance was created out of a concern for the decline of sportsmanship and ethical conduct and a rise in a win-at-all-costs attitude in athletics. The organization seeks to promote a sports culture that values learning respect for self, other, and the game itself.

The Mendelson Center for Sports, Character and Community
University of Notre Dame
10 IEI Building
Notre Dame, Indiana 46556
www.nd.edu/~cscc/

Established at the University of Notre Dame, the primary goal of the center is to bring social scientists and sports practitioners together in order to build character and promote civic responsibility through sports.

The Positive Coaching Alliance (PAC)
Department of Athletics
Stanford University
Stanford, California 94305–6150
www.positivecoach.org

Housed at Stanford University, the principal mission of the alliance is to create a positive culture in which kids love to play a particular sport. This is done by creating an environment in which players, coaches, and parents respect each other and honor the games they play.

The Student Athlete Survival Guide
A-Game
P.O. Box 34867
Los Angeles, CA 90034
www.A-Game.com

The guide and A-Game are designed to help high school and college athletes and parents navigate through scholastic and collegiate athletics. This is done by giving evidence of both good and bad decisions that athletes have made in the past.

P.E. 4 Life
1150 17th St. NW Suite 407
Washington, D.C. 20036
www.PE4LIFE.org

This organization is an advocacy group that serves as a collective voice for promoting the renewal of physical education programs in the United States. The mission of the organization is to establish daily physical education classes in all schools and to focus specifically on fitness activities that can be used throughout one's life.

Sports Leadership Institute
Adelphi University
1 South Ave.
Garden City, New York 11530
www.adelphi.edu/communityservices/sli/background.html

The mission of this institute is to implement leadership programs in high schools and elementary schools. In particular the institute seeks to stimulate student leadership primarily in the areas of substance abuse prevention, bullying, teasing, and sportsmanship.

Coalition on Intercollegiate Athletics
Indiana University
Bloomington, Indiana 47405–7000
http://www.iub.edu/~bfc/COIA/COIA.html

The goal of this group is to advocate for reform of intercollegiate athletics. It was created by collegiate faculty senate leaders at Bowl Championship Series conference schools.

Josephson Institute of Ethics
9841 Airport Boulevard
Suite 300
Los Angeles, CA 90045
http://www.charactercounts.org/

The institute is a nonprofit, nonpartisan, nonsectarian character education framework that teaches the six pillars of character: trustworthiness, respect, responsibility, fairness, caring, and citizenship. Thousands of schools, community groups, and nonprofit organizations comprise the character counts coalition. A special emphasis has been placed upon teaching the six pillars of character to young athletes.

INDEX

Abba, Chuck Jr., *ix*, 177–178
Abba, Chuck Sr., 92, 177
Academic corruption: exploitation and, 231–235; in college, *xvi-xvii*, 177–182, 183–189, 267–268; in high school, 63, 234
Ali, Muhammed, 216
Albany City Rocks, 54, 67–70, 141
Albany Times-Union, 45, 75–76, 97, 137–139, 141–142, 158, 170–171, 173, 204
Amateur Athletic Union (AAU): basketball and 67–70; failures of, 21, 54; growth of, 9
Amherst College, 177–178
America East Conference, 203
American sports: history of, 5–11; media Coverage of 6, 10; pickup games and, 2
Anabolic steroids: and addiction potential, 153; and nandrolone, 155; and Steve Courson, 153–155; and widespread usage in sports, 238–240
Anderson, Marty, 23
Anterior cruciate ligament (ACL) injuries, 128–131, 271
Aplin, Nick, *x*, 215–216, 218
Arena Football League (AFL), 9
Athlete misbehavior/entitlement, *xvii*, 75–78, 170–175, 240–242, 270–271
Athletic scholarships: pressure on academic and social life, 159–162; pressure to obtain, 26–27, 42, 61–65; pressure to retain, 159–161, 181, 233; probability of obtaining, 231
Australia: academic performance compared to Americans, 226; Australian Institute of Sports (AIS), 221, 224; Australian Sports Commission (ASC), 221; comparison to American sports, 223–225; Disability Sports Program, 221; discovery of, 219–220; economy of, 220–221; government in, 220; Indigenous Sports Program, 221; National Sporting Organizations, 222;

Olympics in, 221–222, sports in, 220–227; sports in colleges, 222; Women in Sports Program, 221
Averill Park, NY, and hazing 76–78

Baseball Weekly, 10
Battle, Sean, *ix*
Beaton, Scott, 203
Beekman, Josh, 138–140
Benedict, Jeff, 242
Bensel-Meyers, Linda, *x, xi*, 183–189
Berkow, Ira, 169, 234
Bethlehem, NY, 22, 84, 100
Bethlehem Basketball Club, 47
Bethlehem Central School District: athletic budget and, 100–103; football team and, 90–93; National Honor Society and, 99; national recognition and, 100; sports hall of fame and, 95–97; Suburban Council rules and, 84–89
Bianchi, Vince, 47
Big East Conference, 269
Bigelow, Bob, *ii, ix, x*, 2, 51, 231, 243, 250
Bird, Sue, 163
Bishop, Joe, 25
Blatnick, Jeff, 97
Blouin, Ross, 26
Boeheim, Jim, 68, 142
Bonds, Bobby, 242
Borzykowski, Mark *ix*
Borzykowski, Mort, *ix*
Borzykowski, Ross, *ix*
Boston Amateur Basketball Club (BABC), 67–70
Boston Celtics, 14, 19–20
Boston College, 158, 162, 269
Boston Globe, 10, 96
Boucher, Bob, 26
Bowen, William, 233, 235, 250
Bradley, Bill 42
Braverman, Jesse, 84–89
Bresnahan, Leo *ix*
Briggs, Kenneth, 97

Brookings Institute, 252
Brown, Dale, *x*
Brown, Ted, 21
Burden, Luther "Ticky", 97–98
Burian, Jarka, 202
Burnett, Josh, *ix*
Burnout, 132–137
Business Week, 269
Byers, Walter, 235, 250

Calhoun, Jim, 68
Calipari, John 178
Camby, Marcus, 178–179
Canisius College, 271
Cape Cod Baseball League, 272
Capeless, Rich, *ix*
Capital District Sports Hall of Fame, 97
Capital District Youth Basketball League
    (CDYBL): history and development
    of, 47–60; playing time issues in,
    56–57; playoffs in, 57; problem coaches
    in, 48–50; recreational leagues and, 58;
    teaching basic skills in, 51–53, 55
Carter, Joe, 198
Caruso, Richard, 197–199
Cash, Swin 163
Center for Disease Control and Prevention
    (CDCP), 271
Center for Economic Growth (CEG), 204
Center for the Study of Sport in Society, 289
Chromium picolainate, 269
Cincinnatti, University of, 179, 269
Cioffi, Lou, 77
Citizenship Through Sports Alliance
    (CTSA), 290
Cleary, Bill, 208, 234–235
Club system of sports: adoption of in the
    US, 102–103, 254; in Australia,
    220–227
Coaching: misbehavior of, 196–199, 271;
    philosophy during the 50s and 60s,
    23–28; philosophy during 90s, 63;
    qualifications for, 88; salaries in
    colleges, 236
Coalition on Intercollegiate Athletics
    (COIA), 292
Colorado, University of, 271
College sports, history of, 6
College Sports Council (CSC), 285
Collegiate Athletes Coalition (CAC), 287
Collegiate athlete recruiting, 61–66, 67–70,
    138–144

Colorado Rockies, 193
Commercialism: in collegiate sports,
    177–182, 189, 235–237, 268–269; in
    high school sports, 90–93, 236; myths
    regarding effects of athletics on
    educational budgets, 236
Connecticut, University of, 128, 179
Conroy, Pat, *vi*
Conway, Dan, *ix*, 192–193
Conway, Nicole, *x*, 157–165
Corrigan, Lilly, 128–130
Courson, Steve, *x*, 153–155
Cousy, Bob, 20
Cowan, George, 246
Cowart, Virginia, 73, 106, 240
Crossman, Herb, 171
Cushing, Bill, *ix*
Cushing, Will, *ix*
Czajka, Corey, *ix*
Czajka, John, *x*, 130–131

D'Agostino, Joe, 47
Dale City Cowboys, 45
D'Amato, Cus, 97
D'Angelo, Joe, *ix*
Davies, Brian, *x*
Davis, Erin, 132–137
Division I college sports: and academic
    corruption, 178–179; and moving up
    from Division III, 201–206
Division III college sports: and academic
    integrity, 177–182; and declining
    academic standards, 234–235, 269
Dean, Willie, *x*
Deas, Devonaire, 170–175
DelGiacco, Mike, *x*
den Boer, David, *xi*
den Boer, Maria, *xi*
Denver, University of, 188
Depaul University, 269
Dicicco, Tony, *x*
Disneyworld, and Pop Warner
    Championships, 44–46
Doellefeld, Jim, 201
Doran, Steve, *x*
Dowling, William, 169
Downing, Jason, 75
Doyle, Dan, *x*, 249
Drake Group, 180–181, 232, 285
Dubzinski, Walter, 23
Ducket, Rich, 173
Duderstadt, James, 235, 250

Dufort, Bob, 26
Duke University, 179
Duncan, Bob, 23

Early specialization/profesionalization, xvi, 61–65, 87, 132–137, 229–231.
Eaton, Walter, 82
Engh, Fred, *x*, 37, 231, 243, 250
Ephedra, 239, 269
Ericson, Jon, *ii, x, xvi*, 232–233
Erickson, Ray, 17
ESPN, 10, 184, 270

Fast-women.com, interview with Erin Davis, 133–135
Fairfield University, 271
Favre, Brett, 242
Feinstein, John, 168, 235, 240
Fergus Falls Daily Journal, 17
Fergus Falls, Minnesota, 16
Fergus Falls Red Sox, 17
Fiedler, Matt, *x*
Fine, Aubrey, 249
Fitness-based sports, *xvii*, 102–103
Florida State University, 173
Fonda-Fultonville, New York, and jock culture, 75–76
Footlocker Championships, 132
Ford, Bob, 203
Forth, Craig, 140–143
Freeh, Steve, 195, 272–273
Funding high school sports, 87
Furchtgott-Roth, Diana, 244

Gardner, Massachusetts, 21
Gardner High School, and sports hall of fame, 96–97
Gardner News, 23
Garrett, Jason, 196
Garrett, Jim, 196–199
Gavora, Jessica, 244
Gallagher, Seamus, *x*
Gearan, Jack, *x*
Gearan, Jay, *ix*
Gearan, Mark, *ix*, 97
Gearan, Mike, *x*
Gerber, Chris, *x*
Gerdy, John, *vi*, 3, 73, 168, 250
Gill, Erik, *x*
Gilley, Wade, 184
Gingras, Dave, 26
Golf Digest, 10

Grasso, Mike, *x*
Gray, Michael, *x*
Gutman, Jason, *x*

Hacker, Colleen, 249
Hazing, 76–78, 271
Hart, Jim, 141, 174
Havlichek, John, 20
Health/Fitness: and club sports, 124–126; and competitive sports, 120–123; and lifetime activites, 115–117; epidemic of declining, 10, 111–115; 245–247; in colleges, 123–124; in high schools, 102, 109–127; relationship to reforms to improve, 260; US statistics on, 109–110
Heinsohn, Tom, 20
High school basketball: in the 60s, 25–26; in the 90s, 26–28; and lack of team play, 39–43; and recruiting/transferring, 79–83; and scholarship chase, 67–70; needed reforms in, 254, 258–260; overemphasis on winning, 170–175
High school football: and educational relevance, 88–89, 93; and hazing, 76–78; and long seasons, 90–93
High school sports: athletic budgets and, 100–103; commercialism of, 93; comparison to 60s, 23–28; educational relevance of, 88–89, 93; funding of, 87; long seasons and, 87; growing expectations for, 88; hall of fames and, 95–99; history of, 7; reforms and, 258–260
Hitter, Tom, x
Hjeltnes, Erik, x
Hogan, Pete, x, 110–127
Holmes, Henry, 26
Hoop Scoop Online, 173
Hopkins, Mike, 141
Howley, Dan, 138–139
Hughes, Pat, x
Huma, Ramogi, x
Hunter, Geoff, x

Indiana High School Basketball, 10
Institute for Diversity and Ethics in Sport, 289
Institute for International Sport (IIS), 286
Institute for Preventative Sports Medicine (IPSM), 286
Institute for the Study of Youth Sports (YSI), 289

International Management Group (IMG), 8
Intramural athletics, 87
Isenberg, Marc, *x*, 238, 250
Ivy League, 181, 289

James, Lebron, 270
Janda, David, *x*, 106, 245
Jandris, Ed, 26
Jim Rome Show, 10
Jones, K.C., 20
Jones, Sam, 20
Jarvis, Mike, 68
Jock culture, 75–78, 87, 170–175
Jock curriculum, 63–64, 180, 232
Johnson, Russell, 170
Jordan, Michael, 216, 242
Josephson Institute of Ethics, 292

Kester, Marv, 17
Knight Commission on Intercollegiate
    Athletics, *vi*, 288
Koslowski, Eddie, 21
Kosoc, Nate, x
Kralovec, Etta, 72, 209, 250
Kranick, Art, 133, 135–136
Kranick, Linda, 133, 135–136
Kuchenbecker, Shari, 249
Knight, Bob, 271

Lajoie, Ron, 21
Lappas, Steve, 68
Layden, Joe, 170
Layden, Tim, 107
Layne, Mitchel, *x*
Lefkowitz, Bernard, 242
Levin, Sarah, 235, 250
Levy, Gene, 97
Lieberman, Hadassah Freilich, 96
Linstruth, Geoff, *x*
Lipsyte, Robert, *i, vi, ix*, 237–238, 242, 251
Little League Baseball: all-stars, 41–42;
    challenger division of, 9; history of, 7;
    needed reforms in, 252–254; partici-
    pation in, 8; television playoffs, 27
Longman, Jere, 244
Lonstad, Sonny, 17
Loparado, Nick, 197–199
Los Angeles Times, 10
Louisville, University of, 269
Lucier, Mike, 26
Lyons, Paul, 171

MacArthur, Douglas, *vi*
Maine, University of, 269
Major League Baseball (MLB), growth of,
    5–6, 9
Major League Lacrosse, 10
Malone, Karl, 32
Mancini, Alex, 75
Mara, Wellington, 204
March Madness, 180–182
Marotta, Chris, *x*
Marquette University, 269
Massachusetts, University of, and academic
    corruption, 178–179
Mayben, Emmanuel "Tiki", 173–175
McGreevy, Tom, 77
McGuire, Mark, 216
McNall, Joe, 45
McNeil, Lloyd, 21
McInerney, Rory, *x*
McKellick, Gordon, *x*
Media hype: and ESPN coverage of
    recruiting, 270; and Lebron James,
    270; and signing day, 138–143;
    problems with, xvii; reforms to
    combat, 261–262; responsibility for,
    242–243
Mendelson Center for Sports, Character,
    and Community, 290
Mexicalli Halcones, 45
Miami, University of, 269
Mickey Walker's All-Stars, 68
Mickey Mantle Baseball, 85–86
Microsoft, 269
Milford, NH, 19
Minneapolis Millers, 17
Minneapolis Star Tribune, 242
Miracle, Andrew, 72, 107, 245, 250
Most, Johnny, 20
MSG, 10
Musella, David, *x*
Murphy, Shane, 2, 21
Myer, Chris, *x*

Naismith, James, 41
Nandrolone, 155
National Alliance for Youth Sports (NAYS),
    285
National Basketball Association (NBA): and
    college sports, 194; and need for
    aminor league system, 255; growth of
    6, 9; probability of getting into, 231;

National Coalition Against Violent Athletes (NCAVA), 287
National Collegiate Athletic Association: as monopoly, 269; history of, 7–8; problems associated with, 231–238; reform of, 255–258; television contract, 10, 131
National Federation of State High Schools (NFSHS), 98
National Football League (NFL): and college sports, 194; growth of, 6, 9; need for minor developmental league, 255; performance enhancing drugs and, 153–155; probability of getting to, 231; National Hockey League (NHL), growth of 6, 9
National Institute for Sports Reform (NISR), v, xiii, 247, 251–252, 273–274, 281–283
National Institute of Drug Abuse (NIDA), 153
National Professional Indoor Soccer League, 9
National Student Athletes Rights Movement, 287
National Women's Basketball League, 128, 163
New Bedford Buddies, 68
New England Small College Athletic Conference (NESCAC), 178–179
Newburgh Free Academy, 91
Newsweek, 100
New York Gauchos, 69
New York Giants, summer training camp at SUNY-Albany, 204–206
New York Road Runners, xi
New York State Public High School Athletic Association (NYSPHSAA): and coaching, 85; and recruiting/ transferring, 81–83
New York Times, 10, 132, 169, 230, 234, 244, 246
North Carolina, University of, 179
North Rockland, 92
Nutritional supplements, 239
Nuwer, Hank, 242

O'Connor, Pat, x
Ohio Baseball, 10
Oklahoma, University of, 269
Old Dominion College, 272

Olen, Ken, 19–21
Olympic athletes, probability of becoming, 231
OPEC, 269
Ottaway, Celina, 158–162
Otter Yearbook, 16
Overtraining, 133–135

Papile, Leo, 68
Parental misbehavior, 39–43, 240–242
Parisi, Mark, x
Parental pressure on athletes, 26–27, 42, 61–65, 230
Patriot League, 181, 288
Paul Robeson Research Center for Academic and Athletic Prowess, 270, 290
P.E. 4 Life, 291
Pepper, Dottie, 97
Performance enhancing drugs: and problems with usage in sports, 87, 238–240, 269; and usage by Steve Courson, 153–155; high school cross country and, 135; reform measures and, 260–261
Peters, Mark, x, 224–225
Physical education, declining emphasis on, 110–127; 246
Pitaniello, Dennis, x
Point spreads, xvii, 145–151, 238
Pop Warner Football: and needed reforms, 252–253; history of, 7; Little Scholars Program and, 45; participation in, 8; problems with 44–46, 229–231; televised playoffs of, 27, 44–46
Porter, David, 238
Porto, Brian, x, 235, 237, 250
Positive Coaching Alliance (PCA), 291
Powell, Robert, 36
Proctor, Jon, 19–21
Professional sports, expansion of, 5–6, 9
Providence College, and Title IX, 190–194

Quatraro, Matt, x, 272–273

Raftery, Bill, 69
Ralph, Shea, 128
Ramsey, Frank, 20
Recreational sports, xvii, 117–127, 220, 260
Recruiting, of high school athletes, 79–83, 87, 138–143

Redmond, Cathy, *x*
Reed, Ken, *x*
Rees, Roger, 72, 107, 245, 250
Reo, Armand, 174
Reuning, Dean, 198
Richards, Milt, 201
Riley, Pat, 97
Riverside Church, 69
Roberts, Alan, *x*, 223
Robinson, Steve, 171
Rosen, Larry, 173
Rosenfeld, Alvin, 37, 230
Rotundi, Marcus, *x*
Rowan, Brian, *x*
Ruland, Jeff, 172
Russell, Al, *ix*
Russell, Bill, 20
Russell, Kevin, *x*, 31
Rutgers 1000, 287

Sachs, Michael, 249
Sack, Allen, *x*, 188, 208, 235, 250
Sage, Marcia, *x*
St. Johns University, 271
St. Lucia, Cathy, *x*
St. Lucia, Chuck, *x*
St. Lucia, Ericka, 129–130
St. Thomas Moore Academy, 171
Salzberg, Charles, 249
Sanders, Tom, 20
Schenectady City School District Sports
    Hall of Fame, 95
Scholastic recruiting, 79–83, 87
School athletic budgets, 100–108
Sears, Steve, 19–21
Sears Directors Cups, and Williams College,
    179
Sgambelluri, Steve, *x*
Sharman, Bill, 20
Sheehan, Richard, 237
Sheehy, Harry, 249
Shenendehowa High School, and recruiting,
    81
Shonka, Kristy, 45
Shulman, James, 233, 235, 250
Siarnacki, Jack, 26
Siena College, 271
Signing day, media attention on, 138–143
Singapore: comparison to American sports,
    217; economy of, 210–212; educational
    system in, 212–213; government in,

210; Olympic sports in 215–216; sports
    in, 213–219
Singelais, Mark, 141–142
Sitterly, Jeff, 173–174
Skinner, Al, 141
Smith, Dan, 213–214
Smith, Kate, 129–130
Smith, Reverend William, 190–191
Sneaker money, 69–70
Snyder, Kyle, *x*
Sobol, Thomas, 136
Soccer, participation in, 8
Sodergren, John, 90–93
Soronen, Bill, *x*
Soronen, Mike, *x*
South Troy Pop Warner Football, 45–46
Southern Florida, University of, 269
Sperber, Murray, 235, 237, 250
Sports ethics and values, 39–43
Sports Ethics Institute (SEI), 286
Sports gambling: continued problems with,
    237–238; on college campuses,
    145–151; reform measures to combat,
    260
Sports Illustrated, 2, 6, 10, 208, 234, 270
Sports Illustrated for Kids, 10
Sports injury: and ACL, 128–131; in-
    creasing problems with, 244–245; reform
    measures to prevent, 262
Sport Magazine, 6
Sporting News, 10
Sports hall of fames: in high schools, 95–97;
    Albany Capital District, 97–98
Sports Leadership Institute, 291
Sportsmanship: declining levels of, 39–43,
    47–60, 87, 240–242, 270–271; measures
    to improve, 262
Sports reform problems: commercialism,
    177–182, 182–189, 190–194, 235–237,
    268–269; declining health and fitness,
    109–127, 245–247, 271; erosion of
    sports values, 29–33, 39–43, 195–200;
    exploitation and academic corruption,
    62–67, 79–83, 84–89, 183–189,
    231–235, 267; financing of athletics,
    100–103; gambling, 145–152, 237–238,
    269–270; performance enhancing
    drugs, 153–156, 238–240, 260–261,
    269; specialization/early professionali-
    zation, 13–18, 29–33, 44–46, 47–60,
    61–67; sports injury, 128–131, 244–245,

271; sportsmanship, 75–78, 170–176, 195–200, 240–242, 270–271; Title IX, 157–165, 190–194 243–244, 271; unbalanced media coverage, 95–99, 138–144, 242–243, 270

Sports reform proposals: to control athlete, coach, parent and fan misbehavior, 262; to control excesses in intercollegiate sports, 255–258; to control excesses in youth and amateur sports, 252–253; to create a national sports commission, 251; to create a sports reform think tank, 251; to control athlete, coach, parent and fan misbehavior, 262; to curb media hype of young athletes, 261; to curb performance enhancing drugs, 260–261; to curb sports gambling, 260; to educate parents, 263–264; to prevent sports injury, 262; to promote club sports, 254; to promote interscholastic sports reform, 258–260; to promote intramural/recreational/ fitness-based activities, 260; to promote minor professional leagues, 255; to resolve inequity in opportunity, 263

Sportspages.com, 267

Sports participation, statistics on, 8

Stagg, Amos Alonso, Jr, 195

Stagg, Amos Alonso, Sr, 195

Staniels, Tim, *x*

Staurowksy, Ellen, *x*, 235, 250

Stautner, Ernie, 97

Steen, Ivan, 202

Steurwald, Brent, 91

Stockton, John, 32

Stolba, Christina, 244

Student-athlete, derivation and misuse of term, 179–181

Student Athlete Survival Guide, 291

Suburban Council Championships, 41

Suburban Council coaching rules, 84–89

SUNY-Albany, and moving to Division Sports, 201–206

Superprep, 10, 139

Susquehanna Today, 197–199

Susquehanna University, and naming of the sports complex, 195–200

Sutherland, John, 26

Svare, Bruce: sports participation, *xv*, 5, 13–22; in Milford, NH, 19–21; in Gardner, Massachusetts, 21–28, at

Susquehanna University, 195; biography of, 279–280

Svare, John, *ix*, 15, 30, 31

Svare, Mark, *ix*, 15, 29–30, 98

Svare, Maryalice, *ix*

Svare, Myron: as a father, *xi*, 13–18, 20; as an athlete, 15–18

Syracuse University, 179, 141–142

Telander, Rick, *i*, *ix*

Teamwork, 24–25, 29–33, 40–41

Tennessee, University of, and academic corruption, 183–189

Tennis, 10

Tetrahydrogestrinone (THG), 269

Texas, University of, 269

Thompson, Jim, *x*, 250

Title IX: Americans With Disabilities Act, 9; and cutting men's sports, 190–194, 243–244, 271; and high schools, 87; and pressure on female athletes, 157–165; legislation, 9; reform proposals for, 263

Thornton Center, University of Tennessee, 184

Thorpe, Aaron, *x*

Throwback athletes, declining numbers, 29–32; definition of, 29; examples of, 30–32 Transfer of high school athletes, 62–63, 80–83, 258–260

Troy Boys Club, 174

Troy High School, 14, 174

Tulloch, Matt, *x*

Unequal sports opportunities, 243–244

Ungerleider, Steve, 240

United States Basketball League (USBL), 9

United States Postal Service, 269

USA Today, 10, 81

US News and World Report, and college academic rankings, 206

User fees, 101, 259–260

Venter, Ryan, *x*

Venter, Tom, *ix*

Violence in sports, xvii, 39–43, 75–78, 240–242, 262, 270–271

Virginia Tech University, 269

Vulcan Classic, 132

Wake Forest College, 192

Walters, Kara, 163
Warner, Mari, 204
Washington Post, 10
WBZ Radio, 20
Weiner, Jay, *i, ix*, 242
Welsh, Tim, 193
Wenger, Chris, *x*
Wenger, Tim, *x*
Wetzel, Dan, 237
Wexler, Arnie, 238
Winchendon Prep School, 175
Wing, Matt, *x*
Winston-Salem State College, 173
Winterhoff, Matt, *x*
Winterhoff, Mark, *x*
Wojtukiewics, Bob, 26
Wolf, Rick, 2, 249
Wolff, Alexander, *i, ix*, 73
Woman's National Basketball Association
    (WNBA), 9, 128
Woman's Sports Foundation, 290
Woman's Sports and Fitness, 10
World Team Tennis, 9

Wright, Robin, 185
Wright, Steve, *x*, 215–216
WFAN Radio, 10
WRKO Radio, 19

Xavier University, 179

Yeager, Don, 237
Yearbooks, high school, space devoted to
    Sports, 103
Yesalis, Chuck, *i-ii, ix, x*, 73, 106, 230,
    238–239, 240
Yew, Lee Kuan, 210
Young Mens Christian Association (YMCA),
    7
Youth/amateur sports: Capital District Youth
    Basketball League, 47–60; failures of,
    3; history of, 7; Little League Baseball,
    7–9, 27, 41–42; Pop Warner Football,
    7–8, 27, 44–46; reform of 252–253
Yovine, Brian, *ix*

Zimbalist, Andrew, 235, 237

Quick Order Form

FAX Orders: Fax this form to 518-439-7284.

Postal Orders: Send this form to Sports Reform Press, Bordalice Publishing, Inc., 218 Murray Ave., Delmar, New York 12054

Internet Orders: Please log on to www.bordalicepublishing.com

Please send _____ copy(s) of the following book(s):

_____

Please send to:

Name:_____

Address:_____

City:_____State:_____Zip:_____

Telephone:_____

Email Address:_____

Cost of each book: $19.95

Sales Tax: Please add 8.25% for books shipped to New York addresses

Shipping is by priority mail
U.S.: $4.00 for first book and $2.00 for each additional book.

International: $9.00 for first book and $5.00 for each additional book.

Payment: _____ Cheque _____ Credit Card:

_____Visa _____ MasterCard _____American Express _____Discover

Card number:_____

Name on card:_____Exp. Date:_____